Latino Spin

Latino Spin

Public Image and the
Whitewashing of Race

Arlene Dávila

NEW YORK UNIVERSITY PRESS
New York and London

NEW YORK UNIVERSITY PRESS
New York and London
www.nyupress.org

Library of Congress Cataloging-in-Publication Data

Dávila, Arlene M., 1965–
Latino spin : public image and the whitewashing of race /
Arlene Davila.
p. cm.
Includes bibliographical references and index.
ISBN-13: 978-0-8147-2006-6 (cl : alk. paper)
ISBN-10: 0-8147-2006-4 (cl : alk. paper)
ISBN-13: 978-0-8147-2007-3 (pb : alk. paper)
ISBN-10: 0-8147-2007-2 (pb : alk. paper)
1. Hispanic Americans—Social conditions.
2. United States—Race relations. I. Title.
E184.S75D3553   2008
973'.0468—dc22   2008027818

New York University Press books are printed on acid-free paper,
and their binding materials are chosen for strength and durability.
We strive to use environmentally responsible suppliers and materials
to the greatest extent possible in publishing our books.

Manufactured in the United States of America
c 10 9 8 7 6 5 4 3 2 1
p 10 9 8 7 6 5 4 3 2 1

Contents

Acknowledgments

Latino Spin grew out of a series of talks, and I thank everyone who so generously allowed me to rehearse and develop these ideas throughout the course of five years. In particular, a keynote address at a graduate-student-organized Latino studies conference at the University of Southern California prompted the chapter on the republicanization of U.S. Latinos; colloquia at the University of Minnesota, Penn State, UCLA, and UC-Irvine led to the chapter on the Latino middle class and on immigrants as consumers, while a presentation to the American Studies and Urban Studies Programs at Brown University resulted in the chapter on East Harlem's Uptown project. I especially thank David Roman, Riv Ellen Prell, Roderick Ferguson, Jane Juffer, Lisa Garcia Bedolla, Deborah Vargas, Cristina Beltrán, Lazaro Lima, Michael Innis-Jimenez, Matt Garcia, and Evelyn Hu-DeHart for the inspiring conversations that led to the completion of this volume.

My long-standing friends and colleagues Linda Alcoff, Steven Gregory, and Elizabeth Chin are constant inspirations for my work. Once again, I thank them for providing valuable insights in more ways than they are even aware of. I trust they may recognize some of our many conversations reflected in this work. I also thank everyone who agreed to be interviewed, and who are identified by name in the following pages, as well as those who provided help but preferred to do so anonymously.

Raymond Plumey, Yasmin Ramirez, Lok Siu, Andrew Ross, Robert Alvarez, Patricia Zavella, Maureen O'Dougherty, Charles Hale, Tomas Lopez Pumarejo, and Adam Green read different chapters of this work in their various renditions and helped correct inaccuracies and push my thinking. I am especially indebted to Jose Sanchez and Mark Sawyer, who read the entire manuscript and provided important ideas for revision.

An earlier version of Chapter 5 was published in *Aztlán* and in *Cultural Anthropology*, and I thank the editors and publishers of those journals for their earlier feedback. I also thank Lee Baker and *Transforming*

Anthropology for providing the forum to publish an earlier version of Chapter 6.

Students in my seminars, Contemporary Ethnic Studies and The Making of Latin@ Culture at NYU were a constant source of insights and ideas. I am grateful to them for providing such enlightening discussions and for bearing with me as I thought through the questions that prompted this work. Thanks are also due to Daniel Nieves, who served as a research assistant during the National Association of Latino Elected Officials (NALEO) 2007 conference, and to my graduate assistant Johana Londoño, who was indispensable throughout this project. Johana provided research assistance and comments on an earlier draft of the manuscript, and helped to assure an altogether smoother publication process. Finally, Stephanie Sadre-Orafai provided invaluable proofreading assistance.

It was a great pleasure to work with Eric Zinner and the staff of NYU Press, especially Ciara McLaughlin. My greatest appreciation goes to them for the care and professionalism they afforded this work from the start.

Lastly, my lovely schnauzers Paco and Tula will never read a word of these pages, but they too must be acknowledged for forcing me to take walks, and to get out of my house and mind, at all the right moments.

Introduction

Illegal, tax burden, patriotic, family-oriented, hard-working, and model consumer—how do we make sense of such contrasting definitions of Latinos? Why do they circulate in concert? Put simply, everyone seems to want an answer to the same question: Are Latinos friends or foes? Since the 2000 census showed Latinos to be the United States' largest minority, there has been a growing debate about their values, political attitudes, and impact on U.S. national identity. Nativist and anti-immigrant groups view Latinos as America's most impending threat. Others see them as the single most important, up and coming ethnic group. In dispute is whether Latinos will mongrelize America, or become the new group on the route to whiteness, the New Italians or Irish Americans; or whether they will become the "new mainstream," or perhaps, the new base for the Republican Party.

These questions are far from new. Nationwide debates about Latinos' place and prospects in U.S. society have been rehearsed for decades, alongside the widespread use of the generic categories of "Hispanics" or "Latinos." Still, I believe that something new is at play within contemporary representations. For one, Latinos are being characterized in a more marketable, sanitized, and compensatory way, which I believe is suggestive of Latinos' shifting place in the politics of race. I'm referring here to representations by politicians, marketers, and writers from all sides of the political spectrum that show Latinos to be the most politically and economically rewarding group, or the focus of a growing middle class and the new "mainstream." Some commentators even suggest Latinos are the answer to America's racial problem, as it is believed they are permanently changing the way Americans talk and think about race.

The highly publicized work of Univision's anchor, Jorge Ramos, *The Latino Wave: How Hispanics Will Elect the Next American President*, for instance, tells us that Latinos have distinct ethos and values; they have the power and ability to shape and transform American society. But there is nothing to fear in this trend. Their conservative values—opposition to abortion, homosexuality, and divorce in greater percentages than Anglo Americans—are the same values "America" cherishes but is so rapidly losing. In Ramos's words: "A nation that emphasizes Latinos' morals and family values while maintaining the prevailing U.S. political and economic processes would, without a doubt, be a healthier and more humane society" (2004: 86).

In other words, at this time of uncertainty, Latinos can give America back to America. Such narratives are also common among marketers and authors who tell us that Latinos are becoming "The New Mainstream," that Latinos' growing impact on music and popular culture constitutes clear signs of their coming of age (Garcia 2004). And let's not forget recent scholarship's turn to Latinos' upward mobility. Works like *La Nueva California* conclude that Latinos behave "more like members of the American middle class than middle-class Americans themselves have [by exhibiting] the most vigorous workforce participation, the lowest public welfare usage; the strongest family structures, the fewest heart attacks; the healthiest babies; and a five-year-longer life expectancy, compared to non-Hispanic whites and African Americans" (Hayes-Bautista 2004: xvi). This is the core of what sociologists have termed the "Latino paradox," or the anomaly that Latinos seem to show better outcomes in overall health than their socioeconomic status would predict. Whether this is also true of other ethnic groups whose recent immigrants are as numerous as they are with Latinos, we are never told. The popular usage of the Latino paradox renders Latinos as the only group whose health is seemingly "buffered" by their culture.[1] Latinos have even been linked to declining rates of violence and crime; living among Hispanic immigrant enclaves has been found to be "protective" for non-Hispanic whites and blacks alike (Sampson 2006; Brooks 2006). Something about the immigrant lifestyle renews America in positive terms, while pundits and scholars tell us that Latinos are the solution to America's racial problems. That almost half of all Latinos identified themselves as white in the last census was considered a sign of their mainstreaming; just as the fact that 43 percent rejected traditional racial categories, checking "some other race," was taken as proof that they are at the crux of transforming the meaning of race itself. Put briefly, next to any news about Latinos' ill effects on society, one is likely to find another news story or research brief telling us that there is something about Latinos we can all learn or profit from.

For the most part, these arguments are generated in direct response to the more common portrayal of Latinos as poor, undocumented, destitute, and burdensome to the "national" community. They have been especially triggered by Samuel Huntington's by now well-publicized tirade about Latinos' inherent threat to America's Anglo-Protestant culture, not to mention by the growing xenophobic attitudes enveloping the immigration debate. In this context, the response has been to show Latinos as just "another ethnic group" that is equally well-equipped to display the "Anglo protestant values" of entrepreneurship, education, and success, and their belonging as undoubtedly American.[2] In other words, these more "marketable" representations evidence a growing consensus among pundits, advocates, and scholars who insist and provide proof that Latinos are not a social liability; that they are moving up and contributing; and that, in fact, their values make them more American than "the Americans."

Yet can these more favorable representations sufficiently subdue the perils and challenges that Latinos are generally believed to pose to the "integrity" of U.S. national identity? What may be some of their intended or unintended consequences with regard to current debates over immigration and social welfare? And most important, what do current representations and debates about Latinos suggest about their place in the contemporary politics of ethnicity and race?

Latino Spin provides a critical Latino studies perspective on the production and circulation of these more marketable contemporary representations of U.S. Latinos. By calling attention to some of the realities they may help skew, it specifically probes what these representations may reveal about the place and role Latinos play in the contemporary politics of race. Another development I examine is their effect on furthering whiteness by helping to consolidate polarities between Latinos and other minorities—most specifically with blacks, who are the unnamed reference against which these representations are made, and also among Latinos themselves along the lines of citizenship, race, and class.

The volume advances some of the themes I have previously explored about the importance of color blindness to the rise of neoliberalism, this time focusing on how the post–civil rights synergy of color blindness and neoliberalism has shaped public debates about Latinos. Indeed, neoliberalism is neither color-blind nor devoid of racism, even though it is predicated on its disavowal of racism—the attending view that the market constitutes the fairest space for upward mobility and that citizens who are entrepreneurial can reign supreme, unencumbered by the pettiness of race, ethnicity, and gender. Hence, in the past 20 years, writers have repeatedly noted transformations in U.S. racial ideologies, namely, the rise of color blindness as the dominant post–civil rights discourse on race. According to this view, race and ethnicity are no longer variables for measuring inequalities; civil rights legislation took care of most of America's institutional racism; and meritocracy reigns supreme (Brown et al. 2005; Bonilla 1998). Together these factors are now said to be responsible for the coming of age of minorities to the national (economic) table. Not surprising, the rise of color blindness has paralleled the rise of neoliberal local, state, and federal policies prioritizing the privatization and deregulation of services, not to mention the transformation of American citizens/subjects. At precisely a time when the state has withdrawn most directly from providing its citizens the basics for social welfare, security, and mobility, groups are increasingly being measured and valued with regard to their marketability, that is, for their value as consumers, and for their ability to become a targetable "niche" constituency for marketers, politicians, and privatization pundits. This discourse of equality in the market, however, is obviously racialized; for it is ultimately about sustaining unequal economic privilege while promoting whiteness and normativity, especially among those groups such as Latinos, who are considered its greatest threat.

The ascendancy of neoliberalism, in turn, has been characterized by a diminished space for discussing issues of social welfare and justice. Poverty has become the ultimate unredeemable liability for which the only response is to emphasize the political rentability and marketability of particular groupings. In a similar vein, issues of race and ethnicity have been marginalized in public discourse. Instead, ethnic and racial groupings are pushed to prove their value as political constituencies and consumers if they are to be welcomed to the national political table. The chapters explore this paradigm shift for discussing Latinidad, highlighting the move from deficiencies in terms of recognition, economic gains, and political standing, to the more marketable paradigm, where Latinos are presented as preeminent regenerators of all things "American." Agreeing with most contemporary critical race theory, I also show that seemingly race-neutral discourses emphasizing Latinos' class mobility and other competencies are never free of racial hierarchies; that they, in fact, may contribute to further white privilege and racial inequalities.

Ultimately, I show that contemporary debates that seem to over-ethnicize or de-ethnicize Latinos—whether by presenting them as a threat or as contributors to the "national community"; by highlighting their growing purchasing power and intrinsic "values"; or because of their coming of age or eagerness to assimilate—are never exempt from racial considerations. These discourses are in fact tied to a larger racial project entailing the very reconfiguration of how we talk or do not talk about race and racial hierarchies in an increasingly racially diversified society. In particular, they point us to the operations of contemporary racism, which increasingly works through cultural euphemisms and categories, anchoring itself—as Etienne Balibar once noted with regard to what he termed "neo-racism"—in the "harmfulness of abolishing frontiers, the incompatibility of lifestyles and traditions" (Balibar 1991). Accordingly, "differences" become "failures" that racialized groupings are forever pressed to redress. It is thus necessary to be critical of many of these more sanitized representations, especially of the ways they are circulated in mainstream society, in order to expose whether they respond more to the political climate than to demographic characteristics of all Latinos, or most Americans for that matter.

My interest then lies less in assessing the veracity of some of the contemporary representations of Latinos, than in understanding the political repercussions of their deployment. Knowledge is always socially positioned and created, and deconstructing representations is never as useful as understanding what accounts for such constructions, and what projects and interests are being advanced through them. This is especially so when such knowledge is presented and treated as facts that apply indiscriminately to as highly diversified a population as are Latinos. In other words, my purpose is not to refute or challenge the conclusions advanced by marketers, researchers, academics, or any other "Latinologist," a category from which I am not excluded. Anyone who writes or takes positions about the state of Latinos is not exempt from having their views taken as "expert accounts," or used in public opinion debates, despite our very best intentions to maintain control of how our studies and representations are interpreted and publicly circulated. My own work on Hispanic marketing (Dávila 2001b) has been used for marketing purposes, even though I wrote it as a critical examination of the hierarchies of representation that are attendant in the industry. My NYU website picture is now posted in the Association of Hispanic Advertising Agencies as one of the "scholars" consulted for their Latino Identity Project because I met with the researchers, though I had no control over the output, received no payment, and had no knowledge that my picture would be posted as a "scholarly endorsement."

Hence, I am considerably less interested in the conclusions advanced by scholars, commentators, or writers than in extricating "Latino spin"; that is, in exploring why some knowledges become attendant over others, and how these, in turn, create reality and meaning. I borrow the term "spin" from Stuart Ewen, who defines it as the "customized manufacture of public discourse," that takes place not necessarily through the content of a given poll, study, or writing, but rather by its selective publication, circulation, and deployment (Ewen 1996). Ewen asks how democracy is affected when public opinion is reduced to surveys and sound bites determined by commercial considerations. For my part, I ask how the pressure to look good—as a profitable and attractive people/constituency—has shaped a "people" and their place in U.S. racial hierarchies. The ensuing understandings of Latinos become evident in the discussions by politicians, pollsters, and marketers I discuss in Chapters 1 through 3. But they also operate and affect local politics and decisions about what constitutes a proper Latino museum exhibition or the rightful place of Latino studies in the academy, or what urban development should look like, as discussed in Chapters 4 through 6. Each chapter examines the types of representations of Latinos that become attendant to the strategies of political parties, or the curatorial direction of Latino museums or urban planning agendas, and most important, I examine the impact these depictions may have on the politics of whitening and race.

In exploring these issues, I do not claim to hold the final expertise on the various and intersecting fields of study I touch upon, such as institutional politics, art history, and urban planning. Instead, I have signaled existing bodies of work in these fields that complicate the dominant spin. My intention is not to question the empirical claims that are being made about Latinos. Rather, I explore the selective dominance of some interpretations over others. This is what I refer to as "spin." Additionally, I examine these "marketable" discourses, well aware that they are not representative of the dominant discourse about Latinos. It is well known that this discourse generally presents them as intruders and as a "brown tide" most threatening to America's racial and cultural makeup (Santa Ana 2002). A quick turn to AM radio talk shows or Lou Dobbs confirms the continued preeminence of these views. I am also well aware that Latino spin strives primarily in institutional spaces; that it is not representative of what we may find at the grassroots level, where we are likely to find more oppositional and progressive definitions of Latinidad. I focus on these more marketable representations, however, because they are central to the national conversation about the future of Latinos, and because they are likely to become more widespread in the current neoliberal climate so keen on distinguishing the "good" from the "bad" Latino.

One last clarification concerns my use of Latinos, instead of using Latinos/as or Latin@s, which are becoming common gender-neutral options, especially in academic writing. I purposefully use "Latinos" to signify the ubiquitous use of this term by the media and the mainstream press, which neither signals nor marks differences in gender, race, ethnicity, and other variables when making nationwide generalizations. My goal, it should be clear, is not to reproduce gender hierarchies, but rather to signal how this dominant generic designation also contributes to the whitewashing of this group.

Turning to the politics of whiteness, my analysis recognizes the centrality of projecting model minority values of hard work, family values and so on, to seemingly worthy "others." These values, said to make Americans "American," have long been used to frame the trajectory by which minority groups can claim to belong to the nation, turning some groups into living proof of the ideals of individualism and meritocracy at the core of the U.S. national ideology. Most perniciously, this is a process in which ethnic group after ethnic group has been pressed to distance itself from African Americans, or else has been distanced from "blackness" by others. Indeed, whiteness is never static, both in terms of who is classified as white and how its content is defined, and it is this changing aspect that makes it so pervasive and enduring, irrespective of the demographic shifts underlying the United States' growing diversity. This process has been documented among European ethnics, such as the Irish and Jews, as well as in relation to the honorary white status that has been situationally awarded to some Asian-American groups. At the same time, Latinos are not just any ethnic immigrant group in this country. Unlike most immigrant ethnic groups, however, Latinos share a history of occupation, invasion, and colonization by the United States. In the words of journalist Juan Gonzalez (2001), they constitute America's "Harvest of Empire" and, consequently, the United States has never solely represented a space of refuge or opportunity for most Latinos. And let us not forget that Latinos are a primarily non-European mixed, brown and black racialized people. That is, while many Latinos who are white or light-skinned do enjoy the privileges of whiteness, as a group, they are not so easily "whitened." Their "assimilation" and insertion in the United States presents challenges insofar as it demands a reassessment of U.S. history and its troubled engagement with its Latin American "backyard." Arguments about the particularities of Latinos' "assimilation," or lack thereof, are uninformed if they ignore the challenges Latinos' racialized history and status present to their wholehearted acceptance as undoubtedly "American." This status is never assured by their social and political gains, but rather remains contingent on the larger political and historical climate.

With all this said, representations emphasizing Latinos' upward mobility and coming of age are not merely inventions. Neither should they be discounted as a marketing ploy advanced by actors seeking to control their image. The power and attraction of these images lie in exposing what has remained largely unmentionable: the real diversification that exists among Latinos, along the lines of class, education, race, citizenship, and nationality, among other variables. Indeed, as a nationwide, undifferentiated group, Latinos are still primarily a working-class community, lagging in education, wealth, and access to services and infrastructure. A great percentage are undocumented and susceptible to draconian immigration policies barring them from ever achieving the American dream. However, many Latinos have moved up and continue to do so. Many are aligning with progressive politics and with the political and economic interests of new immigrants and the working poor. But others are purposely or unwittingly distancing themselves from their less fortunate types, be it from undocumented immigrants or from African Americans, as they climb the rungs of American-ness and claim status as "middle class" or "American citizens."

In the present landscape, it is hence increasingly difficult to summon the monolithic "imagined working-class community" of the late 1960s and 1970s. Then, differences around gender, sexual preferences, race, and class were largely subjugated as part of what art historian Tomas Ybarra-Frausto has termed the necessary "strategic essentialism" of the 1970s, so central to bringing attention to Latinos' racialization (Ybarra-Frausto and Dear 1999). Today, the task of mobilizing all Latinos alongside other people of color is just as important, but it is more daunting than ever. If the essentialisms of the past which were built on Latinos' putative homogeneity of class (working class and poor), nationality (Chicano or Puerto Rican), political affiliation (Democratic), citizenship (undocumented), religion (Catholic), residential patterns (urban), sexuality (heterosexual), and race (mestizo or "brown") were never held entirely true, they are far more difficult to sustain now. The political and social climates have changed significantly, while multiple accounts of Latinos' diversity have reached the mainstream. Making the greatest impact among these accounts is the current trickling of Latino celebrities achieving "success" in everyday culture. As a marketer was more than eager to remind me: "Everyone wants to be a Hispanic today, people are learning salsa, there's a hispanicization of American culture, look at the Latin Grammys!" Glossy commercial images take center stage in the American media landscape, making it especially difficult to grapple with Latinos' differentiation in critical ways.

Contrary to the optimism of my marketing friend, however, glossy images can only go so far; the complexity of race in contemporary society is real and requires examination. In this context, we can no longer take simple refuge in appeals to a common Latinidad; concepts of "mestizaje" or transnational Latinidad are not inherently inclusive. Black and indigenous Latinos are not exempted from racial discrimination by well-meaning appeals to mestizaje from non-Latinos and Latinos alike. Turning the map of Latin America upside down, one may discover a top-down racial hierarchy of Latinidad, not dissimilar to the hierarchies that lead many Mexican immigrants from northern Mexico to look down upon their southern "indigenous" counterparts. All the while, throughout U.S. cities, Latino elites, whether wittingly or not, help to exacerbate gentrification, as they distance themselves from their less fortunate counterparts. Complex historical, social, economic, and political dynamics underwrite these distinctions. But so do contemporary representations by well-meaning Latino pundits, planners, curators, and scholars intent on projecting Latinos in the most "positive" light possible. Such predicaments force us to recognize how differences along the lines of region, class, citizenship, place, and race may be emphasized or eluded, as we assert ourselves, or become inserted by others in the shifting politics of race.

Most pressing, I argue that a lack of critical examination of Latinos' "coming-of-age" discourses can facilitate their co-optation into racist projects and policies that affect Latinos and all Americans. And I stress *all* Americans, because it is only by placing Latinos at the center of U.S. race relations that I believe we can begin to discover shared interests and purposes, not only among Latino groups and other racialized groupings, but foremost between Latinos and the fate of all Americans. The immigration debate is relevant here, especially when we realize that citizenship has never shielded racially marked Latinos from being suspected as "immigrants"—just as it has never shielded racial minorities from second-class citizenship status.

This is why it is necessary to see the current immigration and citizenship debate as one that affects all Latinos and people of color, a debate that affects all Americans in general. To think that those of us with citizenship are waived from the racial intolerance and chauvinism triggered by the immigration debate is to be fooled into believing that citizenship has, in fact, provided equal benefits and entitlements to all Americans irrespective of race, gender, class, or sexual orientation. Even white heterosexual Anglo-Saxons should be wary of how they are affected by the immigration and citizenship debate. By fetishizing citizenship as a guarantor of privileges, the immigration debate veils the civil liberties that are increasingly denied to all. In a similar way, ignoring the contexts in which to think about Latinos as a unified category or to theorize about distinctions of race, class, citizenship, and nationality is to facilitate their co-optation into projects that may be detrimental to the general social welfare. These include projects that sustain neoliberal policies which legitimate a diminished social service network, from a living wage to health services to affordable housing, and that further divide the upwardly mobile from those who are not, or simply cannot.

I am also especially concerned with the political uses and effects of current representations of U.S. Latinos in relation to the present and future prospects for intra-racial and ethnic coalitions. In this regard, I interrogate the effects these more "marketable" Latino representations may have on Latinos' relations with African Americans; a choice by no means intended to obscure the political importance of other ethnic groups, such as Asian Americans, nor to draw strict boundaries between blacks and Latinos as static and isolated groupings. As the attending category of Afro-Latino or black Latinos suggests, many Latinos stand at the crossroads of U.S. racial/ethnic boundaries in ways that make it difficult, if not oftentimes irrelevant, to differentiate between the two. My intention instead is to confront and destabilize the primacy that is increasingly given to polarized black and Latino relations and contests in public discourse.[3] After all, it is African Americans who are employed as the named and unnamed reference against which Latinos are positioned as a new model minority, as the "people" that will not threaten, but rather will reinvigorate, American values. This requires that we explore the invisibility vested by the U.S. black and white racial binary on Latinos and other ethnic groups in the United States. And just as attentively, we need to examine how public discourse on Latinos may be sustaining this very binary.

Naming the Projects of Latinos' Racialization

To understand the multiple projects involved in Latinos' racialization requires foregrounding the difficulties of theorizing issues of race among Latinos. For Latino/Hispanic denotes not a race, but an ethnic group comprising people of different racial backgrounds. Granted, arguments have been made to the contrary. The great percentage of Latinos that selected "some other race" in the last census has been interpreted as a sign that Latino ethnicity has been racialized and that Latinos see themselves as a distinct race beyond black, white, and Asian (Haney-Lopez 2005). The number of Latinos identifying in this manner has steadily increased, in direct proportion to a decline in the number of Latinos who identify as white, from 64 percent in 1980, to 54 percent in 1990, to the present 48 percent (ibid. 2005). Hence, it is not so much a process of "whitening" but of "Latinization" that is most evidenced by the census, a trend that sustains Latinos' role in the "browning" of America. Accordingly, Latinos' rapid demographic growth will render whites into a numeral minority and transform the U.S. bipolar racial system into a tripartite or stratified system analogous to that found in Latin America. This development, in turn, has been linked to new forms of subordination and racial blurring as middle categories become stand-ins for honorary white status privilege (Bonilla-Silva 2003). Alternatively, the growing recognition of mixed racial categories has been interpreted as a challenge to binary racial hierarchies, and as a medium for extending more inclusive and critical notions of mestizaje (Perez-Torres 2006).[4]

On the other side of the spectrum is the view that Latinos are becoming the "new mainstream," either following a similar path to Euro-Americans, assimilating and becoming white or, even more optimistically, entirely transforming and expanding the meaning of what's considered "mainstream."[5] Latinos' dumbfounding response to the question of race in the 2000 census was seen as a telling sign of these contradictory processes. That 48 percent, almost half, of all Latinos identified as white was taken as a sign of their mainstreaming; that 43 percent rejected traditional racial categories and checked "some other race" is viewed as proof that they are at the crux of transforming the meaning of race itself.

What is at stake, for commentators and pundits from all sides of the political spectrum, is the meaning of America itself. Is America whitening or browning? This is a problematic question for prioritizing America's racial makeup as its most pressing dilemma, above and beyond any other economic, social, or political issue. Are the fears of anti-immigrant and white supremacist groups about the future of America's "dominant Anglo-Saxon protestant identity" hereby confirmed? Can Hispanics be considered a racial minority if they're no longer a minority; if, in fact, they define themselves either in white or in nonracial terms? How will these trends affect social advocacy on behalf of Latinos? And, what impact will they have on the future of multiracial and ethnic coalitions?

These are important and challenging questions, but they are also extremely disabling. For one, they presuppose an either/or scenario of mainstreaming and racialization that may be applicable to the totality of the Latino population that the scholarship and the empirical record cannot, and in fact does not sustain. This is why sociologists have advanced the concept of "segmented assimilation" to highlight the different ways second-generation immigrants assimilate, and to accommodate the reality that some Latino immigrants do move up, but that others assimilate in a downward fashion; that mobility in one generation can be reversible and affected by race, education, and parental background, among other variables (Portes and Rumbaut 2001). Unfortunately, a lack of longitudinal works looking at trends across generations has facilitated the dominance of arguments based largely on the anecdotal or observational information by middle class scholars and commentators (Telles 2006a). One of the most comprehensive forthcoming studies on the topic, however, bears witness to the continued challenges Latino immigrants face; challenges that make the European assimilation model largely inapplicable to Latinos. The study focusing on four generations of Mexican Americans from 1965 to 2000 shows that Mexican Americans have had steady rates of assimilation with regard to language acquisition, intermarriage, religion, and political affiliation, but not with regard to education and social mobility (Telles 2006a). Accounting for these differences is the racialization to which Mexican Americans continue to be subjected, as well as deficiencies in public education and the lack of a market for middle-rung jobs that do not require higher education. These key important factors setting Mexican Americans, and many Latinos, apart from the experiences of previous European immigrants are consistently downplayed by most of the immigration/assimilation arguments that reach the mainstream.

Latino Spin maintains that Latinos are simultaneously subjected to processes of whitening and racialization and that dichotomous frameworks reducing the fate of the totality of the Latino population to one or another process, especially on the bases of a single variable—be it how Latinos identify racially, or whether they speak Spanish or convert to Protestantism—are simply disabling and reductive. Instead, I propose that Latinos' racialization and their so-called whitening need to be seen as constitutive of one another, but without ever losing sight of the continued preeminence of racial hierarchies. In other words, the ways and manners that, as a group, Latinos are inserted into numerous debates and into contemporary institutions are in fact racially implicated and coded and, more often than not, implicated in furthering normativity. But this process takes place not by whitening or mainstreaming Latinos, but rather, by strategically including and excluding them from that very process. What is most pernicious is that this happens in ways that are not directly or recognizably coded in racial terms, rendering the ongoing racialization of Latinos that accompanies their so-called mainstreaming to be easily dismissed by many cheerleaders of Latinos' coming of age. This is why I am foremost critical of arguments that uphold Latinos' "whitening," in analogous ways to Euro-American groupings (Waterston 2006). In my view, this position ignores the multiple ways in which Latinos are subordinated even when they are supposedly joining the ranks of mainstream culture. These chapters call attention to this process by showing the continued subordination of all that is Latino in the world of art museums, urban planning, academia, and institutional politics that takes place just as Latinidad becomes seemingly central to these spaces.

These arguments will become clearer in the following chapters. But first, it is important to foreground that Latinos encompass people who are phenotypically white, Asian, and black, which means that Latinos of European background are not "whitening"—they are phenotypically white; just as many Latinos are in fact phenotypically black. This is often overlooked due to the simultaneous racialization of the term "Latino" and because both the whiteness of white Latinos and the blackness of Afro-Latinos is oftentimes blurred in public discourse. Such blurring is evidenced by the coinage of non-Hispanic white to categorize "authentic" whites and by the tendency to describe white Latinos as light-skinned not white, and by the total erasure of black Latinos in dominant media representations (Rodriguez 2000). Put simply, Latinos' racial background is consistently trumped by their "Latinidad." At the same time, it is important not to lose sight of the fact that the path toward whitening is not equally open to all Latinos and that those who are white do not face the same level of racial discrimination as Latinos of indigenous and African backgrounds.

A study by the Pew Hispanic Center recently brought attention to this by showing that Latinos who identified as whites have higher levels of education and income and lower rates of unemployment than those who identified as "some other race" (Tafoya 2004). The differences were not staggering. Self-identified Hispanics' social indicators lagged behind those of non-Hispanic whites. Still, the study, perceptively entitled "Shades of Belonging," evidenced the interplay between "whiteness" and privilege among Latinos. It concluded that Latinos' choice to identify as white in the 2000 census is less of a reflection of permanent markers such as skin color than of characteristics that can vary such as economic status and political enfranchisement. For instance, the study found that social context and place mattered in the way Latinos self-identified racially; hence, the 63 percent native-born Latinos of Mexican descent who defined themselves as white in Texas versus the 45 percent who did elsewhere; or the 91 percent native-born Cuban Latinos who identified as white in Florida, versus the 66 percent who did outside of Florida. Even more poignant is the example of Puerto Ricans, of whom 81 percent of island residents identified as white, whereas only 46 percent identified as such on the mainland.[6] The spuriousness of these numbers was not lost on Puerto Rican scholars, who were quick to note that the island of Puerto Rico came out "whiter" than the U.S. population, where only 75 percent identified as white. This in turn triggered debates about the island's racism and subjugation of its African heritage.[7] Obviously then, knowing the percentage of Latinos who identify as white, black, or as some other race is only part of a story, which beyond phenotype is complicated by a range of social, historical, and regional variables.

Latinos' self-identification as white or in nonracial terms, however, stands as the primary reason behind arguments that it is simply a matter of time before Latinos become white. See, for instance, George Yancy's (2003) suggestive title *Who Is White?: Latinos, Asians, and the New Black/Nonblack Divide,* in which he argues that Latinos and other nonblack racial minorities will soon join the cap of whiteness—that insofar as they separate from blacks, they will assimilate into majority status. At the crux of his argument is the meaning of assimilation, which he defines as the experience of thinning one's racial identity and of approaching racial issues from a dominant perspective. Simply put, assimilation is a matter of "thinking like white," as Yancy believes that Latinos can join majority status simply by self-identifying as white. I agree with him that whiteness is not a biological or phenotypical reality, but rather a social, cultural, political, and economic process and project. As such, it is indeed possible for non-European ethnic groupings to be incorporated into this project. Moreover, racial categories are not static, the meaning of white has changed since the turn of the century and will continue to change, and will likely expand to incorporate groups that are currently defined as nonwhite. This was the case with American Jews, the Irish, and other European immigrants, as evidenced by numerous works showing the historical processes and context that led to the American construction of whiteness; especially how it was invariably constructed in direct reference to blacks (Brodkin 1999; Roediger 1999). Already, even if only categorically, Mexicans were regarded as white prior to the 1930s, as were many Latin Americans in the United States prior to the official 1970s institutionalization of "Hispanic" to include all peoples of Spanish heritage and origin (Rodriguez 2000). That their categorical inclusion as white paralleled their subjection to the most direct forms of racism, stemming from U.S. Westward expansion, however, should serve as a warning about the problems of equating racial classification as "white" with racial status, not to mention about the limited application of the European whiteness paradigm when non-European racial and ethnic groups are concerned (Acuña 2006).

Indeed, while race is a cultural and social construct, it is important to never lose sight of the visibility of race. However defined, the pervasiveness of race stems from the static notions of nature, biology, phenotype, and visibility on which it is based. Additionally, race operates through global and regionally defined hierarchies marked by the European conquest and empire of non-European peoples. These are the same hierarchies that have informed and justified the historical subjugation of blacks and Native Americans and their descendants, as well as the fate of many Hispanic Caribbeans, Latin American and Pacific islanders who underwent conquest and colonization on U.S. soil or in their home countries. In other words, unlike Irish and other Euro ethnics, Latinos are brown and black. Yes, many are white, but the majority have colored skin. They are especially "colored" through processes of conquest and colonization and through their direct experiences with U.S. empire. This realization informs the distinctions some writers have made between regular migrants and those who are most appropriately recognized as "colonial migrants," or "colonial/racial subjects of empire," in order to more accurately account for immigrants' different experiences of incorporation into the United States (Grosfoguel et al. 2006). As they note, the conditions shaping peoples' incorporation can vary across Latino groupings, but most of all, are distinct from most European immigrants' experiences upon coming to the United States. Then, there is the important issue of proximity. Latin America's location has historically rendered Latinos a far greater threat to the United States' racial, cultural, and linguistic borders than their spatially buffered Europeans could ever be. These significant differences, however, are consistently veiled when the European whiteness paradigm is uncritically applied to non-European racial and ethnic groups, especially to those whose histories place them in direct contact with the United States' expansion and empire.

The European model of assimilation is also limiting for furthering the dominant black/white binary that has historically hindered the understanding of multiracial pan-ethnic groups. In this model, groups such as Latinos and Asian Americans are reduced to "spectators" of real race relations—defined only in "black and white" terms—and interesting only insofar as they are shown to be moving closer to the "white" or "black" side of the binary (Park and Park 1999). As critics have noted, this binary obfuscates how race operates in a multiracial and multi-ethnic and transnational world, and the distinctive histories that hinder the easy inclusion of Latino and Asian Americans into any of these two binary groupings.

The most misguided proposition in discussions about where Latinos fit racially in the United States, however, is the view that we can equate categorical identifications with empirical experiences of race and racism. In other words, that self-identification as "white" translates to majority status, or that rejecting traditional categories of race, as Latinos did in the census, indicates a lack of awareness of race, or freedom from racism. The most direct evidence to challenge this point comes from Latin America, where arguments that racism does not exist there because racial categories are trumped by national identifications have been consistently disproved. It is true that Latin America and the United States differ in their racial ideologies—Latin American racial categories have long been characterized graduated and fluid as opposed to the more static bipolar binary of the United States, while national identifications in Latin America have historically skewed and prevented the widespread politicization of race and ethnicity–based categorizations. However, and notwithstanding the pollyanna-like views shared by many Latin American nationalist leaders and laypeople alike, race and racism are very much alive in Latin America, strengthened by the very silence that has characterized discussions of race in the area.[8] In other words, if one is black or dark-skinned in Latin

America, identifying oneself in national rather than racial terms—as Mexican, Puerto Rican, or Dominican, or else as trigueño, indio claro, or indio oscuro or by any other racial euphemistic classification—does not shield one from racism, however "mild" or different from U.S. racism it is said to be. In an equal manner, neither is one shielded from racism in the United States by identifying as "white" if one is not visually and culturally recognized in this manner.

Such racial politics highlight the importance of "culture" in terms of the intangible but very real markers of language, dress, demeanor, and cultural capital that, in addition to phenotype, make race so pervasive in everyday life. For instance, the extensive literature on colonialism has pointed out the multiple ways in which language, sexual behavior, comportment, hygiene, religion, dress, accent, and a zillion other cultural "competencies" have functioned to differentiate and identify the "intermediary" brown and colored, and for these to claim status vis-à-vis each other under the specter of a European cultural hegemony (Stoler 2002; Williams 1991). Indeed, pervasive "cultural" markers such as these were used to distinguish those who were deemed more likely and better equipped to climb the rungs of civilization, from those destined to ride on its coattails and doomed to have their positive comportment in matters of dress, jobs, accent, cuisine, and so on, regarded as suspect, derivative, and inauthentic at best (Williams 1993). In other words, racism and racialization have always entailed pressures to conform to dominant frameworks of "normalcy," a state that is always associated as the natural attribute of the powerful groups in society; namely, of those who most closely resemble dominant Western-based national/cultural/linguistic canons of civilization at play.

This is why the concept of ethnorace is so useful when thinking about Latinos (Alcoff 2005; Goldberg 1993). This concept allows us to be attentive to processes of racialization and racism that may be obviated when we focus simply on "race," which in the United States is so easily subsumed to the dominant black and white binary. For more often than not, this binary effectively veils Latinos' and other groups' experiences of racialization, while blinding us to forms of racialization that take place alongside or beyond "race." Such is especially the case when nativism becomes a primary axis of racialization, positing white Americans as the only true "natives," with blacks and citizens with the "longest citizenship pedigree" following suit; and all of them together, as the victims of the ongoing "conquest" by undocumented (colored) folk (Sawyer 2005). At the same time, my intention is not to challenge "race" as an analytical concept, as advocates of color blindness would have us do, even to the point of altogether avoiding racial identifiers from the U.S. census. Instead, I recognize that race is central to the ethnorace conjunction; it is the ultimate qualifier reminding us that phenotypically inscribed racial difference is the paramount variable affecting people's racialization. Yet the concept of ethnorace allows us to acknowledge that, while some members of a particular ethnic group may be visibly white, by mere membership in a racialized grouping, their whiteness remains suspect and conditional, rather than a de facto guarantor of unmarked mainstream status—especially when considerations of class, language competence, and cultural capital are considered. In an equal manner, the whitening of members of an ethnorace does not translate to the "contributions" of the totality of the group as defined in relation to the dominant national identity. Instead, the "model" in the "model minority" remains a slippery attribute.

Chapter Road Map

To grapple with these issues, the following chapters examine some of the multiple projects in which "Latinos" as a monolithic group are homogenized in public discourse and within the projects of political parties, Latino think tanks, of museums, and even of the corporate university. I examine these spaces with an eye to the politics and exclusions that increasingly are involved in the contemporary production, circulation, and consumption of Latinidad. Specifically I am concerned with the different ways in which Latinos are being co-opted into a larger project of whitening that, far from welcoming them to the rungs of whiteness, has in fact contributed to the marginalization of many Latinos, and people of color in general. To this end, some chapters examine representations aimed at national consumption, such as the political advertisements for the 2004 election. Others provide careful consideration of some of the institutional spaces and interests involved in the production of Latinidad, such as Latino-specific museums and Latino studies programs in the corporate university. But altogether, they question the relevant applicability of Latino/a as a unitary ethnic category, some of the invisibilities they bear, and the contexts and spaces that may demand attention to other variables, such as those of race, citizenship status, and class. I believe this kind of examination is indispensable if we are to avoid treating Latinos as a simple "floating signifier," devoid of real content, substance, and politics,[9] and if we are to advance more empowering and inclusive projects in their name or their behalf.

The first three chapters gathered in Part I, The Politics of Latino Spin, are informed by debates on Latinos' current and future place in the United States from media resources, forums, and seminars organized by local and national groups, corporations, and political think tanks that I have been following during the past five years. These chapters also draw from interviews with researchers, advocates, and politicians involved in Latino advocacy as well as from my own experience as a resident and active participant in New York City's Latino scene. Chapter 1 looks at think tanks' and public policy researchers' growing interest in the existence of a long obscured segment of the Latino population: the middle class. This is an important move for bringing attention to Latinos' class heterogeneity. But I also explore the implications of defining a vibrant and growing Latino middle class at the very same time that most people in the middle class are more accurately tagged as "squeezed," indebted, and disappearing. I show how the uncritical celebration of the "Latino middle class" masks the ongoing economic inequities and uncertainties experienced by most Americans.

Chapter 2 turns to the spin that dominated discussions of the Latino electorate in the 2004 elections, and how it facilitated their insertion and mainstreaming in the agenda of these parties, especially that of the Republican Party, which drew a record number of Latino votes. By exposing problems in the polling of Latinos, the limited numbers of Latinos who are registered and actually vote, I show why it is utterly misleading to make generalizations about the Latino electorate. Foremost, I examine some of the problems of subordinating and reducing Latinos' political views to "traditional values." Finally, Chapter 3 underscores the conflicting portrayal of immigrants as economic liabilities, and conversely, as a business opportunity and foundation for future markets. In particular, I explore the compensatory discourses about Latinos as the summa plus consumer that have arisen in response to the growing debate over immigration. This chapter also updates my earlier examination of Hispanic marketing (Dávila 2001b). Latinos have since become even more relegated to being mere "consumers" rather than active participants in the highly profitable media and market economy that has continued to grow exponentially. Latinos' marketability does not represent their "coming of age," I argue, but rather sustains the ongoing conglomeration of media outlets that remain out of their reach.

The three chapters in Part II, Political Economy: Spaces and Institutions, turn to in-depth case studies that show how the pressure to present

Latinos in the most mainstream manner possible can be so easily co-opted into endeavors that lead to social inequalities. I focus on three spaces involved in the representation of Latinos: Latino/Latin American museums, ethnic studies programs in the entrepreneurial university, and Latino-themed urban development. These are spaces with which I am familiar from previous research, and where I have been more directly exposed to the political economy of Latinidad. My hope is that readers who are familiar with other institutions and spaces making claims to generic "Latino" projects can find relevant lessons in these chapters about some of the larger implications involved in the production of more mainstreamed definitions of Latinidad.

In these chapters, we see Latino spin operating as the preferred glossy version of Latinos that these spaces seek to project or attract, although more often than not, the end result is projects that are distanced from Latinos' needs and everyday reality. At the same time, these chapters include more ethnographic accounts of Latinos as active communities that are constantly maneuvering and challenging dominant representations as they struggle for space and political representation.

Chapter 4 examines the largest upcoming development in New York City's East Harlem, and its proposed execution of a Latino/theme component as an entry point to examining the level of inclusivity, or lack thereof, of development pitches that it is claimed will be representative of particular communities. By examining the local struggles around this project, this chapter warns that the so-called Latinization of American cities is built on thin air. Instead, the displacement of Latinos and people of color from urban centers is directly related to the eradication of working and middle classes from the new racially and class-exclusive neoliberal city, and that it implicates us all. I also suggest that urban planning be considered the ultimate public relations tool, a medium to accommodate and appease populations, rather than a tool for democracy and representation in the development of contemporary cities.

Chapter 5 turns to the controversy over the transformations experienced by El Museo del Barrio and other Latino institutions facing changing social, economic, and political conditions in an era of rapid privatization and globalization. This includes a sharpening of the already tense relationship between museums and communities now compounded by neoliberal trends leading to the mainstreaming and bureaucratization of these spaces, and sometimes to a narrowing of what is considered appropriate "Latin" art programming.

Finally, Chapter 6 examines some of the subtle ways in which Latino studies, and other ethnic studies, are becoming mainstreamed, but also newly subordinated in the very process. It explores whether there is room for critical ethnic studies in the corporate university where ethnic studies have been subject to cost-cutting schemes and delegitimized as passé in the current neoliberal climate, sometimes functioning as diversity management tools to provide multicultural literacy.

I conclude this work with some final words on the dangers of wishful thinking. I explore the impact that sanitized representations of Latinos as more American than Americans may have on the state of Latinos and African-American relations, as African Americans serve as their never mentioned but always present reference. I consider what may be at stake when only compensatory "positive" spin dominates public advocacy, including the same spaces conceived to confront and challenge racism. When the current climate turns everyone into agents of color blindness, then what? I propose that we don't get to this point, and that we do so by recognizing, and most important by critically rejecting and passing on Latino spin.

PART I

The Politics of Latino Spin

1

Here Comes the
Latino Middle Class

As recently as a decade ago, it was unimaginable to talk openly about middle-class Latinos. But now, this topic is present with a vengeance. With the marketing industry touting the profitability of Latinos as a market, and political parties touting their vibrancy as the "new electorate," poverty is more than ever a political liability, almost entirely obviated from the national agenda. Thus, when in 2004 a study by the Puerto Rican Legal Defense and Education Fund (PRLDEF) showed that 26 percent of all Puerto Ricans, almost three times the national average, live in poverty, people were not amused. In the words of Angelo Falcón, then senior policy executive of the center: "I could not believe the reactions to this report. Not the feedback we got fifteen years ago. Even our own Puerto Rican politicians were telling us to bury the story, that I was making us look bad." Instead, he was prompted to highlight the good news also shown in the report, that a higher percentage of Puerto Ricans have earned bachelors' degrees, a higher rate than the Latino average, and that nearly 20 percent of Puerto Ricans hold managerial jobs which is a higher rate than the Latino average. This is one instance where the prophets of doom are silenced by the cheerleaders of Latino accomplishment in the process of controlling Latinos' image, in this case that of Puerto Ricans. Attention from marketers and politicians comes to those who are moving up the ladder. What credibility or rentability as voters and consumers can a poor community possibly attract?

This concern to control Latinos' image is far from new. For as long as Latino leaders have organized publicly, there has been debate about the best way to project a more mainstream identity for themselves and their constituency in order to command greater political legitimacy. The issue I'm concerned with here is the seemingly growing consensus on the need to project Latinos as an upwardly mobile constituency alongside the lack of debate about the social and political consequences of such positive projections. In other words, what is at stake when a veteran marketer could so easily assert during an interview that they have won the battle over images? As he explained: "In the 1970s, politicians and scholars were crying poverty making it impossible for us to sell this market, but 30 years later we've won the battle." Or, in the poignant words of Mike Nieves, deputy chief of staff at the New York City Council, the "Perfumados (the perfumed ones) are in; the *titeres* (thugs) holding a flag are totally out." That he would contrast the so-called perfumed ones to "thugs" is telling of the legitimacy lost by whoever is not a professional or upwardly mobile when representing Latinos as a constituency—especially if "holding a flag."

This is the central point that this chapter questions: the confluence of interests that are now intent on reshaping Latinos' image around more marketable, mainstreamed, and upscale definitions in light of the renewed urgency in public debate about Latinos' current and future impact on this country. In what follows, I examine these dynamics by looking at the growing public turn to Latinos' upward mobility. I do not debate this trend—insofar as the entire Latino population has grown, an argument that any of its sectors has grown is impossible to contest. The comments of Roberto Suro, the then director of the Pew Hispanic Center, one of the most important Latino think tanks, come to mind: "insofar [as] the entire Latino population has grown one could even state that the number of freckle faced Latinos has grown and be in the right." What I am concerned with then is the growing overemphasis of discussion and debate about this particular subsector, especially with regard to current debates over immigration and over Latinos' future mobility or lack thereof.

Discovering the Middle Class: The Role of Marketers and Latino Think Tanks

We need to start with the marketing industry which, dependent as it is on advertising monies, has been a leading force in projecting Latinos' buying power and their middle-class status. This has been in direct contrast with the appeals of Latino politicians and scholars whose assessments have necessarily and predictably been more dire, though as I note here, there have also been noticeable changes in their positions. Marketers, however, have always pushed for Latinos' buying power, and for the existence of what the Euro RSCG Latino advertising firm has recently termed the Hispanic "prosumer," the proactive, affluent, and influential Latino whose behaviors evidence future consumer trends. Even brokerage firms such as Merrill Lynch are now targeting the "rapidly growing Hispanic middle and upper class," a far cry from the basic food and personal item product companies that have historically targeted Latinos (Rifkin 1999).

Indeed, the entire business of Hispanic marketing has been central to the concept of the "Hispanic market" and of Hispanics as a people with spending money, not just as the downward poor. Since the early 1960s, this task has been primarily undertaken by native-born, educated, middle-class Mexican Americans in the West, and by Cuban marketing entrepreneurs arriving in New York post–Castro's revolution who founded the first Hispanic advertising agencies. And not unlike today, this task was invested with demands for inclusion and equal participation in the economy. As I note elsewhere, this was the case with the Cuban entrepreneurs who lacked direct experience with U.S. racism prior to their arrival and were quick to project their own middle-class identity onto a newly emergent "Hispanic market" as part of their own claims to belonging as non-minorities in this country. It was also the case with second- and third-generation middle-class Mexican Americans eager to challenge the discrimination that tainted their status. Jesus Chavarria, who founded *Hispanic Business* in 1979, spoke to this when explaining his rationale for founding the magazine:

I knew there was a Hispanic middle class since the 1950s cause there were lawyers, doctors, merchants who had a clear standing but that standing was always affected by this issue of status and civil rights; and this translated into the 60s and 70s which was the first time there was a national consciousness of being Hispanic in America. This prompted me to do a publication that addressed Hispanic issues beyond identity and social services. My concern was how do we become stakeholders in this country. How do we become entrepreneurs? Thus from its inception HB was all about the middle class. It described the struggle of a community that had achieved increased well being and wanted to become part of society, and make that society realize their contribution to the common well and wealth of the nation.

Through their many articles highlighting growing trends in the income, education, and occupational status of Latinos, *Hispanic Business* would indeed be at the forefront of projecting the image of the middle-class Latino. This was important to challenge the view that Latinos are an economic burden, the same view that has long constituted a rationale for challenging immigration and Latinos. Still, it was not until 1994 that it dedicated an issue to the coming out of the "silent minority," confronting the national focus on working-class, new immigrant, primarily Spanish-language Hispanics by highlighting the "silent minority" with enough power to exert influence in national and international politics (Zate 1994).

A similar impetus for recognition and empowerment was also behind one of the first major studies on the Latino middle class, "The Latino Middle Class: Myth, Reality and Potential," conducted by the Tomas Rivera Policy Institute (TRPI), another highly influential Latino think tank. The study was funded by Univision, the largest Spanish TV network and one of the most influential players in defining the parameters of the Hispanic market, under its former president Henry Cisneros, whose connections as former secretary of housing helped secure additional corporate sponsors. The project presented TRPI an opportunity to challenge anti-immigrant arguments and policies as Proposition 187, by neutralizing anti-immigrant sentiment with evidence that Latinos were doing well and moving up, and consequently, that there was little cause for mainstream society's concern. Univision, for its part, gained "objective" research from a nonpartisan think tank documenting the strength of the Latino consumer it could now quote in its marketing pitches. Commercial and policy interests came harmoniously together, if for different reasons.

This confluence of corporate and nonprofit advocacy interests marks an important development in the processes of shaping contemporary representations of Latinidad. It is evident in the involvement of Latino marketers as "experts" in national presidential campaigns, and in the growing co-sponsorship of research by private corporations, especially in the growing involvement of Univision in polls and research, as in the 2004 *Washington Post*/Univision/TRPI poll on Latino voters or in NALEO's Latino voter mobilization project, or in the Tomas Rivera Institute Research on Latinos' TV viewing habits. Not that corporate sponsorship of Latino advocacy organization is new. By the 1970s, companies such as Coors Brewery, Sears, and Exxon were actively involved in Hispanic organizations, such as the League of United Latin American Citizens, known as LULAC (Marquez 1993). What is new is the growing importance of the corporate sector in light of diminishing funding by government and private foundations. Also new is the larger political and economic context favoring emphasis on upwardly mobile constituencies, at the cost of the working poor. All the while, even the most auspicious-sounding report

states that when taken as a group, Latinos are still overwhelmingly working and lower middle class, that the poor almost tripled during the same
time there was a growth in the Latino middle class, and that the gap between Latino households and all U.S. households has actually widened
during the same period.

Granted, Latinos have always been more heterogeneous than their
public representations. Whatever its size, a Latino middle class has always existed, though it has been largely understudied and absent from
public view. The issue, then, is not whether middle-class Latinos exist
and are thriving, but rather, why are we hearing so much about an ever-
present segment of the Latino population, and most significantly to what
end. Indeed, we know that Mexican-American elites in the Southwest
have long represented themselves as Hispanics to distinguish themselves
from the poor Mexican immigrants, while we have read important accounts of how middle- and upper-middle-class Cubans have been fueling
Miami's economy for decades (Portes and Stepic 1993; Montejano 1987).
Middle-class Latinos have also been behind the founding of advocacy
institutions and organizations projecting a strong middle-class stance to
challenge their subordination and stake a rightful place in mainstream
society. One of the oldest political organizations, LULAC, founded in
1929, was in fact the product of middle-class Mexican Americans intent on asserting their entitlements as citizens of the United States, an
accommodating stance that also involved their distancing themselves
from Mexican immigrants (Marquez 1993). A similar accommodating
stance characterized other Mexican-American organizations, akin to
the outlook of some Puerto Rican organizations of the same period in
the East.[1] In other words, geographical and historical differences aside,
efforts at distinguishing and defining a Latino middle class have been
abiding, especially as a means of challenging Latinos' status as foreign
and un-American irrespective of their achievements, gains, and citizenship status.

The radicalization of Latino social movements in the 1960s and 1970s,
however, would dramatically center poverty, economic and political enfranchisement, and self-determination in the national Latino agenda.
Still, an accommodating stance was never altogether abandoned. After
all, ethnic advocacy organizations have never operated free from mainstream society nor government and private funding sources, a position
that would undoubtedly limit their critique of the economic and political structures of mainstream society. This explains why many of the civil

rights organizations founded in the late 1960s, such as MALDEF and NCLR, have been accused of elitism and have been criticized for their dependency on government and corporate interests and for emphasizing Latinos' rights rather than the much-needed economic and political transformations (Marquez 2003). These tensions were evident in the highly corporate-sponsored annual conferences of the National Council of La Raza that I attended in 2005 and 2006. Then, it was not uncommon to find delegates openly frustrated with multiple interests as varied as the U.S. Marines, political parties, the Mexican government, and major corporations that gather there to sing Latinos' praises. The corporate-inscribed pens, note pads, mugs, and other freebies laid out at the elaborate luncheon tables were simply not enough to curb my luncheon partners' frustration; their local constituencies did not quite match the glossy images so lauded by the speakers during their "Latino love fest" luncheon speeches.

The political movements of the late 1960s and 1970s, however, unavoidably instilled a renewed activism around community and working-class empowerment, foregrounding poverty into the Latino political agenda as never before. The Great Society programs of the times also contributed to this trend by helping to turn poverty and social programs into a political commodity. Indeed, the range of social programs and resources associated with the Great Society may have had limited effects on structural economic transformations, and may have functioned more to regulate and govern, rather than to empower the poor. But they also provided invaluable resources for Latinos and other minorities. In the then primarily Puerto Rican New York City's East Harlem, Great Society programs strengthened a bourgeoning Puerto Rican middle class, while leading to the rise of minority power blocks around the control of government funds (Sanchez 2007). One result is that government funds created incentives for consolidating "poverty" and marginality, though not necessarily for fostering a critical working-class politics into the Latino political agenda.[2]

Also contributing to the politicization of Latino poverty at this time was the onset of university programs in Chicano and Puerto Rican— now Latino—studies. After all, these programs were the direct product of social struggles for inclusion and representation in the academy, and exposing inequalities and bringing about social equality were seen as part of this mission. Let us remember that by this juncture, Latino poverty had long been pathologized through numerous "culture of poverty" arguments and was in dire need of critical analysis to account for the historical and structural inequalities that produced it. Within the nascent Chicano, Puerto Rican, and later Latino studies programs, pedagogy and research were therefore necessarily tied to a larger social equity agenda. Interestingly, despite the considerable amount of research on the Latino working class and the poor, there would be a dearth of scholarly attention in the documentation and research of issues related to class differentiation among Latinos. This is in sharp contrast to the African-American studies literature, where the black middle class has been the subject of more consistent scholarly attention; a disparity I believe is linked to the historical hyper-privileging of "culture" and language as defining elements of Latinidad.[3] There had been important studies that examined the Mexican middle class in the Southwest, and some of Cubans, whose preferred immigrant status soon made them synonymous with middle- and upper-class Latinos. But in general, if Latinos and class were discussed, it was the working class, if not the poor, that was assumed to be the norm.

The result was a monolithic "imagined working-class community" where differences around gender, sexual preferences, race, and class were largely subjugated as part of what Tomas Ybarra-Frausto has termed the necessary strategic essentialism of the times (1999). In an interview, he recalled the pressures exerted on him and the generation of college-educated Chicanos coming of age in the 1960s by the romanticization of the working class, "We all felt great pressure to be cholos because the only identity that was legitimate was that of the rural or urban poor. And people felt guilty to be middle class. We ended up sabotaging our own mobility." There were consequences with this trend, he noted. In his view, alliances with upwardly mobile groups that would lead to a stronger movement were never fostered, while class suspicions were aggravated by the politics of racial authenticity.

The hegemony of this Latino monolithic "imagined working-class community" explains the uproar created by two of the most important works speaking about or on behalf of the Latino middle class from the 1980s onward: Richard Rodriguez's *Hunger of Memory* (1982), and Linda Chavez's *Out of the Barrio: Toward a New Politics of Hispanic Assimilation* (1991). Both personal and autobiographical, these works differed in tone and political repercussion. Rodriguez's indigenous "brownness" has always tempered his views about assimilation; and in his latest book "Brown" maintains a firm eye on the trilogy of class, ethnicity, and race; while Chavez still prides herself in her conservative assimilationist views and in being "the most hated Hispanic in America," a tag incorporated into the title of her latest autobiography. Rodriguez's work is rife with pain, the pain of becoming distanced from his family and culture by formal education, the pain of misrecognition, and the clash between his upwardly mobile disposition and his status as "underprivileged" minority student. Chavez, less reflective of her own ascent, takes shots at the entire Latino advocacy system that facilitated her mobility. What these works shared was a critique of the caging of Hispanic identity around narrow conventions of authenticity espoused at the time. Both espoused the view that empowerment can only come through assimilation, and both censure Latinos' culture and the Spanish language as culprits for their ghettoization. As such, these books were immediately controversial. Puerto Rican intellectuals, in particular, were especially angered at Chavez's representation of their community as "the Puerto Rican exception," the group whose poverty challenged all rational explanations, leaving only them to blame for their status.[4]

Controversies aside, these authors were extremely influential in challenging orthodoxies of Latinidad—the notion that true Latinos are always liberal, poor, needy, etc.—opening up the door to numerous exposés on the emerging middle class. Even critics of these works I spoke with credited them with opening discussion on the Latino middle class throughout the 1990s, marking a turn away from dominant representations by both the mainstream press and most Latino advocates and scholars. Henry Pachon, president of TRPI, identified additional factors that fueled this turn, among them the booming 1990s economy and the growth of the Latino population. But most important, he attributed the budding attention to the middle class to a growing intolerance among Latino middle-class researchers with the stereotypical and unilateral portrayal of Latinos as poverty-stricken. This last point is worth underscoring: the very middle-class background, or current middle-class status, of most Latino researchers, journalists, and other Latinologists speaking for or on behalf of Latinos. At odds with dominant representations of Latinos as needy and poor, middle-class writers have been especially prone to the "corrective image mode" in order to correct images in which they simply do not recognize themselves, and that many blame for their subordination.

Indeed, the problem of self-image was identified by the veteran civil rights activist and former president of the NCLR, Raul Yzaguirre, as the greatest challenge of his 30-year career with the organization. During an interview at La Raza's 2006 meeting, he explained his struggle to correct Latinos' image and the awe such corrective images invariably produced. As he noted:

We have to understand and internalize that Hispanics are the hardest working of Americans, the most patriotic of Americans, the most family oriented and entrepreneurial of Americans. Everything that is supposed to be uniquely American we embody. We originated these arguments a long time ago and I'm happy that they are being picked up but they are not picked up enough. The average American does not hear these arguments. When I make them to an Anglo audience they say, wow! They are surprised to learn that Hispanics have higher participation in the labor force, that they work more hours per week. These are surprising facts.

In his view, Latinos had to internalize these more positive representations, and the world of advocacy had to be at the vanguard of creating a paradigm shift in how Latinos are represented and talked about.

The shift to the Latino middle class should additionally be seen in relation to larger trends in the world of advocacy and social policy. After the disbanding of social welfare for Welfare to Work Programs in 1996, public policy think tanks saw poverty literally fall from grace as a policy issue that could garner funding support. José Garcia, a senior researcher at Demos, a New York City–based non–partisan policy think tank, explained: "The working and the middle class became easier to sell after the 1990s. There were new buzzwords in the world of policy and advocacy and all programs had to deal with 'entrepreneurship,' with 'access' and 'asset' building." Thus, by the 1990s, the more "legitimate," though equally filled-with-spin world of policy think tanks, would join marketers in producing influential studies and exposés on the Latino middle class. Produced by more legitimate nonpartisan and noncommercial sources, these studies lent greater legitimacy to the existence of a middle class, attracting the immediate attention of the mainstream press. In particular, in 1996 the Los Angeles–based pundit and commentator Gregory Rodriguez authored "The Emerging Latino Middle Class" for the Pepperdine University Institute for Public Policy with the sponsorship of AT&T and other individual and corporate sponsors, followed by the already mentioned groundbreaking study, "The Latino Middle Class: Myth, Reality and Potential" (2001), by the Tomas Rivera Policy Institute.

Rodriguez's study was especially influential. It was covered nationwide by major newspapers, such as the *Los Angeles Times*, the *New York Times*, the *Washington Post*, the *Wall Street Journal* and others, while earning him accolades from *The Economist* for "decisively changing the understanding of the Latino experience in the United States."[5] This was so, even when the study was intentionally focused on middle-class Latinos in Southern California and was not meant to provide a picture of Latinos nationwide! Indeed, as we shall see later, the fact is that while these studies' executive summary and conclusions on the Latino middle class highlight progress and upward mobility, upon closer scrutiny they all show a more complex picture, because the story is unavoidably more complex. However, this is not at all how these studies were received and covered by the mainstream press, and, we could safely assume, by the wider public. Furthermore, seldom were the gains of the Latino middle class compared with that of other groups. What was emphasized instead is the overall improvement in their status, consistently described as "remarkable." Whether this media coverage represents complicity with the current penchant for stories of peoples' consumer value, or is a matter of simplicity–the simplicity demanded by the parameters of media coverage, especially of Latinos—is hard to say. The striking point is that these reports were enthusiastically received by the mainstream press, with headlines always confidently positive of Latinos' coming of age: "Latinos in California: the Next Italians (*Economist* 1996); "More Hispanic Households in the U.S. Are Joining Middle Class, Study Says" (*Wall Street Journal* 2001); "Southern California's Boom Is Latino-Led; Rising Middle Class Spearheads Region's Economic and Cultural Transformation" (*Washington Post* 1997); "Latinos Can Look to an Italian Legacy" (*Los Angeles Times* 1996); "Latinos to Shed Minority Status" (*Daily News of Los Angeles* 2004); "Hispanic as Victim Label Is Inaccurate" (*San Antonio Express* 2001).

During a phone interview, Rodriguez expressed his surprise and pleasure with the reception of his study. Echoing what I was told by other middle-class Latino writers and researchers, he was frustrated with the deficits and dysfunctions framework that has characterized most Latino research. He had lived through the transformations of Southern California and felt that no one was looking into the social mobility achieved by an important and largely overlooked sector of the Latino community. Hence his report acknowledges Latino poverty. No report can hide this fact, especially among the foreign-born. But his primary motivation was to shift the debate about Latinos away from their dysfunctions to their contributions, and most important to counter the dominant view of Latinos as poor, uneducated, and unassimilated to U.S. society by highlighting their political and economic coming of age. Indeed, this is a view that he continues to promote through numerous studies, editorials, commentaries, and research reports, as evidenced by the following headlines: "From

Newcomers to New Americans: The Successful Integration of Immigrants into American Society" (a publication for the National Immigration Forum, 1999); "Latinos: No Longer Society's Victims" (LAT 2002); "Suburbia Gains an Accent" (LAT 2003); "150 Years Later, Latinos Finally Hit the Mainstream (NYT 2001); and "Why We're the New Irish" in *Newsweek* magazine, among others. In these reports Latinos are shown moving up, intermarrying with whites, joining the mainstream, and in less need of affirmative action and protective policies. Latinos are unjustly seen as a "minority," goes the thinking; rather, they should be seen as an immigrant group that is unavoidably slated to join the mainstream.

Even international research organizations such as RAND Corporation have joined the fore. With the headline "Rand study shows Hispanic immigrants move up economic, educational ladder as quickly as other immigrant groups," Rand's website announces the study of James Smith, one of its chief economists, arguing that there is no reason to be pessimistic about Hispanics' assimilation and mobility; that they are more than well positioned to reproduce the experience of European immigrants (Smith 2003). Isolating Latinos across generations, the study shows educational gains among Latinos that would not be evident if different generational cohorts had been combined. But can we truly compare Latinos' mobility to that of European immigrants based on their generational educational gains? I doubt that the numbers of years of education in the 1900s and in today's highly technical and symbolic economy can be so easily compared in terms of economic outcomes. Perhaps "Want assimilation? Improve schools" would have made an equally if not more appropriate headline.

Exposés on the Latino middle class, however, have not ceased to be controversial. For one, just as the earlier emphasis on poverty cemented an "imagined working-class Latino community" in the public imagination, the stress on middle-class Latinos is equally implicated in another essentializing move. After all, whether we are talking about the poor or the middle class, we are nevertheless talking about an undifferentiated conglomerate–Latinos, whose treatment as such presupposes essentialized statements about an entire group of people, be it around one class identity or another.

This predicament explains the public stir over TRPI's 2001 study. When it was first released, this study became one of the most highly circulated in the media, attracting accolades for bringing attention to a long silenced story, but also receiving many criticisms. A critic who spoke to me in anonymity said that this study represented the "corporatization" of Latino policy think tanks, not only because it represented a corporate-sponsored research, but because of the greater marketability of conducting research on the middle class. In other words, this is research that, in addition to a social policy value, had a distinct marketing value, especially for corporate America, the media, and potential advertisers. Yet production of more "marketable" research was seen to pose risks to the autonomy and legitimacy of Latino think tanks.

Henry Pachon, director of the TRPI, is fully aware of these concerns. He himself has marveled at the circulation of his studies and the commercial ends that they may serve. As he explained, the TRPI website lists a variety of publicly downloadable reports focusing on all areas of Latino advocacy, from health to education. As of 2006, however, the most downloaded report was "El Sueño de su casa: The Homeownership Potential of Mexican American Families" (2004), a study funded by the mortgage lender Freddie Mac, whose popularity Pachon attributed to the growing interest in the Latino market among mortgage lenders and people in the home ownership industry. I could not help but wonder whether readers were following TRPI's prompts to find solutions to current obstacles in Latino homeownership identified in the report, or whether it was predatory lenders who are aggressively targeting Latinos who were coveting the study.[6] I wondered, well aware that it is industries interested in tapping the Latino market that often emerge as the major financial supporters and consumers of the research and educational events organized by many policy think tanks. A case in point is TRPI's spring 2007 conference, "Growth Strategies for Corporate America: Increasing Wealth in the Latino Community." The conference gathered some of the top corporate, financial, and Hispanic community–oriented companies "to shed light and discuss the needs of the next significantly affluent generation in America" and was marketed and specifically recommended to "senior executives in the banking, finance, and real estate industries."[7]

The point is that corporate/research collaborations are not without contention. They can increase the impact of a particular study, but not without raising concerns about the autonomy of Latino think tanks or the efficacy of Latino advocacy. This is particularly true when economic and social lags and needs identified in particular studies are overshadowed by interpretations of achievement and progress or economic opportunities, in ways that limit the efficacy of Latino research. This impasse strikes at the crux of the matter. For the issue is not whether a Latino middle class exists, but rather the fact that its exposure is so unavoidably politicized.

Because they constitute too much of a political and economically sought after base, their treatment is inescapably loaded with social consequences for all Latinos.

The Politics of Region, Citizenship, and Class

Before turning to these questions, I want to reflect on the relative dominance of Western and Southwestern–based Mexican-American intellectuals, pundits, and entrepreneurs in bringing the Latino middle class to public attention. In part, this is to be expected, considering Mexican Americans' longer history in these areas, and subsequently their greater numbers and longer history of class polarization and diversification. This history informs the growth of Latino middle-class hubs where Latinos currently outnumber whites, like those that Rodriguez saw develop in Southern California and whose existence he was so keen to expose in his study. In contrast, we cannot talk about a Cuban enclave in South Florida until after 1959, whereas in the Northeast, Latino middle-class enclaves are a much more recent phenomenon, fed primarily by out-migration and resettlement from urban centers like New York (Torres 2006).

The preponderance of Western-based interlocutors of the Latino middle class, however, points also to important regional differences with regard to the interplay of citizenship and class. Namely, I believe that it points to a key standby for signifying class: citizenship status. Class differences obviously have been at play among Puerto Rican immigrants in New York. But as a primarily working-class immigration of colonial citizens, class differences were less exacerbated by differences in citizenship status, at least during the city's first Latinization era composed almost primarily of Puerto Ricans. In other words, whether poor, working class, middle class, educated, or recently arrived, Puerto Ricans have come to this country as citizens, however compromised that citizenship may have turned out to be. For their part, it is well known that the first large wave of Cuban immigrants were primarily middle and upper class, that is, considerably homogenous in terms of class and level of education. Although they lacked American citizenship, they were welcomed as political immigrants, affording them access to an expedited path to citizenship. In other words, not until the large-scale immigration of South and Central Americans, and most recently of Mexicans from the 1980s onward, would citizenship status emerge as a potential axis of differentiation among the first Latino migration waves to the Eastern United States.[8] The case of

Dominicans merits qualification, given that their shared Caribbean background with Puerto Ricans provided a buffer to their citizenship status, at least at first—many could and did pass for Puerto Ricans. In contrast, class and citizenship have been inexorably linked in the West, where the constant flow of undocumented immigration has long represented a consistent threat to the citizenship and status claim of the U.S.-born and the upwardly mobile (Gutierrez 1995).

The point here is that the extent of class polarization, and the meaning of class among Latinos, and hence the interest in studying the middle class, cannot be analyzed independently of the level of immigration and diversification of Latino populations in particular locations. That is, issues of nationality, class, race, citizenship status, and generational differences, and the accompanying issues of authenticity and legitimacy that are always triggered by these variables, are inexorably tied to social hierarchies. I am referring here to the "just when we're becoming upward mobile here comes a new round of newcomers to taint our image as foreign, undocumented, Spanish speaking and poor" threat that immigration represents, not solely to mainstream society's "Americanness" but to the Americanness and the very image of the upwardly mobile Latino. Add to this the disregard of the U.S.-born Latino often held by recent immigrants with respect to issues of cultural pollution and authenticity, and we could then begin to appreciate the many factors straining the relationship between class and immigration status. I'm referring here to beliefs about the levels of cultural capital, ability, and cultural sensibilities and propensity that each group (immigrant and U.S.-born) has often associated with each other and how it is believed to affect ideas of who is more or less able to achieve middle-class status.

The concern from Puerto Rican leaders about the report on Puerto Rican poverty at the start of this chapter provides a good example of this. As I soon learned, these reactions were most of all informed by the abundance of negative images of themselves that Puerto Ricans have to confront on a daily basis, which had become especially common since the 1990s, simultaneous to the growing diversification of the city's Latino population. In this context, these images are not only circulated by the mainstream, but increasingly, by other Latinos intent on staking a higher claim in the city's ethnic order of Latinidad by differentiating themselves from Puerto Ricans and increasingly from Dominicans. As explained by an editor of *El Diario-La Prensa*, which received numerous complaints about how Puerto Ricans were portrayed in the PRLDEF's study:

We're no longer alone in New York and people come here with bias against Puerto Ricans. We don't need our institutions to say we're poor when we already have Colombians and Venezuelans and Argentineans with this bias against Puerto Ricans. When Puerto Ricans are being trashed there's a lot of pressure and we're put in the defense. How could we be poorer when we have been here the longest, is what people think. I've been in the same room with newcomers who say to my face that "los puertorriqueños matan el espanol" (Puerto Ricans kill the Spanish language). The only comfort for us is that there are also Dominicans if not we'd be the only ones being dumped.

The editor's comments point to important variables involved in class and status differentiation, and to the contexts that lead to their expression and politicization. Indeed, as many approaches to class analyses exist, we know that class is not only a matter of economic standing, but also of the cultural capital or competencies some groups are seen to be able to wrest or not on the basis of their background, occupation, histories, and consumer power. We know that there is an injury to class, making its perception an extremely slippery concept; and that we humans, as status-deciphering machines, are forever coming up with new codes for reading and masking it.[9] Among Latinos, variables as diverse as nationality or citizenship status complicate the picture, not to mention that class allotments are sometimes regionally specific and can vary situationally.[10] In other words, the hierarchies drawn around economic and cultural capital in the Southwest, or along the border, or in New York City, are often specific to the ethnic and migration status of the makeup of the Latino populations in these regions and cannot be so easily equated with each other. Similarly, as I've discussed elsewhere, cultural and economic capital are often inverted among foreign- and native-born Latinos—foreign-born immigrants, who are the most economically vulnerable, are also presented in mainstream discourse as the most equipped for upward mobility because of their immigrant aspirational stance and greater conservatism and hence supposed complicity with the status quo.

This is all to say that it is not solely the upper-class Latino who is presented as conservative or as having the most cultural capital—the stereotype of the rich Cuban immigrant comes to mind here—but also the most modest recent arrival, if for different reasons. Put simply, social hierarchies among Latinos are messy at best. Awareness that our views and living experiences of class are informed by our own position, and by the contexts we maneuver, should at least make us acknowledge that encompassing reports of a homogenous Latino middle class will never be revealing nor enough.

Defining the Slippery Object

With this warning, reports on class status are most often statistically driven and hence necessarily unconcerned with people's experiences of class. Who then falls statistically within the Latino middle class? The first thing to keep in mind is that while the U.S. census has formulas to define poverty according to thresholds of income and family size and ages of members, there is nevertheless no official definition of the "middle class," a most convenient omission feeding the ideological dominance of the middle class as constitutive of American identity. This is one of the reasons why it is often said that class in America is simply "a state of mind." For instance, while in 2002 the median household income was $42,409, with the middle 20 percent of the country earning between $40,000 and $95,000 a year, a study by the National Opinion Research Center quoted in the *Washington Times* found that 50 percent of Americans with annual family income of $20,000 to $40,000 called themselves "working class" or "middle class," as did 38 percent of individuals with family incomes of $40,000 to $60,000 and 16.8 percent with family incomes of more than $110,000 annually (Baker 2003). More recent polls confirm these findings. The *New York Times* 2005 series on class found that 45 percent of respondents felt they had improved class standing since growing up. Only 1 percent and 7 percent described themselves as upper and lower class respectively. The majority was in the "middle" (Scott and Leonhardt 2005). It is obvious then that class is not solely about income, but that variables as diverse as location, region, family size, education levels, and profession, not to mention the much less studied variables of race, ethnicity, and gender, continuously affect people's self-positioning as "middle class."

In addition to the factors mentioned above, it is also especially important to account for the transnational experiences and the different reference frames that foreign-born immigrants sometimes bring to bear when defining class identities in the United States. As put forth in the evocative statements of an unnamed immigrant informant in Philip Rodriguez's 2004 documentary "Los Angeles Now": "In this country, there are only two classes, the upper class and the middle class. But there are no poor. Because here if one works you have the right to an apartment.

No poor

The apartment by law has carpet, air conditioning, heat, stove, refrigerator and with a little bit of sacrifice, with ten dollars at a garage sale you can find a TV. And with a little more sacrifice, a little car. That's a rich man's life in Latin America." This statement is revealing on many fronts—first for showing the different definitions for measuring class that exist among immigrants and U.S.-born Latinos—who would certainly demand a lot more than a second-hand TV set to define themselves as middle class—and second, for anchoring class so clearly with modern consumption. In fact, if anything has made class "a state of mind," it is contemporary consumption, affected by the availability of cheap consumer goods and credit, which aggressively sustain the belief that there are "no poor."

This may explain the little outrage and public attention attracted by the declining lifestyle and shrinking status of the middle class, all the while the comforts long associated with middle-class status—such as owning a home, sending kids to college, saving for retirement—increasingly disappear. Their foe is the much publicized outsourcing, unemployment and underemployment, and escalating prices for gas, shelter, and health care fueled by privatization policies which continue to affect people's chances for upward mobility. In other words, upward mobility is more difficult today than ever, as we were recently told by three special reports on the middle class by the *New York Times*, the *LA Times*, and the *Wall Street Journal* (Gosselin 2004; Scott and Leonhardt 2005). Why, then, we must ask, is the Latino middle class being touted as "vibrant" and growing at the very same time that "squeezed" and "disappearing" are much more accurate tags for the "middle class"? This to me is the relevant question, that emphasis on this subsector of the Latino population would come at the very time that the middle-class status of all households is least secure and most predicated on debt and credit. This issue is quite central because, while family income may have risen, so has credit card debt, and the cost of credit, especially among minority families (Silva and Epstein 2005). Headlines on how minorities were most affected by the subprime loan scandal are quite familiar. Indeed, it is unquestionable that income and education levels have risen throughout the years. It is the disparities that remain unchanged and continue to widen, and make the concept of middle class questionable at best, that need to be critically challenged.

Noteworthy spin on the Latino middle class emerges from studies that measure it according to household rather than individual income, veiling the fact that the Latino middle class is made up less of individuals' upward mobility than of households' resource and labor pooling. Income definitions have also varied, but generally studies use the median income for all U.S. households as the threshold for defining the Latino middle class. Thus, the TRPI study defined the Latino middle class in 2001 as those households with incomes above $40,000, a cutoff approximating the average U.S. household income in 1998. Two years later, *Hispanic Business* defined the middle class as ranging from about $32,600 to $81,500, figures drawn from doubling the poverty threshold income for Latinos in 2002 at the lower end, and multiplying it five times to get to the higher figure (*Hispanic Business* 2003). In other words, what is increasingly defined as the Latino middle class is never too far from the median household earnings for all U.S. households; except that this income is more stretched in the average Latino household, which averages 3.4 persons as opposed to 2.4 persons for non-Hispanic households (Consumer Expenditure Survey 2001). What is more, while the Latino middle class has grown, so have poor and working-class Latino sectors. Despite its enthusiastic coverage in the mainstream press, the Tomas Rivera study, for instance, is explicit in showing that while middle-class Latino households grew almost 80 percent from 1979 to 1989, from 1.5 to 2.7 million, the number of households at the poverty level more than doubled from 1.2 in 1979 to 2.6 in 1998, a factor attributed to immigration. And let's not forget about location. While Latinos' residential patterns have diversified, they are still largely concentrated in major urban centers, where living costs are higher, and housing entirely prohibitive, as any "middle-class" New Yorker can readily attest.

Indeed, when comparing the Latino and white middle classes, studies invariably show that the gap between Latino and white households achieving middle-class status has actually increased. The Tomas Rivera Study on the Latino middle class shows that 60 percent of Anglo households had achieved middle-class status compared to 40 percent of Latino; while income disparities between Latinos and all U.S. households widened during the same period (TRPI 2001: 1).

Who then is the Latino middle class? The fact is that by desegregating the U.S.-born Latinos from the immigrants, a different picture emerges. The TRPI states that U.S.-born Latinos have 30 percent higher incomes and two to three years' more schooling than immigrants. And upon closer examination, there is even great diversity among U.S.-born subgroups: "U.S. born Cubans and Central and South Americans meet or exceed the education levels of Whites, whereas even third-generation Mexican Americans have high school dropout rates double or triple those of Anglos" (p.

2). Likewise, the greatest percentages in income growth were seen among Latinos in the highest income brackets. A similar picture emerges from the study *Hispanic Business* conducted in 2003, where Latinos are described as a "young set, wealthier and more numerous than ever," though closer reading again shows disparities in the incomes of the U.S.-born and immigrant Latino, and great disparities in the education and income levels of some subgroups (*Hispanic Business* 2003). In other words, the stratification Latinos are undergoing is not very different than that which exists in the entire population, where we see the fastest growth at the higher levels of income, and a widening of the gap between the have-tons, the have-some, and the have-very-little. It is therefore important that variables of citizenship, region, race, and nationality be added to this picture if a full picture of the Latino middle class is to ever emerge.

Warning: Succeed at Your Own Peril

As seen, Latinos' class diversification has finally come to light, complicating their continued treatment as a homogenous aggregate. And contrary to how the Latino population has long been described, there are sectors that are moving up, while some are moving far faster than others. A recent study on "The Wealth of Hispanic Households: 1996-2002" by the Pew Hispanic Center confirmed these disparities when it pointed out that while "Hispanic households have less than ten cents for every dollar in wealth owned by white households . . . the wealthiest 25 percent of Hispanic and Black Households own 93 percent of the total wealth of each group" (Kochhar 2004). The study is particularly important because it looks at a moment of economic downturn, the 2001 recession, and exposes the extreme vulnerability of Latinos' middle-class status, due to its very little net worth.

But I do not want to end this chapter with bad news. What I meant to examine are the positive prospects and upward mobility that many Latinos are unavoidably achieving. Indeed, who does not like to revel in good news? What individual who is successful, and goes through the day encountering images of upward mobility among our people, would prefer studies and portraits of poverty and economic failure? I have talked to enough marketers and pundits to know that dreams and aspirations are always in; talk of poverty and injustice is always a downer. Still, I would like to conclude by suggesting that unabashed enthusiasm over the upwardly mobile Latino is premature and problematic. The obvious reason is that it naturalizes as normal what remains an out-of-reach dream for so many. Another is that underplaying economic inequalities may leave us with less rather than more middle-class people in years to come.

But, most important, I want to call attention to some messages that are implicit within current discussions of the Latino middle class. As stated, study after study of the Latino middle class reminds us that Latinos are moving up and making remarkable progress economically and educationally. It is the continuous arrival of poor immigrants with no education and few skills that skews their progress, invariably bringing down statistics for all Latinos. First, it is important to not lose sight of the divisive anti-immigrant sentiments that may be triggered by these findings, which feed into the same fears latent among many upwardly mobile Latinos; the sentiment that their upward mobility and Americanness is continually threatened by newcomers "tainting" their image. These sentiments are alive and well, and are behind the growing support for anti-immigrant measures by Latinos and non-Latinos alike. This is a message that perpetuates existing divides along citizenship status, lengths of stay, and achievement among Latinos while erasing the larger social and economic policies that affect the relative mobility of all.

The most troublesome problem, however, is that matters of race and ethnicity are effectively erased within discussion of class and mobility among Latinos. Statistically based and driven, they divorce Latinos from the everyday experience of class and status. Dynamics such as those I repeatedly observed among middle-class Puerto Ricans in East Harlem remain in the background. As documented in *Barrio Dreams*, Puerto Rican development enthusiasts failed to benefit from their communities' "development" in ways similar to whites and non-raced developers. They were repeatedly confronted with the fact that their education and middle-class "status" was tempered by a "tainted" heritage that made it difficult for them to cash in on their culture, or promote Puerto Rican tourism in the area. In other words, hierarchies of race and ethnicity continue to complicate the prospects of a Latino middle class to begin with. And it is only by acknowledging, not by denying or underplaying these hierarchies in our studies, that we can better assess the meaning of upward mobility for Latinos and other ethnic minorities in this country.

The problem is that many of the studies on the Latino middle class have the unfortunate if unintended consequences of dismissing racism and discrimination as a thing of the past, for they show that it is not discrimination that keeps people down. If you isolate native-born Latinos, you'll see them moving up the ladder in ways analogous to the progress enjoyed by former European immigrants. As said earlier, conflating the economic, social, and cultural contexts faced by old and new immigrants is extremely problematic. The flows, continuity, and extent of immigration are different, as are the racial and ethnic backgrounds of immigrants, the economic conditions and labor markets encountered among other variables debated by sociologists (Alba and Nee 2003). All of these variables are obviated when we apply the European immigrant analogy to Latinos. Emphasis on middle-class Latinos also requires that we subtract almost 40 percent of the total Latino population who are immigrants to uphold the reality of this construct. In other words, immigrants are again used as the scapegoat and the main impediment to a true appreciation of Latinos' upward mobility, displacing the myriad issues that affect Latinos' incorporation into the new economy, not to mention everyone's chances for upward mobility. Most notably, this story of upward mobility entirely obviates discrimination as Latinos are conflated with Europeans—all we need to do is once again factor out the immigrants!

Ultimately then, the coming of age and public recognition of Latino middle classes is a welcomed and much needed development. It is about time that we acknowledge this long missing segment of the Latino population, of which we have much more to learn about its attitudes, directions, and sentiments, and not solely as an aggregate statistic, but as a living reality. But we also must be cautious about how middle-class Latinos are discussed and the ends for which they are celebrated in the current context, where there is less and less room for even raising issues of equity; where only positively spun stories can be told. So we must determine how we can best acknowledge the upward mobility of some, without ever ignoring that discussion of a "Latino middle class" operates in a larger field where the very possibility of a middle class as a living and accessible reality is rapidly and assuredly being narrowed.

2

Latinos: "The New Republicans (They Just Don't Know It)"

> In Hispanic immigrants we are absorbing immigrants who are easily assimilable—Westerners, Christians, and capitalists who appreciate the value of a free and law-based society.
>
> —Leslie Sanchez (2007)

Are Latinos America's scapegoats, or the belle of the ball? For two years now, the immigration debate has dominated public discussion of Latinos: Brown faces are out there. Immigration and Latinos represent what is wrong with America. We must do something—Now. With the coming 2008 presidential election, however, Latinos emerge as the belle of the ball. We are told that Latinos are the swingiest of the swing voters: the one decisive constituency. Pundits claim that, unlike African Americans, Latinos are not married to any political party. Anyone can get them.

By now, arguments about how Latinos voted in the 2008 presidential elections are likely on the rise, as are theories about what their voting trends suggest about Latinos' character, values, and political dispositions. The democratic primaries gave ample evidence of this trend when Latinos were deemed racist if they voted for Clinton and sexist if they supported Obama. I suspect that similar sweeping arguments will be forming by the publication of this book, and in circulation for years to come. This chapter suggests that such arguments are most productively seen as public spin rather than as statements about the complexity of Latinos' aspirations and realities, and that they are most revealing of the contradictory place that Latinos are increasingly given in the public imagination as America's political darlings and scapegoats. Such is the case when Latinos become the embodiment of what, depending on where we stand in the political spectrum, we may fear and praise most in the American electorate, whether it is patriotism, family values, conservatism, racism, and so forth. Put simply, I suggest that praise and censure of the Latino electorate are, in fact, of little consequence to Latinos' political standing. I make this point by turning back to the 2004 election, which political pundits generally regard as having marked Latinos' coming of age, in light of the ensuing debate over immigration.

Democrats and Republicans have been courting Latinos for decades. But it was during the 2004 elections that Latinos emerged as the ultimate swing voter after this traditionally democratic constituency backed the Republican Party in unprecedented numbers. Indeed, the 2004 elections were undoubtedly unique and controversial. Whether it was values or issues, or the Iraq war, or Bush's popularity, that influenced voters was debated for months after the election. But among Latino political pundits, it was the "Latino realignment" with Republicans that stirred the most controversy. The debate was set off by figures from the National Election (NEP) exit poll which reported that Bush had received 44 or 45 percent of the Latino vote, a greater percentage than had been predicted and a significant increase from 2000. Similar figures were soon quoted in flagship newspapers like the *Los Angeles Times* and the *New York Times*, to the consternation and surprise of mainstream and Latino pundits alike.

The Republican "landslide" was quickly disputed by Latino political scientists and by the advocacy community. It's all spin, as determined most forcefully in a report by the William C. Velasquez Institute, the research arm of the Southwest Voter Registration Education Project. Latinos had supported John Kerry by a 65 percent to 33 percent margin; the discrepancy could be accounted for by methodological failures in the polling of Latinos.[1] Namely, the NEP poll's reliance on general market sampling measures was biased toward suburban and rural areas, rather than the metropolitan areas where Latinos are more concentrated, whereas relative to the greater Latino population, a greater percentage of the NEP sample had completed at least a bachelor's degree and fewer identified themselves as being of Mexican ancestry. Later it was also revealed that the NEP sample had an overrepresentation of Cubans in Miami-Dade County, who are predominantly Republican (Suro et al. 2005). All these methodological sampling factors had preselected Republican Latinos, if not entirely provided an incomplete picture of the electorate.

The actual breakdown of Latino votes cast may remain forever contested—although most national trade publications showed Bush capturing roughly 40 percent of the vote. What was not contested is that Latinos showed a shift increase—of whatever size—toward President Bush. Also uncontested is that this increase had taken on a life of its own, as it became widely circulated, exposed, and spun: Latinos are turning Republican and this is due to their inherently conservative values. Democrats—Watch out!

Latinos' characterization as conservative and culture-bound is not new. These views have long been used to marginalize them, by rendering them unequipped for modernity and progress. Below, I suggest that something similar takes place when they're characterized as such in the political sphere. Latinos are also a heterogeneous population. Many have been Republicans and many are becoming Republicans; and later I offer some possible reasons for this trend. But most of all, I want to argue that in the current neoconservative context, the spin about Latinos' cultural values takes on new meanings and functions, especially in relation to their so-called turn to the Republican Party. In this context, debate over Latinos' political views should be seen as part of a larger trend for realigning spirituality, morality, values, and ethnicity along politico partisan and ideological lines, a trend that is currently at the very heart of American cultural politics. In other words, reducing the complexity of Latinos' experience to a narrow set of conservative values parallels a current narrowing of the meaning of what is American. The spin over Latino political values is hence less indicative of Latinos' views than it is an expanded projection of the "good all-American values" of family, faith, and country onto a population that is still seen to represent a threat to the American polity. This threat was neatly captured in the *Newsweek* feature headline published after Villarraigosa's victory in Los Angeles, "And How Hispanics Will *Change* American Politics" (my italics). Are Latinos not part of that "America" they are supposedly said to change and affect? In other words, a Latino victory is celebrated, but the specter of their foreignness remains, as Latinos are presented as a threat that could "change our system." Or, read between the lines, Latinos remain unreliable, undiscriminating, and faulty voters, and more dangerously, they make ill-equipped elected officials unable to ever be representative of American society. Briefly then, I want to express skepticism about current celebrations of Latinos as the new "swing" voters, and as inherent holders of "American" values. I want to suggest that these arguments need to be seen in light of larger neoliberal trends where "values" have become preeminently marketable and where emphasis on Latinos'

natural conservative "American values" surface as the preeminent medium to temper the threat their demographic growth is seen to present.
In this context, what Latinos might contribute to the future of American
electoral politics, especially with regard to issues of citizenship and social
equity, is effectively narrowed.

On Polls and Polling

> There's more polling on Latinos, but if you look at the questions
> carefully, you can figure out whether they are trying to get at what
> Latinos think, or whether they are trying to get a response to say
> what Latinos think. . . . people are not interested in the answers.
> They are interested in polarizing the responses to make a point.
> —Clarissa Martinez, National Council of La Raza

The debate over the coveted Latino vote started months if not years before
the 2004 election. Since the 1980s, Latinos have been consistently discovered and rediscovered by the media and pundocracy prior to each presidential election, only to be dismissed quickly thereafter (De Sipio and de
la Garza 2002; Leal et al. 2005). But the 2004 elections were marked by
an unprecedented number of Latino polls and studies, which solidified
the spin over the "sleeping" Latino giant. Among them were polls by the
Washington Post, by Univision and the Tomas Rivera Policy Institute, by
the New Democrat Network, by the Hispanic Federation and Zogby International, by Univision and NALEO, to name a few. This is a significant
development if we consider that the first national opinion survey focusing
on Latino politics, the Latino National Political Survey, was conducted as
late as 1989 (Garcia et al. 1989). This study provided the first look at Latinos' political values, and identified important and enduring theoretical
and methodological problems in the polling of Latinos. Among them are
the difficulties of achieving a representative Hispanic sample; determining
what type of attention should be paid to national subgroups; in what language or languages polls should be conducted; and in what percentages
each grouping should be included. In fact, the debate over the NEP exit
poll figures suggests that difficulties in the polling of Latinos have become
exacerbated by the current abundance of "official" and professionally conducted Latino polls. The result is that, more and more, what is known
about the Latino electorate is contingent and conducive to speculation, as
all poll-derived conclusions can arguably be said to be.

Indeed, the accuracy of all types of opinion polls and surveys has long been debated and challenged. Writers have criticized the constructed nature of polls, the methodological quandaries that affect them, and the multiple interests that shape them, not to mention that how the nature of the sample is defined and recruited can impact their result (MacFarquhar 2004). Then there's the key issue of how questions are worded and posed. As explained by Clarissa Martinez, a researcher from NCLR at a panel on Latino voters at the Center for American Progress: "If you look at issue of immigration in particular, there are a lot of apples to oranges comparisons. It is not the same to ask someone if they favor a path to legalization or immediate deportation. It is not the same to ask someone if they prefer open borders or legalization, no one in this country favors open borders, even the NCLR does not favor open borders regardless of what some people may say!" Researchers have also noted the adverse effects polling has had on democracy by limiting public discussion to opinion snapshots of predetermined subjects (Champagne 2004; Lewis 2001; Ewen 1996). What remains uncontested, however, is the power of polls and polling. Such power is not limited to reflecting reality, but most significantly includes the shaping of self-conscious subjects and "averaged Americans" through their measurement and open discussion of all aspects of Americans' behaviors, tastes, and opinions (Igo 2007).

The issues at play in Latino polls, then, are no different than those at play in the polling of any other population segment, except for the political stakes involved. Latino voices are muted, or not included, in general opinion surveys, making "Latino-specific polls" the primary medium for political "Latino representativity." In fact, the current resurgence of Latino polls and research has not entirely quelled lingering skepticism about whether Latinos constitute a viable research object. Once again, Clarissa Martinez described this predicament as follows: "We walk a fine line because when we maintain that the Latino population is not a monolith, people assume that Latinos are all over the place, that you can't have a Latino strategy and be easily dismissed." In other words, the race for Latinos' public opinion parallels the construction and acceptance of Latinos as a grouping with some common interests that people could justifiably refer to for guidance with policy issues.

But this task is becoming increasingly difficult. For one, it is hindered by the very preponderance of pollsters which are increasingly aligned with particular interests. It should not escape us that numbers and statistics are socially constructed, as is any other type of research. My interviewees gave evidence of this when they described research on the Latino electorate as "leftist" or conservative or as aligned with the Democratic or Republican Party. And while some polls are produced by Democratic and Republican polling firms, such as Lake Snell Perry and Associates and the Terrance Group, ironically, it is noncommercial research by Latino nonprofit advocacy organizations, with the most experience with Latino research, whose neutrality seemed to be placed most at stake because of their advocacy history. The result is the highly unfounded view that mainstream pollsters assure objectivity whereas Latino researchers are inherently biased. This is the same view that sustains the greater legitimacy of polling conducted by institutions with the least experience in the polling of Latinos. Latino advocacy organizations are aware of this biased view and often partner with "assembly-line" pollsters of the likes of Zogby when they need to be strategic about how their research will be publicly received.

The fact is that no poll and public opinion survey is ever exempt from charges of partiality. Hence, it is not their veracity but their uses that I find most interesting. In particular, I am interested in the ways in which polls and public opinion may shape Latino political values in the very process of representation. This point is central because the results of most polls are disseminated with the least amount of information to assess their accuracy, or the larger context that leads to particular conclusions. As a researcher in a major company explained: "What we do is provide snapshots of people's opinions. But they are always fluid. At the end of the day it's up to them how they choose to present the data." I want to call attention to the operative word "them," implying the involvement of larger interests in the circulation of the data. And who is "them"? Clients commissioning the research, of course, but also the media intent on the more marketable stories, not to mention political pundits who stand to benefit most from more Latino-targeted efforts. Consequently, more than one interviewee acknowledged that Latinos had become victims of their own success. Once entirely ignored, they now suffer from an overabundance of research, surveys, and reports that are only regarded as valuable for their newsworthiness and political function. Efrain Escobedo, director of Voter Engagement with NALEO Educational Fund, explained: "There's enormous pressure to explain the emergence of this new electorate. But what people want to know is, is this going to change anything? How will this change the country? And what does this mean for the Democrats and the Republicans?" But looking at Latinos only in terms of their political relevance reduces how we look at them, what issues are probed, and in what ways, he went on to explain. For sure, one troubling outcome is the overpoliticization and reduction of Latino issues around politico partisan lines.

Charles Kamasaki, head of the NCLR office of research, made a similar point, though this time emphasizing the "man bites dog" message that tends to dominate coverage of Latino research. This is the tendency to elevate the most obscure statistic, that which most counters conventional wisdom on Latinos because it makes the most newsworthy headline. As he noted: "See, if we tell them that Latinos generally support a progressive agenda, they say, so what? This is not news." He acknowledged that any good research will show nuances and counterintuitive discoveries, especially when comparing different groups across nationality, class, and so on. What he found misleading, however, was the tendency to take nuance for consensus: "That's how you get headlines like 'Latinos have mixed views on immigration,' when in reality Latinos are generally a pro-immigrant group." I was given similar reasons for the preeminence of conservative Latino spokespersons, such as Linda Chavez and the nationally syndicated columnist Ruben Navarrette, Jr. In countering stereotypes that Latinos are inherently liberal, however, these spokespeople stand out, and are readily embraced by the mainstream media. After all, it comes across as more legitimate as well as more provocative if it is a Latino, rather than a non-Latino, who says conservative things about Latinos.

This penchant for newsworthiness explains why, corrective memos on how Latinos really voted in the 2004 election circulated by Latino advocacy organizations notwithstanding, it was the 44–45 percent figures that received the most coverage in the mainstream media. These figures sustain a more marketable picture of Latinos as "the" swing voters, confirming their up and coming position as a profitable political target, in need of more Latino-directed polls, pollsters, and advertising campaigns. Consequently, it is these figures—not the corrected and contested ones—that became "facts" prompting editorials and discussions to frame the debate around particular conventions: That Latinos are turning Republican, that this is a sign of their "maturity" and coming of age, a natural outcome of their upward mobility and assimilation; that Latinos have hard conservative values and morals, that they are leaving Catholicism for evangelicalism, that they care primarily about a charismatic leader, never the issues.[2] The contradictory nature of these portrayals is worth noting: Latinos were said to be moving up, changing status and parties, but never shifting their moral and traditional core values. Absent from these discussions remain the major concerns of the Latino electorate, as confirmed by most research on Latino political attitudes conducted prior to and after the 2004 election: education, the economy, and jobs (Flores 2004; Zogby and Wittman 2004; Suro et al. 2005; NALEO 2004). These issues do not differ from those of the general population, though similarities are never as sexy or newsworthy as are differences, and as a result, are hardly reported.

Yet, the most significant issue veiled by all the hype over the powerful Latino electorate is their continued disenfranchisement. Despite their rapid population growth, Latinos remain overwhelmingly underrepresented in the realm of electoral politics, and notwithstanding recent gains represented by Villarraigosa's victory in California, and the election of two Latino senators—Republican Mel Martinez from Florida and Democrat Ken Salazar from Colorado in 2004, and Democratic Senator Bob Menendez in New Jersey—their representation remains insignificant relative to their numbers. Latino elected officials are also concentrated in local and less powerful branches of government, such as in city council and in the legislative branches. In 1999, they constituted less than 1 percent of all elected officials (Hero et al. 2000), while in 2005 the National Association of Latino Elected and Appointed Officials (NALEO), which has been publishing a more standardized annual roster of Hispanic elected officials since 1996, listed 5,041 Hispanic elected officials. This number is not compared to the total number for elected officials nationwide, making it impossible to assess any gains since 1999. What the roster amply shows is the continued concentration of Latinos in municipal and education school board posts and in Southwestern states, confirming their continued lagging presence at varied and higher levels of government (NALEO 2005).

Most significantly, less than half of all Latinos are registered to vote. This number is partly explained by demographics. Irrespective of ethnic or racial background, the voters more likely to participate in the electoral system are older, more educated, and more affluent. But Latinos lag behind in education and income and have high numbers of youth and noncitizens who are ineligible to vote. Thus, in 2004, only 39 percent of the Latino population was eligible to vote compared to 76 percent of whites and 65 percent of blacks. Likewise, only 18 percent of the total Latino population went to the polls, compared to 51 percent of all whites and 39 percent of all blacks (Suro et al. 2005).

Further contributing to Latinos' disenfranchisement are important differences between eligible voters and the Latino population as a whole.

Latinos are not a monolith, and eligible voters are primarily English-speaking, older, more affluent, and better educated than the Latino population as a whole, making them into a "proxy" for a totality of a population that is largely unlike themselves (Suro et al. 2005). Similar differences in education and income also exist among the general population and those who vote, though the greater gap between those who are eligible to vote and those who are not among Latinos adds to these differences' greater significance when Latinos are concerned. This is one of the reasons why, to the chagrin of pundits, activists, and scholars alike, the highly opinionated political scientist veteran Rodolfo de la Garza has been a vociferous critic of most generalizations about Latinos' political views, to the point of even questioning the power of the Latino electorate. As he explained:

> There's no way of knowing how Latinos voted or would have voted. Statistics are based on those who voted. What happens with those who did not? People will find numbers to support any argument, but there's no empirical data to support that Latinos are such a swing vote or turning Republican. The fact is that there was no election in California, in New York or Texas and that means that 65 percent of Latinos had no reason to vote. How do you explain that? Does that lead to more voter dissatisfaction? Does that mean more Latinos are turning Republican?

His statement adds yet another variable to Latinos' political disenfranchisement—the fact that many Latinos have little incentive to vote because they live in states that are politically overdetermined. These factors combined render nationwide generalizations about Latino political trends and views that are more conjecture than a factual and comprehensive picture of Latinos' political views. Finally, adding to the present conjectural state of knowledge is the preponderance of quantitative surveys over in-depth qualitative studies looking at the range of variables affecting Latinos' political participation. Lisa Bedolla's study of Los Angeles's Latino politics is unique in this regard. Her study documents how variables of gender, history of political organization, and level of nonelectoral participation, citizenship, and generation can have major effects on the level of political participation shown by members of the "same community" (Bedolla 2005). Yet, complexities such as these are not easily contained by a survey, and only surveys can be easily spun by politicians' pundits, adding to their greater marketability and greater popularity with corporate funders and foundations.

Still, even if allowing for a greater "conservatism" among Latinos who vote, people who work with this electorate paint a more complex picture. As I was repeatedly told by people working in Latino political advocacy, Latinos do show conservative social values with regard to abortion, and identification with religion, family, and tradition. They were also described as having a sense of optimism and patriotism, and a sense of waiting to live the American dream, that, in contrast to African Americans, was seen as rendering them particularly open to the optimistic appeals advanced by the Republican Party. As Arturo Vargas from NALEO put it:

> The immigrant experience is very important for this electorate. That they're here because they feel that they can make it in this country. What happens is that if the second generation does not succeed, then after the third and fourth generation, you get a different paradigm; that's when you have realization of discrimination, but that's a different experience from African Americans. In other words, there's no rage, what you hear is the sense of aspiration, maybe they won't make it but they have a sense of aspiration and optimism that colors how they may be willing to vote.

This view obviously presupposes that Latin-American immigrants come as empty vessels filled only with hope, without any preconceived negative ideas about the United States, which is extremely unlikely given the U.S. reputation throughout Latin America. Leaving this point aside, Latinos' sense of aspiration was a commonly agreed upon characteristic of this electorate.

At the same time, Latinos are shown by most polls to have a more liberal view of the role of government, and to support more aggressive federal government in everything from healthcare to affirmative action and the environment. Latinos are also found to be especially concerned with the need to improve education and the economy, and to have a more compassionate view about immigration favoring programs that facilitate family reunification, protection of immigrants such as the passage of the DREAM Act, than the "average" population.[3]

It is interesting to note that it was not Latinos' liberal stance toward government that received the most coverage after the 2004 elections, but rather how their values are turning them invariably to the right, or how their voting patterns differ significantly from African Americans. The debate about Latinos' religious conversion to non-Catholic Christianity is relevant here. In editorials in the *New York Times* and in public debates, it was said that Latinos voted Republican because the Republican Party went to church and courted born-again Christians (Curiel 2004; Elliot 2004). Suddenly, Latinos were described as fleeing the Catholic Church and moving to evangelical sects in herds. Political scientists confirmed that non-Catholic Christians favored President Bush, unlike Catholic Latinos, who voted predominantly Democrat. But they also warned that this trend was far from the huge religion gap it was presented to be; for non-Catholic Christians constitute only 18 percent of the Latino electorate (Leal et al. 2005). A mere two years earlier, a nationwide poll examining changes in religious identification in the Hispanic community from 1990 to 2001, whose results were highly circulated in the mainstream press, had also shown that the "fastest-growing religion among Hispanics is no religion at all" (Kornblum 2002). The majority still identified as Catholics, but the percentages are dropping, while the greatest growth was among groups who were said to believe in God but to have no religion at all (to 13 percent from 6 percent), representing the same secular trends that exist in the general population. Did Latinos experience mass overnight conversions during the 2004 elections? A more likely scenario is that the overemphasis on the role played by Latino born-again Christians, and the importance of this one sector of the Latino electorate, is directly related and informed by the spin attracted by the Christian right at the national level.

Also hidden from view is the fact that Latino voting patterns were not that different from the general population, which also voted Republican whether in their own best interest or not. Why they did led to much speculation. For some it was the specificity of a war election that swayed voters. Or it was the outcome of what Thomas Frank has termed the "great backlash" conservatism that dominated the national stage. This was not the first year, he noted, in which voters were mobilized through explosive social issues, and where cultural anger was marshaled and "married" to pro-business economic policies (Frank 2005). Unlike Latinos, however, the general electorate was not so easily reduced to snapshots of conservatism and values. Populations in the so-called red states were; but that Latinos—who overwhelmingly reside in the so-called more liberal blue states—were as well indicates that something else was at play in their portrayal as inherently conservative. Specifically, what got most coverage is that which made Latinos a more marketable constituency; namely, the views that are most likely to calm mainstream fears of the "awakening" giant the Latino electorate was said to be, and that most easily aligned Latinos with the dominant neoconservative political climate. This trend exposes the irrelevance of debating whether Latinos are "Democrats" or "Republicans." In both instances, the debate over Latino political values is accompanied by a restraint in what they are allowed to bring to the table of institutional politics: a value-laden, easily swayed, and highly marketable political constituency.

Courting the "Awakening" Giant

The synergy between preconceived ideas about the Latino electorate and the attendant political climate is evident in the almost identical Latino advertising strategies developed by the two main parties. It is important to discuss advertising, because the 2004 campaign was characterized by a significant increase in spending in this area and by a general consensus from both parties that advertising was central to swaying the Latino vote. In public forums, pundits from the Democratic Party regretted having taken the Latino electorate for granted; just as Republicans attributed their success among Latinos to their aggressive grassroots recruitment and advertising.

Signs of the Republican Party's grassroots strategies were evident during the 2005 NALEO conference in Puerto Rico, in the questions posed by two audience members to Victor Carrillo, chairman of the Railroad Commission of Texas, the one Republican speaker, during a bipartisan panel on electoral politics. One attendee noted that Republicans were "hassling the cream of the crop, the best and the brightest of our community." A restaurant owner, he himself had been courted multiple times by his local Republican Central Committee. Another denounced the challenge posed by statewide Republican appointees like Carrillo: appointing Republican Latinos to state posts facilitates their future election to that very post over and above any contending democratic candidates. They have jumped the hoops of race, and the general electorate is more likely to accept and vote for them if they had been previously appointed, noted the attendee. Indeed, the Benetton style of the Bush presidency is well known, more blacks and Latinos were appointed to high-level Cabinet positions, instilling a specter of representability like never before.

The fact is that Latinos historically have been aligned with the Democratic Party, an alignment that has also contributed to Latinos' disenfranchisement by making them an assured base block that has been only minimally courted by Republicans and Democrats alike. This trend has made of Latinos a generally neglected constituency, adding a significant dimension to the debate over their so-called political conversion to the Republican Party. Namely, that Latinos have been failed by the two parties, that many are aware of this, and that their shift from one party to another may be guided less by ideological than by practical considerations. I had ample evidence of this when writing about gentrification in East Harlem, where long-time Latino democratic leaders, like state senator Olga Méndez, were purposefully turning Republican if not denouncing the Democratic Party's failure to acknowledge and provide resources for local Latino leaders. They felt they could obtain resources more easily from a party that sought to court them, instead of take them for granted. In other words, their shift had less to do with a political ideological conversion than with practical considerations. This point was also made by veteran political strategist Sergio Bendixen when sharing the comments of a Dominican participant in a focus group session on Latinos' views about the parties. As he noted, in the words of this focus group participant, the Republican Party was "like her brand new boyfriend who sends her flowers and chocolates, and takes her to dinner and calls her every night to tell her how much he loves her." In contrast, the Democratic Party appeared to her as "her ex-husband who just sends her a check every month." Too bad that the new boyfriend will soon become an old lover; too bad also that he is not bound to send her a check every month, I quickly thought, until I appreciated the very revealing analogy. It drew me back to Puerto Rico, where plebiscites for the island's political status are popularly known as "beauty pageants." Boyfriends and beauty pageants: perceptive labels to expose the whimsical, arbitrary, unequal, and ultimately disengaged relationship between the electorate and the institutional parties. But the point here is far more simple: that unlike the Democratic Party, the Republican Party has been romancing Hispanics and launching aggressive new efforts to court them.

The GOP's luring of Latino voters dates from the 1960s when it developed its Southwest strategy geared primarily to white-collar Mexican-American professionals. It peaked in the 1980s when it began to develop more nationwide campaigns working consistently with Lionel Sosa, a marketing guru and founder of one of the largest Hispanic marketing agencies (Subervi 2008), and consolidated around the election of George Bush in the 2000 election, when a "dream team" of Hispanic marketing professionals and pollsters was put in place (Sanchez 2007).

Sosa, well known as a premier broker and marketer of Latino cultural values, enjoys retelling of his first encounter with Ronald Reagan, when the soon-to-be president told him that it would be a "breeze" to convert Latinos to Republicans, because "Hispanics are Republicans, they just don't know it." Sosa credits Reagan for coming up with the format he has since followed for every presidential race: showing how similar Latinos and Republicans are because of their conservative values. Most significantly, Sosa is a firm believer that character rules over issues or party, in other words, that the candidate who can present him/herself as a trustworthy, likable, family person and of good moral value and sharing Latino values can win irrespective of the issues. The tactic, then: to highlight the candidate's character over the issues, and most important, as noted in the photocopied PowerPoint presentation he readily shared with me, to "portray and treat Latinos as equal American citizens, not as helpless victims in need of government aid." As he noted, conservative values are more directly aligned with Latinos' cultural core; that in itself gives Republicans a political edge.

Sosa's strategy touches on familiar territory: the old marketing adage that Latinos will come your way—buy your product, vote for your candidate, etc.—if you push the right cultural buttons. This view is not only Sosa's, but underlines the entire business of ethnic and Hispanic marketing, which elsewhere I've shown to be predicated on a narrow and monolithic version of Latino culture. Accordingly, Latinos' marketability as a political constituency stems not solely from their fluidity as the so-called new swing voter block, but most importantly from their culture, which makes them a more easily managed constituency. This view pervades most Latino political strategists beyond party affiliation. It is shared by Sergio Bendixen, a political strategist consultant for the New Democrat Network who believes that Latinos voted Republican not because they're predisposed to conservative views, but because Republicans have developed more sophisticated ways to win Latinos' hearts and minds. In other words, it is a matter of engaging them and communicating with them in a culturally sensitive way and in Spanish to convince Latinos "to come your way."

The ironies of this culture-driven strategy were perceptively noted by Antonio Gonzalez from the Southwest Voter Registration Education Project during a panel held at Demos, a nonpartisan, nonprofit, New York–based research organization, to discuss the debate over the National Latino Exit Poll: "To say that Latinos are swing voters attracts Republican attention. It's a business strategy. But if you're also saying that they are smart and selective [or swing voters], they're going to rethink this and figure it out. Because you're telling them they argue with one side on the issues but vote with another. It's a bad message because it says to them [the parties] that you don't need to invest in the issues. That we can be had for a song."

And songs they had. According to Adam Segal, director of the Hispanic Voter Project at John Hopkins University, Spanish-language TV ads by both presidential candidates tripled in 2004. Campaigns started much earlier, and were more aggressive and directed. They were still limited in scope and concentrated in battleground states, representing, in his words, a type of "bikini politics" that covered only essential parts of the electorate (Segal 2004). Latinos in California and New York, uncontested Democratic states, for instance, remained unaddressed by either party. Nonetheless, the significant increment in political advertising efforts was plainly evident, especially when contrasted to the parties' hands-off approach toward black voters. For, unlike with African-American voters, strategists can court Latinos and run parallel and synergistic strategies in Spanish-language media without alienating their base of white voters. In Spanish-language TV, they could broadcast ads like "Nuestro Pais, Nuestro Presidente" (our country, our president) where flags from Latin American countries (such as Puerto Rico, Mexico, Dominican Republic, Nicaragua), are waved openly before a final shot of the U.S. flag. This double spin ad where "our country" refers ambiguously yet directly to Latinos' attachment to both the United States and their home countries would never fly on the mainstream English-language networks without entirely maddening the anti-immigrant Republican base.

Campaign-wise, there were predictable differences in how the two political parties addressed Latinos. As in the general market campaigns, Republicans questioned Kerry's persona and the Democratic Party for providing fewer opportunities and choices and more taxes, while the Democrats raised questions about Bush's record in service and his broken promises to Latinos. Additionally, ads differed in the general address, tone, and treatment to their constituency. Democratic ads were more likely to address Latinos as a community with needs in health care, education, income, etc., whereas Republicans focused on aspirational images of Latinos as either participant, or else as guaranteed future stakeholders in the "American dream." Ads by the New Democratic Network produced as part of their "Hispanic Project," to counter the more aggressive Republican strategy toward Latinos, are good examples here. The ads were not directed to selling Kerry or any specific candidate, but rather the

Democratic Party as the party that can deliver to Latinos. This included a number of didactic ads about the gains in civil rights and social services gained under the Democratic Party in the past (as in "Scrapbook," where a grandmother answers her grandson's query of "what is a democrat?" or in "History," where past democratic presidents such as Roosevelt, Kennedy, and Carter are hailed for the peace and prosperity they helped bring about). This strategy, however, was flawed on a number of counts. For instance, Marcelo Gaete, a director of programs at NALEO, noted that the strategy failed to connect with voters representing the two biggest sources of growth: naturalized citizens and youth. As he explained: These voters have little to no relationship with the Democratic Party's programs of the 1960s and could not relate to the nostalgic message, not to mention that encouraging young voters to vote like their grandmother is destined to backfire.[4] In contrast, Republican ads emphasized opportunities, and showed Latinos making it, while touching on Latino pride. They were also more geared to the present and focused a lot more on Bush as a candidate, which political pundits for both parties agreed had produced more effective and targeted ads.

These general differences notwithstanding, both parties' reliance on Latinos' supposedly "surefire" cultural buttons of communality, hard work, and family is strikingly similar.[5] And if the Bush campaign was more successful in attracting voters—which political pundits attributed to his more culturally sensitive approach to Latinos—I want to suggest it was not because he pushed the right "Latino cultural buttons." A better conclusion is that as a long ignored and marginalized constituency, Latinos reacted to their more direct and aggressive courting by the Republican Party, which was not limited to messages, but included grassroots appeals. For the core of both parties' message to Latinos is noticeably similar and equally enmeshed in the old adages about Latinos as a "traditional" people. Most significantly, these messages link Latinos to a neoconservative political agenda irrespective of party affiliation while positioning them at the margins of "America." In particular, I want to call attention to a striking trend: the presentation of Latinos as bearers of the same values revered and promoted by America. But this was done by limiting values to conservative, "model minority" qualities, while reinforcing and reinscribing hierarchies of belonging by legitimating who is the rightful owner of whatever is regarded as "American."

Two political advertising executions exemplify this cultureless approach and the hierarchies they help engender. Both were conceived as recruiting videos to be viewed during parties and rallies. At around five to six minutes, they are longer than regular ads and provide good examples of the parties' philosophy for targeting Latinos and their common reliance on culture triggers. The first is Lionel Sosa's brainchild: "President Bush on the Latino Spirit" first aired during the Republican Convention and was narrated by Bush himself. Part of the "Nos Conocemos" strategy, it presents Bush as familiar with Latinos, an admirer of their spirit.

> George W. Bush: "About 15 years before the civil war, much of the American west was northern Mexico. The people who lived here weren't called Latinos or Hispanics, they were Mexican citizens. Until all that land became part of the United States. After that many of them were treated as foreigners in their own land. Yet they did not choose to run. They stayed. This was their home. They worked, raised families, and built communities. Their sweat, tenacity and heart helped build this country. They suffered discrimination and injustice, to be sure. Yet an inherent optimism, born on the faith of God kept them on course. . . . Today there are over 40 million Latinos in the United States. That's 10 million more than the number of Canadians in Canada. If the United States' Hispanic population were a Latin American country, it would be the third largest, but it would also be the richest. That richness is best seen at the core of the Latino spirit. It has to do with values, strong conservative values. A belief that family comes first. That family helps one another. Latino parents instill in their children a strong work ethic, faith in God, patriotism, personal responsibility, determination. These values are my values. I live by them and I lead by them. . . . Every year, Latinos add to this country's wealth and to their own. Latino income and educational levels are getting higher every day. Hispanic home ownership is at an all-time high. Hispanic small business growth leads all other categories of small business growth.

The positive message of mobility and coming of age is complemented by a collage of aged black and white photographs—yellowed by time, or by sepia tone—in the historical section of the ad, countered with brightly colored takes of rosy-cheeked, light-skinned, and upwardly mobile Latinos in the present. In both the past and the present, however, it is intimate family portraits and pictures of Latinos at work that dominate. We see children doing homework, families boarding an SUV, posing for a family portrait, raising the American flag, as well as a grandmother greeting her family, small business owners tending to clients, Latinos in suits,

Fig. 1a, 1b, and 1c. Stills from Bush 2004 "Nos Conocemos" (We Know Each Other) advertising campaign targeting Latinos featuring patriotic upwardly mobile Latinos. Campaign by Lionel Sosa.

etc. Statements by U.S. treasurer Rosario Marin and allusions to the appointment of Alberto Gonzalez, and Hector Barreto, director of the Small Business Administration, reinforce the message that Republicans have delivered unique opportunities to Latinos. The video ends with a blessing by Ms. Marin to the president: "Vaya con Dios" (Go with God), and the president's response: "Nos Conocemos" (We know each other). Notice the identification of Latinos' cultural values (faith, family, patriotism, optimism, work ethic, etc.) and most significantly how these values are also identified as the same values Bush lives by—in other words, as inherently American (or Republican) values. Narrated by the president himself, the ad is very explicit about what outcome is produced by these values (success) and who commands, bestows value to values, and represents them more clearly: "I live by them, I lead by them." In other words, Latino-positive values are validated as such by Bush—by America in a move that rhetorically positions Latinos outside that "America" especially if "their" values do not lead to an upwardly mobile outcome.

Remarks by Ken Mehlman, chairman of the Republic National Committee during NALEO's 2005 annual conference, are evocative of this message. Evoking the "Nos Conocemos" campaign, Mehlman placed great emphasis on the commonalities of values and interests between Republicans and Latinos: "Your interests are our interests . . . your cause is our cause. We welcome your pride of country, your love of family, your faith in God. We welcome your contributions. Mi partido es su partido (My party is your party)." Yes, Latinos' contributions and patriotism, family and faith were praised by Mehlman. But the group that is welcoming and extending praise is well established—the unnamed yet very well-known "We" to which Mehlman, not Latinos, so clearly belong.

A similar approach is found in Kerry's "Un Futuro Mejor" (A Better Future), a longer ad distributed alongside an "Action Toolkit" or "Paquete de Activism," which in its length and use provides a good counterpart to "Nos Conocemos." The ad is narrated by Henry Cisneros, former secretary of Housing and Urban Development during the Clinton administration.

> Henry Cisneros: Les presentamos a John Kerry. A list of what is important to John Kerry reads like a list of what's important to the Latino community. . . . Kerry understands that the family is one of the most important things in our lives. Family is there to give us strength, when we need it, just as we give of our strength when our family is in need.

Fig. 2a, 2b, 2c, and 2d. Stills from Kerry 2004 "La Graduación" advertising campaign targeting Latinos, featuring a proud grandmother on graduation day. Campaign by Chambers López & Gaitán LLC.

Kerry: Working families all across our country are living by the oldest and the greatest American values.

Ed Pastor, Congressman from Arizona: Yo apoyo a John Kerry porque respeta los valores de las familias Latinas (I support John Kerry because he respects the values of Latino families).

Woman: Supporting Latinos is more than speaking the language. You have to understand our cultural values. You have to understand how important family is.

Cisneros: John Kerry has worked, and will continue to work, toward making families stronger, removing those things that hold them back, giving them what they need to grow and prosper.

Kerry: Values that built America. Strong families, deep faith.

Cisneros: Our faith is what guides us. Telling us what's right. With faith as his guiding principle, John Kerry will unite our country again with the rest of the world, and bring the American people together, one nation under God. (Segal 2004)

Once again, vague allusions to Latino cultural values of strong families and deep faith are made and in turn presented as tantamount to the very values that "built America."

But it is Kerry who once again establishes the Americanness of these values, and who identifies what the values that "built America" are, and who praises Latinos for exhibiting them also.

Marking Difference/Making America

I've expressed skepticism about Latino pollsters, shown the actual disenfranchisement of this so-called new sleeping giant and some of the ways that so-called Latino values were used in the past election. I believe this all boils down to a simple point: Latinos are at the heart of the remaking of America. But not in the optimistic ways described by political pundits. Praise and discussion of Latino values in the mainstream press does not signal that mainstream society has finally gained respect for the "Latino spirit." Instead, we can only be sure that the so-called Latino spirit is being used in novel and new ways, most notably for politico partisan ends, in ways that support a narrow definition of what is patriotically American.

The contradictions of the summa plus conservative Latino are perhaps most clearly evident in the work of Univision's news anchor, Jorge Ramos: *The Latino Wave: How Hispanics Will Elect the Next American President*

(2004). In it, and repeating the national spin about the Latino electorate, Ramos predicted that Latinos were sure to elect the next American president. In contrast to the more "established" voting patterns and attitudes of blacks, he noted, Latinos are less loyal to party than to issues; issues like homosexuality, abortion, divorce, and gay marriage have and can continue to attract them to the Republican Party. Ramos goes on to make a strong argument about the power of Latinos in shaping American society, and about their distinct ethos and values, involving "morals and family values that differ distinctively from the rest of the American population" (85). Latinos are coming of age, he tells us, and rapidly integrating, while never assimilating, into "American" society. Yet there is nothing to fear in this trend, for Latinos can exert a force of positive change in "America." Their conservative values, opposition to abortion, homosexuality, and divorce in greater percentages than Anglo-Americans, instill the same values America cherishes but is so rapidly losing. Or, in his words: "A nation that emphasizes Latinos' morals and family values while maintaining the prevailing U.S. political and economic processes would, without a doubt, be a healthier and more humane society" (86). That is, Latinos will give America back to America, as Latinos values are once again represented as archetypically American, but only in extremely narrow and conservative terms.

In this way, emergent representations of Latinos are best seen as reiterations of the so-called American values, of family, democracy, upward mobility, and workmanship through the praise of those rendered to be the greatest threats to these very values, and that as such are positioned in most need of direction and guidance. We should not lose sight of the fact that it is the same people who are regularly represented as "takers," not givers, to the nation, through welfare, illegal immigration, and crime that are being described as family oriented and traditional, and increasingly as "middle class." These are undeniably good all-American values that we are repeatedly told compound the fabric of American culture. Yet these are values that Latinos are constantly tied to, but that are never asserted about whites. Perhaps that is because they are never suspected of lacking them? unlike Latinos and minorities?

The point is that behind the cultural distinctiveness of the Latino electorate touted in public discourses lie more commonalities with dominant American values than differences. These representations then need to be seen for what they do: accommodate Latinos by establishing or else by marking differences, in the very process of establishing commonalities.

Even the most antithetical "American" values Latinos are said to exhibit, such as love of their home culture and the Spanish language, can be seen in this manner. Rather than antithetical to "American" culture, and in sharp contrast to Huntington's view, Latin culture and the Spanish language have been central "Americanizing" tools. One way is by providing the justification for Latinos' exclusion from the national community in a way analogous to how race has functioned among African Americans. Americanization, we have to remember, has never meant the equal incorporation of individuals into the national community, but rather their ordering and placement within it. This is a process that has been historically informed by the extent to which individual groups resemble U.S. dominant norms around gender, sexuality, race, ethnicity, religion, and class favoring the dominant white Anglo-Saxon Protestant American ethos. In other words, Americanization does not erase differences as much as it feeds from these differences, and uses them as the very basis for the differential ranking of individuals and groupings. I believe that culture and language among Latinos functions this way insofar as even the most "Americanized" Latino is always considered to belong less to the national community on the basis of his/her intangible "culture." The myth of the dominant white Anglo-Saxon Protestant ethos, and of its putative continued concrete existence despite the browning of America, is predicated on these types of exclusions.

CODA

A lot has happened since the political parties' public courting of Latino voters in the 2004 election. The war on terror has been accompanied by a growing xenophobia and by a myriad of anti-immigrant groups and measures, from the Minutemen to Protect Arizona Now and Protect America Now, which have imparted a troublesome, strong "Us versus Them" rhetoric to the debate over immigration. Even more "immigration-friendly" measures were imbued by this rhetoric. The "Border Protection, Antiterrorism, and Illegal Immigration Control Act of 2005," better known as the Sensenbrenner Bill-H.R. 4437, for instance, included measures criminalizing immigrants and those who help them, while more "sensible" compromise bills by the Senate included a provision making English the national language, and making naturalization a far more costly and inaccessible process. No wonder the LA-based grassroots activist group "La Coalicion 25 de Marzo" termed it the "bondage slavery bill."

Fig. 3. A demonstrator at the 2006 conference of the National Council of La Raza. Photo by the author.

Yet, as these pages go to print, news about the parties' increasingly aggressive battle for Latino voters once again dominate the airwaves. It's mid-July, Spanish language political commercials are on the rise, and advertising veteran Lionel Sosa assures me that this is just the start: "You will see that in this election Latinos are more important than soccer moms, than evangelicals, than any other group." His brand new ads are yet to circulate, but the couple he showed me displayed the familiar "Sosa" mark. They tout Latinos' patriotism and bravery during military service, pledge support for more Latino candidates, and masterfully draw on Latinos' upward mobile aspirations. I also browsed through Obama's early ads in YouTube and found ads like "Como Padre" echoing the old culturalist strategy of family and conservatism that has become so common when targeting Latinos, so new yet so desperately similar to previous campaigns, each ad bearing witness to the spuriousness of Latinos' so-called political coming of age.

Just a few months before the political efforts preceding the elections, no one seemed to want to dance with Latinos, as in the apt metaphor of political scientist Jose Sanchez. Latinos appeared as the riskiest constituency with which any party could possibly associate—at least publicly. Now we see a political love fest toward Latinos, facilitated by the targeted world of Hispanic media and advertising which allows the political parties to target this constituency without alienating their mainstream base.

For, far more real than Latinos' move from the "margins to the center" is the mainstreaming of the xenophobic, enforcement-only approach, and the white supremacist views framing the immigration debate and the future of Latinos. It is against this larger context that the political battle over Latinos' political and cultural values should be considered. This is a context that is likely to limit the articulation of "Latino values" with a progressive agenda of change, and with anything that may render Latinos too threatening to the general mainstream. The idea that advancing a progressive agenda is difficult enough without Latinos and immigration foregrounding the issues is one line of thought that is likely to lead to a greater disregard of Latinos and to their treatment as a constituency that merits little courting. Certainly there should be no messages and campaigns that would alienate the general (read white) electorate. A concern, then, is that the Latino pundocracy and the political parties continue to instill the belief that the only way for Latinos to be "American" is by being more American than the Americans. A concern is that these appeals may continue to narrow the content and definition of what is American, making it politically irrelevant if Latinos, or anyone for that matter, "come of age." With these warnings, I nevertheless return to the dream world of political ads. I bring to mind their promise for opportunity and change, and hope that this time their claims serve as a pledge for a real and lasting political coming of age.

3

The Hispanic Consumer

That's "A Lot of Dollars, Cars, Diapers, and Food"

Recognize that in just seven years, the 43 million plus Hispanics in the U.S. today will have spending power equivalent to 60 percent of all 1.3 billion Chinese.

—E-mail sent by the owner of a New York–based Hispanic marketing agency to his client

We are in the business of counting people and we have never cared if you're documented or not. Early on we learned that when we did phone surveys, "American Research Bureau" sounded way too governmental. We needed a name that would not scare the undocumented away, something that sounded more gizmo-ish, more futuristic, that's how we changed our name to Arbitron.

—Pierre Bouvard, president of Sales and Marketing for Arbitron, during a presentation to the National Hispanic Media Coalition, NYC

One of the most intriguing conundrums in contemporary representations of Latinos is their growing preeminence as a so-called booming and profitable market at the same time that they continue to be stereotyped as illegal and a burden to the nation's economic welfare. This contradictory scenario was poignantly evident throughout 2006, at the height of the immigration debate. While editorials bemoaned the threat that Latinos supposedly pose to the integrity of "America's national culture," it was not uncommon to find news in the business section of major national newspapers touting the profitability of this market. On and on, we were told that Latinos have large families and conservative values, that they feel strongly about culturally specific marketing and that they make up a booming and coveted market. *USA Today* headlines, for instance, stated that "Media tune in to ethnic audiences: As immigration rates soar, broadcasters, cable channels, newspapers, magazines take notice" and "Immigrants courted as good customers; Businesses compete to win their loyalty," along with similar news fueled by speculation over the sale of Univision, the largest Spanish-language television network, which was sold in 2007. Exactly which group of investors would get the profitable bounty was a story that appeared repeatedly, right alongside xenophobic editorials and letters to the editors set off by coverage of the immigration debate. One could have easily thought that the objects of so much attention were two entirely different populations—one a liability, the other a profitable market.

Arguably, marketing discourse is one of many other fields articulating public ideas of and for Latinos alongside political parties, strategists, and think tanks. Yet numerous trends point to the growing influence of marketing in the national discourse and debate on U.S. Latinos. Among them is the historical preeminence of economic frameworks within the nationwide debate on immigration. In particular, immigrants' value has long been reduced to their economic contribution, be it as an anonymous workforce, as an economic liability, or as a mass of undifferentiated consumers.[1] There is also the record amount of Hispanic advertising monies spent by corporate America, which, according to HispanicBusiness.com, grew almost 50 percent since 2000, from $2.3 billion to a projected figure of $3.6 billion in 2007. Even the major political parties have increased their advertising budgets. During the 2004 campaign, they paid $14 million in Hispanic advertising, up from $3 million in 2000, which attests to the growing interplay between marketing and national politics in mainstreaming commonplace understandings of Latinos.

Adding to the power of marketing discourse is the general lack of civic leaders relative to the number of marketing pundits who serve as Latino spokespersons. This disparity is poignantly displayed in one of the many frequent articles on Latinos' boom and popularity predating the 2000 census. Following a common trend, a *Newsweek* feature on Latinos' shaping the face of America was supported, not by politicians, nor labor leaders, nor scholarly experts, but rather by Nelly Galán, the then director of programming for Telemundo, the second largest Spanish TV network, and Chrissy Hauberger, founder of *Latina* magazine. Marketing charts and statistics that show the size, growth, and buying power of Latinos from Arbitron and Strategy Research Corporation were also cited, while a blurb describing younger Latinos was titled "Generation Ñ" after the catchy phrase Hispanic marketers coined to describe young, upwardly mobile Latinos. All of this speaks clearly to the paucity of non-marketer spokespersons in the entire feature.[2]

The second point this chapter examines is the stark difference between current commercial representation of Latinos, especially immigrants, as family-oriented, traditional, and religious, and their continued portrayal as unskilled, uneducated, illegal, crime-ridden, and unemployed. I suggest that, at the core of this treatment is a unitary one whereby, irrespective of their history or legal status, Latinos are always potential aliens and outsiders and hence "immigrants." In this context, publicly sanctioned discourses of and about immigrants become relevant not so much for what they communicate about Latinos per se, but rather for what they reveal about the regulation and maintenance of a particular national identity.[3] Specifically, such discourses can be analyzed as functional resources that perform and reiterate the "American values" of democracy, upward mobility, and workmanship through the censure or praise of those rendered in most need of direction and guidance. Images and discourses of immigrants "making it" as consumers, for instance, simultaneously help feed and establish the myth of American democracy safeguarding the attainability of social and economic prosperity for all, while veiling the actual inequalities reproduced on the basis of people's social, cultural, or racial backgrounds that may affect or hinder economic attainment and progress.

These are some of the reasons why my earlier examination of Hispanic marketing concluded that marketing discourse is more revealing of U.S. normative values than of any attributes unique to U.S. Latinos. In what follows, I suggest that marketing continues to function in analogous ways; and moreover, that despite the increased growth and complexity of Hispanic marketing, commercial definitions of Latinos as a market have continued to narrow. This trend responds both to political economic trends within the industry that have favored media conglomeration and solidified the dominance of the Spanish-language media; and to the growing xenophobia that envelops discussion of Latino immigrants which, extending to all Latinos, demands their continued sanitization through positive commercial images.

The Politics of Hispanic Media:
Consolidation, Access, and Ownership

Contemporary marketing thrives on difference, be it along the lines of age, gender, or race, that can be targeted, turned into a market, and sold to corporate America and beyond.[4] Similarly, it is Latinos' supposedly cultural and linguistic uniqueness apart from "mainstream" society, and hence dependence on culturally relevant marketing, that has historically underlined the operations and profitability of Hispanic marketing. As noted in *Latinos Inc.*, this industry's common name of Hispanic Marketing is indicative of its nature and scope: its premise is not only that there are unique differences between "Americans" and Latinos that need to be addressed through culturally distinct advertising, but that it is language, specifically the Spanish language, that constitutes its primary distinguishing variable. Ironically then, it is the highly feared Latino "immigrant," whose putative newcomer status makes him or her more culturally authentic and hence more easily marketable, that has long been construed as the model "Latino" consumer. As we shall see, this involves addressing fears of Latinos' "foreignness" in their presentation as a safe immigrant population that is full of assimilable traits that the greater society can be proud of, but that remain culturally distinct, in their place and with their culture.

Emphasis on the Spanish-speaking consumer is promoted first and foremost by Spanish-language TV, and in particular, by Univision, the most important outlet for nationwide advertisements for the U.S. Latino market. Its 2006 media kit claims that 90 percent of U.S. Hispanics speak Spanish, that two-thirds of U.S. Hispanic adults are foreign-born, and that Univision commands a 34.6 percent share of viewers of the entire Hispanic population, above and beyond all major networks and cable stations, whether in Spanish or English. In so stating, Univision thus provides us with a very good example of what is a common trend in the industry at large: the manipulation of figures and statistics about Latinos to turn them into a profitable and accessible market, and the central role the Spanish-dominant Latinos play in such commercial imaginations. In reality, the 90 percent of Hispanics that are described as Spanish speakers and as the primary audience for Univision range in language competency and include bilingual and mostly English speakers who are not as likely to watch Univision. With regard to the percentage of foreign-born Hispanics, it is significant that this percentage is as high as two-thirds only among the adult population, not among the youth, which is the fastest growing segment of the total Hispanic population. Again, the point here is not Univision's self-serving manipulation of numbers, but rather its construction of the totality of Hispanics out of one of its segments.

Obviously, the portrait of the foreign-born and Spanish-dominant Hispanic who watches only Univision and Spanish-language television has not remained unchallenged. The battle over Latinos' media consumption in Spanish has been at the center of long-standing debates over representation, jobs, and money, and ultimately about determining who can or cannot profit from this market. For one, the dominance of the Spanish-language media universe has long sustained the importation of cheaper media programs from Latin America, while discouraging the production of original programming. Despite all the excitement provoked by *Ugly Betty*, ABC's English-language mega-production of the Colombian-based telenovela *Betty la Fea*, it is worth noting that the show represents a Latin American import, an adaptation of a genre and a script that had already proven successful and profitable. As media scholar Tomas Lopez Pumarejo explained during an interview, the show represents a growing trend in the new international division of media whereby Latin American media is positioned as provider—of genres, scripts, and formats—to American TV producers, who retain commercial control of their execution and distribution for the more profitable U.S. market. All the while, U.S. Latinos' access to and control of the media remain untouched by these arrangements. It is also noteworthy that while *Ugly Betty* revolves around Latino characters, it is not marketed as a "Latino media product" but rather as a general market offering. As such, it is unlikely to have a major impact on Latino media offerings in years to come.

At the crux of the issue is the profitability of the Hispanic marketing/Spanish language diad and its effects on hindering change. One may think that this is a positive development in the current monolingual and anti-Spanish language climate. However, the current state of affairs has sustained a growing conglomeration of Spanish-language media, a narrowing of content, alongside the continued exclusion of Latinos from the media that profits so handsomely from them. The Spanish language/Hispanic marketing is additionally supported by some of the major general market research companies. Nielsen TV ratings, the company that holds a monopoly on TV ratings nationwide and is considered the "gold standard" for TV audience measurements, for instance, has generalized language use as their primary testing variable for this market. In so doing, this company has also been at the center of many debates.

For years, Latino media activists have been critical of Nielsen, bemoaning its lack of transparency; the limited number of households that are measured to determine the viewing habits for the entire Latino population; as well as the lack of young Latinos in their sample, among other criticisms believed to lead to the undercounting and miscounting of minorities. They have also criticized Nielsen's use of language as the primary variable to test this market because it is believed to lead to the over-counting of Spanish-language TV viewers. It would take a major corporation joining in the criticism, however, to bring these issues into the limelight. Namely, in 2004, Rupert Murdoch's News Corporation opposed the introduction of Nielsen's local people's meters, which it feared would show similar trends already documented at the national level: audiences drifting away from network TV and moving to cable, and would have had an impact on the Fox network's advertising rates. The counting of Latino and minority audiences suddenly became a key concern of News Corp. Most specifically, News Corp. was behind the launching of the "Don't Count Us Out" campaign, a grassroots effort that fed from local media activists' concern, but that was actually primarily funded and fueled by Murdoch's News Corp.[5] Marta Garcia from the National Latino Media Council recalled: "All of a sudden we were involved with a major transnational corporation that has largely snubbed the Latino community. They hired all of these lobbyists and we were holding hands with the enemy. And sure enough, the whole thing backfired. FOX [News Corp.] is a client of Nielsen, and when it was no longer convenient to them, they simply dropped us."

Indeed, News Corp. had larger interests than "minority audiences" in mind. A media client dependent on Nielsen, News Corp. had bigger concerns than Nielsen, including gaining greater access of its control of the ratings industry. And as suggested by communications scholar Philip Napoli, minority audiences provided the perfect decoy. In his view, the debacle over Nielsen was ultimately a good example of the media industry's ability to wrap its self-interest in "public interest rhetoric," this time in the civil rights claims of minority groups.[6] News Corp. was hence the biggest winner of the Don't Count Us Out campaign, which turned out to be a perfect example of Latino spinning: the real concerns of minority groups about how they are being measured and about how Nielsen affects their representation, visibility, and power were easily muted.

This example underscores the difficulties Latino media groups face in light of the increased commercialization of Latino audiences. Their lack of power, resources, and access to stakeholders often makes them dependent on larger institutional entities. Such dependency in turn increases the likelihood that their views be dismissed as the interests of governmental, corporate, or not-for-profit stakeholders rather than as genuine Latino concerns, not to mention the potential that "Latino interests" be co-opted for advancing commercial alternatives that exclude them as major beneficiaries and stakeholders.

Research reports were central to the debate over Nielsen's measurement of Latinos. First was the "Latino Television Study" (Rincon and Associates 2004) commissioned by the national Hispanic Media Coalition and produced by Rincon and Associates. The study challenged the home-language measure used by Nielsen as "unstable and inadequate," finding that the audience for English-language television programs was underestimated, while calling for the need for external audits to verify the accuracy of Nielsen estimates.[7] For their part, Nielsen commissioned the Tomas Rivera Policy Institute to review and challenge the report's findings. Not surprisingly, the study, "A Policy Review Paper Assessing the Nielsen and Rincón Study on Latino Television Viewing," concluded that Rincon's findings were unfounded and not supported by the data, prompting a counter-response from the National Latino Media Council which denounced the response as a "not so scholarly exercise to distract industry attention away from their client, Nielsen Media Research."[8]

The political brouhaha over Nielsen shows that the measuring of Latino audiences is inextricably connected to larger economic and media interests, and that controversy over these measurements is not likely to end. In fact, Nielsen's status as proprietary research, and its lack of transparency, will insure that its measurement of Latinos and other minority audiences remains contentious in years to come. In addition, there are enormous economic incentives that hinder innovation and change in the business of measuring Latino audiences. Napoli explained during a telephone interview: "Nielsen is an unregulated monopoly, and they've invested all this money in their systems and training, they have little incentive to change. It's worked all these years without challenges and they are the only game in town and everyone has to sign to their system."

Producers of English-language media have also criticized Nielsen's use of language as their primary sampling variable, proposing instead a system based on the U.S. Census, such as on nativity, or whether Latinos are immigrant or U.S.-born. A chief proponent of this view is Robert Rose, a former Univision employee and executive director of AIM Tell-A-Vision

Group and producer of the English-language, nationally syndicated *Lati-Nation* show. In 2005, Rose launched a very public grassroots campaign to challenge Nielsen's sampling of Latinos. The campaign, "Help! Change TV," is advertised by the image of a young Latina woman whose mouth is taped shut with masking tape inscribed with the word "Nielsen" to dramatize the effects of the company's underrepresentation of U.S.-born Latinos in their language-based sample. The example Rose was eager to share to support his view is that of the show *Ugly Betty*. Despite featuring Latino characters and themes, and being heavily promoted and advertised, the show was shown by Nielsen to have underperformed heavily among Latinos. He was quick to point out that ABC has a much larger pool of potential Hispanic viewers—U.S.-born and presumably English-speaking Latinos make up 60 percent of the population, versus 40 percent foreign born—in addition to more powerful stations in all the major markets (ABC is VHF and Univision is UHF). Despite these differences, however, *Ugly Betty* was found to lag behind Univision's *La Fea Mas Bella*, the Mexican remake of the popular Colombian telenovela, which Nielson found had pulled three to four times the Hispanic ratings over ABC'S *Ugly Betty*.[9] The math simply does not add up, he insisted; it corroborates that sampling methods for Hispanic viewers are flawed and biased in favor of Spanish-language TV. Yet problems of sampling Hispanics go beyond the issue of language, as explained by a researcher working in Hispanic sampling:

> The ugly truth is that everyone cuts corners in terms of sample design and methodology because to do it right would imply the use of greater resources that they are not willing to commit to spend. Most companies are simply not sufficiently committed to the Hispanic market to insure a representative and stable sample size. All the while, they emphasize that they have a nationally representative sample.

Yet, measuring Latino audiences according to nativity, instead of language, as some Nielsen critics propose, presents its own sets of problems. How about accounting for the diversity among the foreign-born, such as between the upper-class immigrant and the undocumented working immigrant? And how about differences between the U.S.-born who is a second, third, or fourth generation—are they all part of the same market? And would this new type of classification backfire in the present nativist context by feeding distinctions between "the rightful" and the "illegal"

Latinos"—that is, those who are U.S.-born and hence more likely to be citizens, and the foreign-born who most likely are not? Will advertisers be scared off from investing in Spanish-language TV if their customers are so readily identified as foreign-born immigrants? At least, the present category of "Spanish-dominant" Latinos refers primarily to the foreign born, without openly signaling it so.

Yet Latinos' linguistic diversity remains a reality, and in a move that would have been unforeseeable when I first began to write about Hispanic marketing, some marketers are taking steps to move away from language. This move is critical if they are to assert their dominion over the bilingual and English-language Latino segment of the market, which is increasingly targeted by general market shops bypassing Hispanic marketing altogether. In addition, this move is part of the industry's strategy to remain competitive amidst a harsher immigration climate. Consider the Association of Hispanic Marketing Agencies' "Latino Cultural Identity Project," an initiative launched in 2006 specifically intended to move away from the industry's reliance on language and acculturation models, which I will turn to later. The project was carried out by AHAA's (Association of Hispanic Advertising Agencies) leadership in consultation with academicians, though, as admitted by Carl Kravetz, the then chair of AHAA, the lack of media alternatives for non–Spanish language ads remains the greatest obstacle to the initiative's success.

Indeed, despite the recent emergence of more English-language, U.S.-produced media—*George Lopez* and *Ugly Betty* in the major networks, and MTV's *Tr3s*, and *LatiNation* and *SiTV* for the younger Latino market, the media universe for the Latino market remains a primarily Spanish language–dominated one made up of imported programming, leaving little room for local talent and sensibilities. Not only are there powerful new Spanish-language media, such as V-Me TV, a Spanish-language, public television station out of New York, which is planning to expand nationally, but Univision has become an even stronger and more dominant player since I began to monitor the growth of Hispanic marketing and media in early 2000. In particular, national media trends favoring conglomeration and concentration of media outlets have facilitated Univision's growth, especially its controversial merger with Hispanic Broadcasting Corporation, the largest owner of Spanish-language radio stations at the time of the 2003 merger. As a result, Univision remains the largest and most dominant player in advertising revenues in the Hispanic market. It is the fifth largest television network and, in the words of Jorge

Reynardus, a New York–based advertising executive, Univision continues to be the "eight hundred pound gorilla in the room and the real engine of this market." Univision owns the top Spanish-language formatted radio station KLVE-FM (Los Angeles), the top Hispanic websites (Univision. com), and the top Spanish-language cable network (Galavision).[10]

Similar trends toward consolidation are visible in all media genres. Less than a handful of investors now dominate Spanish-language newspapers and English-language, Latino-oriented weeklies with companies such as Tribune Co., Knight Ridder (purchased in 2006 by The McClatchy Company), Hearst Corporation, and Impremedia buying out most independent weeklies or launching entirely new publications. These developments have raised serious concerns about the corporatization and dilution of the news and opinion editorials directed at this market.[11] Even equity funds dedicated to investments in the Latino market have joined the fore, assuring the continued commercialization and consolidation of the Hispanic market. The lure is seemingly limitless, as indicated in the marketer's e-mail to his client cited at the start of this chapter, or as noted by Marcos A. Rodriguez, the managing partner of one of these Latino-oriented equity funds, the Palladium Equity Partners. In Rodriguez's words, quoted in the *New York Times*, "investing in the Hispanic market in the United States [is like] investing in an emerging economy like Argentina or Mexico, but without the currency or political risk," following the common trend of presenting the Hispanic market as a nation in and of itself, or as the fifth largest and richest Latin American country.[12]

Concerns over media conglomeration and its effects on limiting diversity and local programming through its reliance on syndicated programming are not limited to Latino/a media. Yet, where Latinos are concerned, the situation is more dire. According to a study by Free Press, conglomeration has led to a decrease in minority ownership of media outlets; minorities make up 33 percent of the U.S. population, yet they own only 3.26 percent of all TV stations; whereas Latinos, who comprise 14 percent, own 1.11 percent of all TV stations.[13] In other words, the seemingly greater number of media offerings for Latinos veils their consignment to being mere consumers, rather than producers or owners of media outlets. It is important to note that neither of the largest Spanish-language TV networks, Univision, Telemundo, and Azteca TV, are Latino owned, but rather are controlled by American investors and corporations, alongside investments from Latin American media moguls. The newest owner of Univision is Egyptian-born, Israeli-raised American media mogul Haim

Saban, the 75th richest businessman according to Forbes, heading a group of American investing companies. Executive positions in Latino media continue to exhibit an ethnic division of labor, as confirmed by Juan Piñon's work on Azteca TV, one of the latest Spanish-language media entrants to the U.S. Latino market. As he found, top positions in production, programming, sales, and news are dominated by Anglo Americans or upper-class Latin Americans and the lower positions are held by U.S. Latinos, whereas there is a hierarchical racial and ethnic distribution of the Latino talent.[14] Speaking loudest about this hierarchy is the pervasive preference for speakers of so-called non-accented Spanish who are light-skinned, and who can be easily marketed in the transnational Spanish-language Latin American media market.

In addition to furthering inequalities in ownership and access to jobs, conglomeration has exacerbated the lack of programming and choice. Indeed, there exist more investors, more Spanish-language radio, and more programming. Communications professor Maria Castañeda estimates that from 2000 to 2004, media outlets for Latinos grew 125 percent. But, as she also notes, there is far less choice, as described below.[15] This was brought vividly to light during the 2006 public hearings on media diversity organized in New York City by the National Hispanic Media Coalition and the Free Press, among other media advocacy groups. There, over 100 attendees provided vivid and emotional testimony about the effects of conglomeration on minority audiences in front of two FCC commissioners and an audience of 400 primarily black and Latino New Yorkers.[16] It was impossible to miss the audience's commonly shared outrage: "Por favor no more blonde-blue eyed-heroines," and "no more imported programming," "no more washed out fake commercial editorials," were some of the many repeated concerns. Similar concerns were being voiced throughout U.S. cities, according to a coordinator involved in the organization of other town hall meetings. Among them, calls for more diverse programming and local news; and for more and fair coverage of our communities; for more politically diverse opinions; for representations that show that "we're more than violence, drugs and poverty"; for staff that knows about us, at least about the history of particular policy debates that affect our communities; alongside cries for local media that would help bring local, state and national emergency alerts; and whatever happened to our music, to Tejano, salsa, bachata, and other genres after all these radio takeovers? And why is Clear Channel Communications not being charged by the FCC for their anti-immigrant slurs?

Fig. 4. One of the hundreds of people who showed up at the New York City FCC hearings. Speakers testified on the need to stop media conglomeration and to demand more local content in the media. Photo courtesy of Free Press.

Unfortunately, these and other important considerations of content remain largely hidden from public view. Foremost, they remain subordinate to the profitability the Spanish-language media universe assures, such as by facilitating the types of consolidations that are increasingly apace in this market. This helps perpetuate the view that Latinos are most touched through Spanish, even if they do not speak it. A recent rendition of this argument is provided in *Hispanic Marketing: A Cultural Perspective* by Felipe and Betty Korzenny (2005). While acknowledging language diversity among Latinos, the authors fall back on the same views, even identifying Spanish as the "emotion-laden" language and English as the more "functionally oriented" language. Whether Spanish is also "functional" and hence deserving of public use and acceptance is never addressed. Instead the Spanish language is once again stereotypically described as the language that communicates most directly and emotionally with the Hispanic consumer, harking back to the dominant rational-Anglo/emotional-Latin Americans dyad made so commonplace by nineteenth-century U.S. and Latin American nationalist ideologies.

Through this and other strategies, conceptualizations of the Hispanic market have tended to anchor themselves in the immigrant, foreign-born, and Spanish-dominant Hispanics, the sector regarded as the most tame, reachable, and most easily moved with the right emotional appeal. These assumptions are evidenced by the comments of one marketer who, when describing the ideal Latino consumer, explained: "We are really talking about two different types of Hispanics. The Hispanic who is Spanish-dominant, the guy that works hard and at night watches a soap opera and goes to sleep, and the Latino." Interestingly, as he continued to elaborate on the distinction between them, he attached a political personality to the Latino but not to the Hispanic. "It is Latinos that politicians are after," he added "they are the ones that make noise and that complain if they don't like something," unlike the Hispanics who, according to him, just "watch soap operas, buy products and work hard." In other words, what surfaced as the most attractive Hispanic characteristic was a concern with material acquisition, not politics; the nonpolitical figure, epitomized as the illegal, the alien, the one that "stays home" and is most afraid of visibility. These traits remain veiled and transposed; they are never mentioned but always implied in the very category of "Hispanic."

Stark distinctions between Hispanics and Latinos, however, are not usually prevalent in the industry. And this move is primarily one of strategy, not ignorance. Years in the business of Hispanic marketing have made both marketers and clients quite sophisticated about Latinos; few can ignore differences regarding acculturation, language use, generation, class, and so forth. But differences remain economically risky. They are increasingly explored in Internet and in alternative media marketing, or in TV ads circulated in some states such as New Mexico, known for their large percentage of English-dominant Latinos. Yet few corporate clients are as invested in Hispanic marketing to explore differences among Latino demographics, and consequently, the putative "authentic" consumer of yesteryear remains the most profitable consumer. This is the one who, according to our discussion above, would more likely be called a Hispanic—used by marketers as a code for immigrants. In projecting the idea of the affluent but culture-bound Hispanic, we thus have one of many mélanges that are constructed in the process of selling the market: a construction involving the higher income of the U.S.-born cloaked in the authenticity of the foreign-born, which is only possible if we ignore the intraclass variation among U.S. Latinos. Never referred to as individuals, but rather as a market and a conglomerate, marketers then repeatedly vouch for its affluence and rapid growth, statistics which, not surprisingly, are never contrasted with income figures for non-Latinos.

The Culture that Makes Us Profitable Is the Culture that "Brings Us Down"

As with language, the market's growth and consolidation have ironically paralleled a constriction, rather than a diversification, of the type of cultural definitions that are generalized about the Latino consumer. The specter of culture looms large in this market where Latinos are regularly characterized as holding "communal values," among other cultural characterizations that additionally represent Latinos as more spontaneous, affectionate, and relaxed about time, as spiritual, and so on. "Anglos," who are their constant reference, in contrast, are said to see themselves as individuals, and to rely on themselves and institutions, rather than on family, and to stress symmetry and democracy in interpersonal and in cross-gender relationships, among other traits sharply contrasted to Latinos'.

These ideas are alive and well notwithstanding the industry's considerably greater complexity since the onset of Hispanic marketing. Consider AHAA's Cultural Identity Project, the first attempt to consolidate a common definition of Latinos' identity across advertising agencies.[17] The project is wrapped around the idiom of scholarship and research. It acknowledges complexity. We are now told that Latino identity "is NOT confined to language and acculturation. Rather, at the *heart* (emphasis mine) of Latino Cultural Identity is a set of complex, adaptable, intricate, and interrelated values that change through time according to the environment and external stimuli." However, it is the "heart" that is regarded as the core of Latino identity, a heart that has four chambers—a unique Interpersonal Orientation, Time and Space Perception, Spirituality and Gender Perception—responsible for its functioning. In other words, we are talking about a fancy new language and terminology for the same old cultural clichés that have long dominated the Latino market, which once again are described as being "radically different from that of non-Latinos" revolving around collectivism, and Familismo, which were once again sharply contrasted to non-Latino American core values, of individualism. "Ours is a collectivist culture in which the goals and interests of the group are emphasized over those of individual members. Our Interpersonal Orientation also drives our acceptance and giving of authority, our dependent relationships, our communication style, and our relaxed sense of privacy."[18]

I won't be so bold as to maintain that efforts to conduct research on "Latino values" or trends are hopeless or destined to fail. Researchers in myriad fields—health, linguistics, psychology, sociology, political science, and even anthropology—have sought to define and better understand human behaviors and attitudes through models and measurements. Instead, I am concerned with the ease with which many scholarly insights can be so easily trivialized in the context of marketing. It is also noteworthy that many generalizations made about Latino consumers are not different from those generalized by the insidious culture of poverty thesis, where Latin culture traits are held responsible for Latinos' "intrinsic" lack of ambition and consequently, their self-imposed status. In fact, based on the writings of key Latino marketing brokers, there is a general recognition that the culture that makes Latinos profitable is the same culture that brings them down.

Lionel Sosa, who has made millions marketing Latino values to corporate America, provides a poignant example of this view. His *Think and Grow Rich: A Latino Choice* (2006), a Latino version of Napoleon Hill's 1937 bestseller *Think and Grow Rich*, maintains that Latino success is a matter of shedding the "cultural baggage derived from our roots." In his view, Latinos can achieve success through Hill's mantra, but only after shedding their common cultural baggage derived from Catholicism, Spanish colonization, and their disposition to respect authority. It is these values that have led Latinos toward a path of shame, suffering, sweat, and sacrifice, rather than toward a path that cultivates the Anglo-American values of independence and individuality. Sosa's theory harks back to centuries-old Hispanophobic views most represented by the infamous Black Legend, which represents Spanish civilization as inherently barbaric, making their descendants prone to criminality, vice, and indolence. This is a view that reverberates in debates over immigration, as evidenced in the words of Representative Tom Tancredo, chairman of the House Immigration Reform Caucus, and others who fear the cultural invasion represents a "scourge" and a "cultural suicide" for Western civilization.[19]

Similar messages of Hispanics' doomed cultural legacy are repeated in numerous self-help and motivational books, which are among the fastest growing genre dominating the category of nonfiction commercial books of "Latino interest." Written by successful Latino "pillars," these books often follow three very predictable formulas. First is when the authors put Latinos down for not pulling up their bootstraps. A recent example is the controversial yet highly publicized "One Nation, One Standard: An Ex-Liberal on How Hispanics Can Succeed Just Like Other Immigrant Groups" (2006) by veteran Puerto Rican former congressman Herman Badillo. Years ago Badillo became infamous for his racist comments against rural Mexican and Dominican immigrants, whose "deficiencies" he blamed for overtaxing the New York City public school system. This time, Badillo is an equal opportunity defamer; he chastises all Latino parents for not caring enough about their children's education. Entirely ignoring discrimination, and the current deficiencies in public education infrastructure and even the growing surveillance that deters undocumented parents from becoming involved in the public school system, Badillo bemoans Latinos for failing to prioritize education and not following the paths of earlier immigrants. His diatribe provides a good example of the pervasiveness of this "blame the victim" formula.

The second dominant nonfiction literary trend is when authors remind us that success comes to Latinos who adopt "mainstream" values of upward mobility, and who keep their self-sabotaging values in check, as we are told by Lionel Sosa's books or by Hispanic businessman Charles Patrick Garcia in *A Message from Garcia: Yes, You Can Succeed* (2006). Then, there is the increasingly popular trend of urging Latinos to draw from their strengths, be it by repackaging their culture in cutesey ways, as does former CBS and FOX anchorman Mario Bosquez in *The Chalupa Rules: A Latino Guide to Gringolandia* (2005), or by strategically taking advantage of their Latino values, such as their innate strengths in relationship building, as we are summoned to do in *The Latino Advantage in the Workplace: Using Who You Are to Get Where You Want to Be* (2006) by Argentinean-born and -raised business consultants Mariela Dabbah and Arturo Poire.

A pervasive Latin/Anglo dyad underlies many of these authors' ponderings, where culture always triumphs among Hispanics, making it irrelevant to identify them by class, nationality, ethnicity, generation, or any other variable, as they are all culturally the same. In a similar manner, a presumed white Anglo America becomes the key symbolic reference in advertisers' conceptualization of the Hispanic consumer, projecting commonalities that override differences of race, class, or ethnicity among Hispanics. One need only talk to advertisers to perceive the strength of these ideas, as I learned

Fig. 5. Collage of recent book covers discussing how Latinos can achieve success in business and life. Photo by Johana Londoño.

after asking some New York advertisers to describe the "average" consumer to which they target their advertisements. These were described, among overtly culturalist characterizations that recycled a view of a "traditional" Hispanic in opposition to "Americans," as people who are "conservative, who care about their culture, who are respectful of their elders and traditions, and who love to eat rice and beans," among other culturalist generalizations. Communicating with Hispanic consumers becomes a matter of communicating with emotion and to the emotions. As simply put by Lionel Sosa, in his first and best-selling book, *The Americano Dream*: "What we're dealing with here is the logic of the heart, not the logic of reason, and the power of its effect on everyone, but especially Latinos is remarkable. . . . Like our homelands we are lush and warm. We are extraordinarily open with each other. We communicate through a touch, a gesture an embrace" (1998: 112).

Ultimately, despite the growing sophistication of Hispanic marketing—more stakeholders, investors, and programming—the view that the Latino market is principally defined by its culture remains unrelenting. It is this view that drives the continuous production of research, surveys, and portraits of the Hispanic consumer; unlike the mainstream consumer—who is targeted in terms of class, generations, or gender—the Latino is continually reduced to an issue of "culture."

I have described the problems of this type of portrayal at great length elsewhere. Suffice it to point here to the continued folklorization of Latinos, part and parcel of their projection as a market that is easily marketable, authentic, and ready for mass consumption. As we have seen, these representations continue to reference the immigrant population—the same

[handwritten margin note: Latinos are continually defined by culture]

population that is constructed as a threat in mainstream society—as the idealized authentic consumer, necessitating its continued sanitization as the market that exhibits the "Nation's" most "positive" values. In other words, the commodification of Latinos presupposes their disciplining into the "right" way of being an "ethnic." This construction presents Latinos as possessing a unique, bounded, and separate culture from U.S. culture, which is simultaneously constructed as homogeneous, white, and "mainstream," not unlike Latino think tanks are said to do, as described in Chapter 1.

The perils of this type of representation were visible during the 2004 election where Latinos were treated as a unique cultural entity, targeted through multiple culturally specific ads. But, as we saw, they were interpellated as equal in values to "mainstream" America because of their so-called core conservative values of family so keenly translated to the anti–gay rights and anti-abortion Republican agenda. In other words, what we have seen is a preponderance of tamer and more publicly palatable appeals and representations of Latinos that are less threatening to an imagined "mainstream." And I am not implying that Latinos' so-called positive American values of family, hard work, and patriotism could not be just as easily inserted into a progressive agenda of change. Images of families marching together during the 2006 pro-immigrant demonstrations on May 1 should decisively give political pundits some alternative ideas of how to deploy Latinos' family values. As noted earlier, however, the xenophobia unleashed by the immigration debate makes me skeptical that Latinos would be portrayed as the active agents they are any time soon, or that their "values" would be too directly associated with an agenda of political or social reform.

I also remain concerned with the selective manipulation of marginality in the construction of the affluent yet authentic ethnic consumer. As we saw, this involved veiling that ethnicity and affluence are antithetical concepts for U.S. minorities. After all, Latinos' supposed cultural differences may render them attractive to marketers, but these differences are more likely to be construed in greater society as an impediment to upward mobility, a mark of their foreignness and hence lack of social or political entitlement. Certainly images of upwardly mobile Latinos can have a positive role by communicating that heritage is not antagonistic to upward mobility, that Latinos are entitled to mobility as they are to their "culture." But images of affluence cannot bring empowerment on their own, especially if they mask the realities of marginality, unemployment, and racism as they sanitize Latinos for public consumption.

From Rags to Riches?
On the Politics of Latino Consumer/Citizenship

> Hispanics embody a hard work ethic; familial responsibility; religious faith; pride; appreciation; and a sincere desire to learn and better themselves. All these make Hispanics ideal consumers and ideal Americans. . . . Legislators and our fellow Americans cannot ignore the influence of immigrants . . . on corporate America's bottom line and on the U.S. economy.
>
> —Association of Hispanic Advertising Agencies,
> "The Dollars and 'Sense' of the Immigration Debate"

In sum, marketing discourse is not without political and economic repercussions. Not only does it offer an extremely narrow means of entry into the "mainstream"; it also prioritizes consumption over income, and spending over employment or economic parity, veiling the ongoing segmentation between those with "real" jobs, and income, and those who lack it. In this context, the only reference for social parity becomes spending, or putative consumer power of individuals, calculated through disembodied bulk estimates, never to be contextualized against the consumption rates of the all too real, powerful groups in society. This fosters my skepticism over the abundance of reports and discussions about Latinos as a market. Yes, Latinos are undoubtedly gaining visibility through such discussions, but only as a market, never as a people. And, "markets" have to be containable and approachable, if they are to be attractive to capital. In this context, the tropes of conservatives for spirituality, family values, and emotion can be studied for what they are: not so much valid descriptions of Latinos, but rather, a projection of dominant society's longing for docile, unthreatening consumers. These preferred subjects may work hard, have values and traditions that American society can be proud of, but must remain unthreateningly in their place, at a distance, with their "culture" as a visible and unquestionable reference to the existence of a white non-raced U.S. world. All the while Latinos remain relegated to consumers, increasingly distanced from access and ownership of Latino-targeted media.

Yet representations and discourses are meaningless without a consideration of the social and historical reference in which they circulate. And considering the preeminent role business sectors play in any public debate on immigration, it is important to acknowledge another side of the critical scenario I have described. I am referring to the role consumer politics may play within contemporary cultural politics, despite their very significant limitations. As Lizabeth Cohen's work on the transformations on consumer politics in postwar America and beyond shows, consumers' political realm has been greatly diminished, from one where consumers could effect social policy transformations to assure consumers' protection and well-being through fair prices and market conditions, to one where their political role is reduced to simply the purchase of products (Cohen 2003). She signals this transformation by distinguishing between "consumer citizens" and "purchaser consumers" which, in her view, does not invalidate the existence of more policy- and structure-oriented consumer politics today. What this distinction does is mark the diminished context in which consumers can assert themselves politically to effect lasting policy change, which is especially true for Latinos.

Undoubtedly, the Hispanic marketing industry has played a central role in raising the visibility of Hispanics in public life, if only by alerting businesses, politicians, unions, and even religious leaders to the need to cater to Latinos, if they are to grow in profits and numbers. The growing realization that Latinos buy products, that they contribute to the economy, not only as producers but as consumers—paying taxes even when they buy a Coca-Cola, as noted by a panelist at a Mexican immigrants forum in New York City—has been an important political gain. It has fueled corporate American's growing interest in the Latino market, and their relatively more positive attitudes toward immigrants. Indeed, as stated by the Association of Hispanic Advertising Agencies position on the immigration debate, Latinos represent "about 6 to 7 million invisible consumers—that's a lot of diapers, a lot of cars, a lot of food . . . and frankly a lot of dollars that can be attributed to the immigrant population,"[20] and this point calls for an assessment of the role consumer politics may be playing within contemporary Latino cultural politics. It is worth returning then to all the hoopla about immigrants' economic value with which I started this chapter.

The excitement over *Business Week's* 2005 cover story, "Embracing Illegals: Companies Are Getting Hooked on the Buying Power of 11 Million Undocumented Immigrants," during La Raza's 2005 annual meeting comes to mind.[21] Amidst discussion of the growing xenophobia raised by the immigration debate, the mood was somber as audience members brought up case after case of immigrant discrimination in their communities, until an audience member brought up the *Business Week* cover. "See, America cannot do without its Latino immigrants," he noted while pointing to the cover, which unmistakably showed a Latin American, most specifically Mexican or Central American, as signaled by the picture of a border fence.

What was cause for much discussion was the cover's bluntly optimistic and idyllic representation of the U.S. business community's hopeful views of undocumented immigrants: an upwardly mobile message of from "rags to shopping" that anyone would gladly embrace for herself. On the left side, we see the stereotypical picture of the undocumented immigrant recently arrived carrying nothing but a bag of clothes. He is in motion, but we can see that he carries a dirty clutch, that his cuffs are rolled up as if to ease the sweat of a night of walking in the desert. The background is dark, gloomy, and dangerous, as signaled by the barbed-wired fence to his back and the spiked cactus at his feet. In contrast, the right side of the cover presents an idyllic sight. We now see three-quarters of his body, evoking perhaps his newly attained assimilation quantum? He's smiling and looking to the distance. He seems happy and content, and in motion, but this time he is moving forward. He is returning from a shopping spree, as signaled by the five colorful shopping bags he carries with confidence and head on, in direct contrast to the dirty bag he once dragged behind him. He is no longer walking among cactuses but along a well-paved white road—the road to whiteness? In the background we see a perfectly manicured lawn and a road of identical and spacious suburban homes. We could assume he lives in one of these homes. He is dressed conservatively in a pin-striped shirt and khaki pants. The sky is bright, and undisturbed by clouds. No wonder the cover made such an impact.

At the 2006 NCLR conference, pride over Latinos' consumer power was quick to resurface. I am reminded of the audience member who, Texan hat in hand, remarked forcefully about the best ways to get the attention of an elected official:

> Our [political] representatives get tired of hearing the violin. If you give them economic numbers they tend to hear better. In your testimony to politicians let them know that the machine they're so afraid of, that immigration is fueling the fastest and largest economy. That if you add the state gross product of the California and Southwest economy we may not need them "si siguen chingando" (if they keep fucking with us).

His comments drew open laughter—people obviously identified with the speaker's comments and with the less sensitive political climate everyone

Fig. 6. The rags to riches cover of Business Week *gave much to talk about at the 2005 annual Conference of the National Association of La Raza. It corroborated that, as an attendee noted, "They can't do without us immigrants."*

must tread that he described so clearly. This is a context in which needs, or "the violin," are considered to be exhausted or exhausting, leaving the numbers game, as in arguments that underscore Latinos' economic might and contributions, as the only viable option for Latino advocacy.

The point is that Latinos are becoming increasingly aware of their economic value and contributions and however simplistic, skewed, and problematic their depiction as consumers has been and continues to be, one must also ask whether this recognition is likely to be politically relevant in years to come. In fact, this awareness may be more significant than ever in present society, where private companies rule the day and where, unlike the state and public sectors, many of them are going out of their way to do business with undocumented immigrants, even accepting alternative forms of ID from undocumented immigrants, such as the Mexican consulate–issued matricula. The financial services industry working in areas such as remittances, bank accounts, credit cards, and home loans is perhaps at the forefront of this trend. And so are media research company giants such as Nielsen and Arbitron, which are in the business of "counting people" and have never distinguished between the documented or not, as noted earlier by Arbitron's Sales and Marketing chief, especially when Spanish radio becomes their major engine for ratings. Smaller retailers, for their part, have been even more aggressive in their courting of Mexican immigrants. The "Pesos for Pizza" promotion launched by Dallas-based Pizza Patron in 2007 may be the best example of this economic move at the local level. The chain's owner received death threats and hate mail for accepting pesos as payment. But he stood his ground, carrying 10–15 percent of the business in pesos, which proved a winning move for the franchise (Kovach 2007). In September 2007, the magazine *DiversityInc* devoted an entire issue to "The Business Case for Immigration," a title that succinctly made the case for the economic and business value of immigrants. Widespread knowledge of the fact that immigrants contribute not only through work but through consumption informed the May 1's "Day Without Immigrants," where immigrants' supporters were urged to not only not work or go to work, but to defer selling and buying. The word is out. Latinos' buying power makes a difference. More specifically, immigrants' buying power makes a difference.

Conservative economists may have disregarded the economic impact of the boycott as insignificant. In their view, the U.S. economy is way too big and complex to be affected by any single sector; it was mainly immigrant businesses and immigrants themselves that were hurt most by the boycott.[22] But if indeed the Hispanic market is an $862 billion market, as AHAA tells us, then a future consumer boycott won't be ignored for long.[23] In this regard, a Hispanic marketer and twenty-five-year industry veteran with whom I discussed the May 1 demonstrations shared interesting insights. He was especially infuriated with the extremely controversial yet mostly hidden measure included in the more "generous" Senate immigration bill making English the official language of the United States. He noted that this is a sentiment most of his colleagues shared, and that has galvanized many to defend the importance of Spanish-language advertising. He had yet to meet one single client, however, that had raised doubts about advertising in Spanish. On the contrary, he felt that clients are more than ever committed to market segmentation, that many had even been awakened by images of crowds of immigrants and Latino supporters incited to march by Spanish-language DJs. In his view, it had been an education for them to see people come out and have a voice. He was even quick to turn the events into a marketing pitch. As he explained: "If Spanish-language advertising can produce these massive crowds, imagine what it can do to their products!"

Briefly then, marketing is likely to be the only place where we may not witness a direct backlash against Latinos, whether undocumented or not. Marketers may be reaching out to the youth, to the "acculturated" and the bilingual market, but they are still largely dependent on immigrants to "refurbish" the base of their market. They also know full well that Hispanic marketing, as we currently know it, will be unavoidably affected by the halt of immigration and the policing and persecution of their market base. And insofar as this is the case, we must question the ascendancy of marketing as a space of presentation. Marketers and corporations may be Latinos' number one cheerleader, but they cheer us solely for buying their products. They reduce us to sanitized representations; their cheers mask Latinos' ongoing relegation to being mere consumers who lack access and ownership in the very media economy that profits from them. If only for these reasons, they cannot ever be our sole, and most powerful, spokespersons.

PART II

Political Economy
Spaces and Institutions

4

The Times-Squaring of El Barrio

On Mega Projects, Spin, and "Community Consent"

It's not every day that you get to re-imagine two entire city blocks . . . and work to create something totally new.
—Daniel Doctoroff, New York City's deputy mayor at a Harlem Chamber of Commerce Economic Development Luncheon

Talk about scale and bulk is good. Desire for cultural components is great. Thinking Green is appropriate. . . . But that's small change. . . . We want a project, but a project that's planned by us, designed by us, and programmed for us. For after this, there is no more. Don't let this massive project be predetermined and solely given to one developer, . . . not at the expense and sacrifice of the people who live and work here.
—Gary Anthony Johnson, member of Community Board 11

That New York City is undergoing a rapid and advanced stage of gentrification and that communities of color are experiencing the greatest burden is a simple understatement. Take the current transformations in East Harlem, a.k.a. Spanish Harlem, or El Barrio, now increasingly also known as SpaHa, among other, more chic names. As is the case all over the city, projects coming to East Harlem are larger in density and design, increasingly fast-tracked and presented as inevitable, triggering debates about the future of the area's cultural identity. Thus, it was not that surprising when the largest commercial and residential development coming to the area planned to include a Latin-themed cultural component in its marketing and execution plans in order to foster public acquiescence for the project.

What follows examines this project, which I discuss with its original working name of "The Uptown N.Y. Project" and what it reveals about how Latin culture is being inserted into urban projects and about the difficulties communities face when attempting to wrest control of these developments. For, more so than with other recent developments, East Harlemites appeared to take considerable control of the Uptown N.Y. Project. In a rare and celebrated victory in 2005, they halted its progress to demand greater community involvement. The end result was the formation of a Community Board 11 Task Force in January 2006, which was limited to making recommendations about the project's contents, and could not halt its inevitable development and potential effects. However, by providing a venue for "community" involvement, the task force brings meaningful attention to the issues at stake when communities contest projects in the face of what is becoming an increasingly inaccessible planning process.

This chapter suggests that urban planning is best considered as a conduit of spin rather than a medium for public debate, and that its primary function is to foster public acquiescence, by creating the spin and the perception of community involvement, consultation, and openness. Planning and urban policy have long been linked to real estate interests. Its pretense of technical knowledge and its purported interest in the greater civic good make planning central to curbing dissent and conflict, all the while real estate and private developers remain inordinately dominant in the planning process (Diaz 2005). Accordingly, writers have exposed the community consultation process as irrelevant or as a process in need of improvement—be it through the training of its members and other measures devoted to assuring increased community accountability (Chait 2001). These failures were amply evident in my previous research on gentrification in East Harlem, where the area's community board was repeatedly consulted but was hardly able to control or shape developments to meet their needs. But now, I suggest, the community planning process functions quite efficiently, if we consider it a public relations tool, or even a marketing focus group vehicle for soliciting "community input," for projects that are fated to be exclusive of local interests and needs. In other words, I propose that planning be considered the ultimate spin. It creates the perception that projects are in fact catering to communities, not solely by fostering a veil of inclusivity but foremost of inevitability and a fait accompli.

Inserting Latinidad in the Luxury City

To understand the Uptown N.Y. Project's significance, it is important to grasp the enormity of its scale, and how it fits within New York City's larger development agenda, and in particular, within the agenda of the newly created Mayoral Commission for the promotion of Latin media and entertainment. First, in terms of scale, the project was slated to cover two city blocks, from 125th to 127th Streets, and the length of an avenue from Second to Third Avenues, making it a massive project by any New York City standard. Most important, the project represents one if not the last opportunity to develop two entirely "empty" contiguous spots along the highly coveted 125th Street Harlem corridor that is a central anchor of any development in Upper Manhattan, linking Harlem as it does from West to East and river to river. As a result, heavy-hitter developers were involved from the beginning. The proposal was developed by Urban Strategic Partners (the same developers formerly involved with the Harlem USA shopping mall in West Harlem), and included a combination of retail, ranging from small outlet stores to destination (read Wal-Mart type) retailers, and approximately 1,500 units of housing in a series of 42-story buildings. An underground bus depot to house over 80 buses also would have been part of the project. In other words, this was a mega-project that left no hot buttons untouched: the prospect of commercial establishments that would squash local businesses, the environmental threat presented by higher traffic and bus emissions that would have exacerbated the area's horrific asthma rates, and the development of more "mixed-used housing" that everyone feared would result in more unaffordable housing.[1]

Yet once again, and following a common trend in neoliberal urban developments, culture became THE hook. One of the most intriguing aspects of gentrification is how communities' opposition to developments is oftentimes tamed by the inclusion of cultural initiatives that allege to be representative of these very same communities. Two evocative examples of this culture-based strategy in the Harlem and Upper Manhattan region are the inclusion of a Heritage Tourism Initiative within the Upper Manhattan Empowerment Zone, and The 125 "River to River" study's emphasis on maintaining and building on Harlem's "historic and existing character" as part of the development plans for the area.[2] Matt Wambua, the deputy mayor's office senior planning consultant for projects in Upper Manhattan and the Bronx, explained: "We want to keep this as a unique corridor,

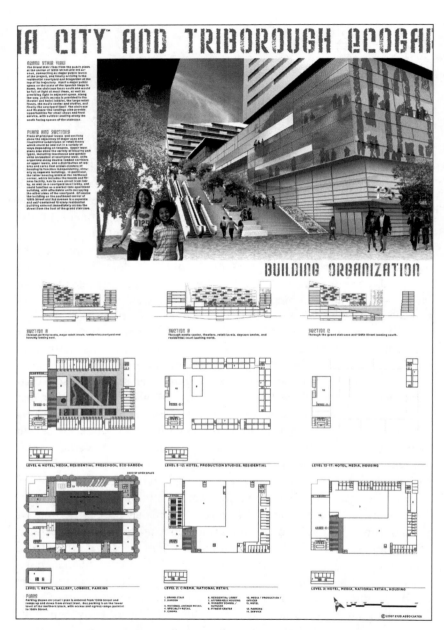

Fig. 7. Above, one of the designs submitted to NYC Office of Economic Development for review. The developer was one of the few that actively incorporated local community concerns and local groups as development partners. The project, however, was disqualified early on. It provides a good example of the massive scope of the project. Courtesy of Ben Zitron.

anchored and rooted in the rich black and Latino tradition, a corridor that could be universally pointed to as the capital of black and Latino arts and culture. We don't want to end up with a corridor that could be anywhere in New Jersey."

Wambua, who is African American and described himself as being especially concerned over the need to bring about more "balanced" gentrification that would lessen displacement of communities of color, considered it a victory that the "River to River" study had achieved a consensus on the need to respect the area's cultural identity. Developers and bureaucrats tend to be "scared to death" to talk about arts and culture because it is too "loaded" with issues of ethnicity, he noted. But this did not apply to him or the deputy mayor's office. In his view, the value a cultural component can add to any given project and to its ability to obtain community support far outweighs the "messiness" that often accompanies the development of any cultural initiative.

As a result, the Uptown N.Y. Project included a "Latino-themed mini-city" featuring performance spaces, recording studios, entertainment spaces, and even talk of housing for artists, in other words, a cultural component strategically informed by previous community debates. For years, the area's Puerto Rican leadership had been complaining that Puerto Ricans and "their culture" had been bypassed by most developments and that East Harlem had not received funding from the Upper Manhattan Empowerment Zone Culture Industry Fund, debates I captured at length in a previous work. Briefly, the debate had fed the frenzy over whether there would ever be any Latino-controlled or -evoking project in the area that would at least symbolically help quench the area's rapid gentrification, leaving residents clamoring for more Latino-specific development. The idea of a Latino-themed component was also informed by East Harlem's long-standing need for more culture and entertainment venues. Proposals for theaters and entertainment venues in East Harlem had circulated for years, to no avail. East Harlem is greatly lacking in culture and entertainment infrastructures, as evident in the poignant example residents were likely to point to: their having to leave the area to watch a film.

These locally stated needs notwithstanding, the Uptown's cultural component was developed with far broader interests in mind. Specifically, the idea was developed in consultation with the Latin Media & Entertainment Commission (LMEC), established by Mayor Bloomberg in 2003 to realize New York's untapped potential as the Capital of Latin Media as part of the administration's strategy for investment diversification in the areas of tourism and entertainment. In particular, the commission was given the mandate of marketing all that New York has to offer to Latin industries throughout the world, mainly, the ability to target "the most diverse and sizable Latino population in the world" as equally as to experience the newest wave of "Latin culture and media entertainment."[3] With Jennifer Lopez and Robert de Niro as honorary chairs, the commission includes artists and actors such as salsa singer Willie Colon and actor Antonio Banderas, Hispanic marketing moguls such as Daisy Exposito and Joe Wiscovitch, along with representatives of the major mainstream entertainment industries such as Time Warner, television stations, and the major Spanish-language media. There's even a Miss Universe among the commissioners, the 2003 winner from the Dominican Republic, Amelia Vega. In other words, the commission's membership provided a "who's who" list that provided the appearance, if not necessarily an assurance, of legitimacy and representativity that symbolically sanctioned its role as advisor to the mayor on business and strategies specific to the Latin media and entertainment industry. The heads of seven city agencies under the direction of the deputy mayor for Economic Development and Rebuilding are also part of the Commission as ex-officio members, strategically connecting the LMEC with all the governmental units involved in issues of planning and development in the city. This citywide membership would ensure an equally citywide, and hence, outward vision at odds with East Harlemites' demand for initiatives that would either come from or be specifically directed to their immediate community.

To understand the workings of the LMEC, however, we first need to delve into the workings of the Bloomberg administration under which it was initially founded. Specifically, we need to consider "the Bloomberg way," as Julian Brash has described the Bloomberg administration's corporate- and technocratic-centered approach to government and urban planning.[4] In this approach, the city is to be conceived and treated as a luxury product to be developed and marketed, the government as a corporation, the mayor as CEO, and businesses, not residents, as its clients. In this new governing context, only a billionaire and the corporate-savvy Bloomberg or his staff, made up of highly educated technocrats, is presented as being the most able to supersede narrow interests for the sake of the global city's greater good. This informs Brash's conclusion that the Bloomberg administration is simultaneously and excessively political and anti-political: political for advancing the interests of a particular class over others, more specifically of the business elites of whom Bloomberg himself is a member, and anti-political for invalidating criticisms of his governing and planning agenda as a rudimentary and self-interested form of politics.

Central to the "Bloomberg way" has been the hiring of staff members who share the mayor's corporate and business background, especially the staff in the most important development positions in his administration, such as the deputy mayor for Economic Development and Rebuilding, Daniel Doctoroff, and the president of the Economic Development Corporation (EDC), Andrew Alper. Bloomberg's corporate-centered approach is also behind some of the most unprecedented levels of centralization, with all development projects and policies placed under Doctoroff's control.[5] This strategy is evident in the inclusion of the heads of key agencies involved in economic development in the LMEC, assuring access and synergy between the mayor's office and the range of Latin entertainment and media industries represented by the commissioners.

But it is not at the level of organization but rather in matters of vision where synergies between "the Bloomberg way" and the workings of the LMEC are most evident. Bloomberg's new investment strategy relies on branding the intangibles of New York City as a luxury product, rather than in lowering the costs of doing business in the city, such as by extending tax incentives to particular industries.[6] The goal was to market the value added and the competitive advantage gained by doing business in New York; in other words, in selling New York for the sake of it being New York, because it is the most efficient place to do business, or because it has the greatest and most educated talent, and so on. Bloomberg has also sought to diversify the type of business that comes to New York, with special emphasis on attracting high-value industries willing and able to capitalize on the value of doing business in New York, such as, among others, media, information technology, tourism, and television and film production.[7]

LMEC's mission of anchoring New York City as the Latin capital was therefore centrally in sync with this larger economic directive of attracting high-value industries, such as business in Latin media and entertainment. Thus, following the Bloomberg administration's penchant for mega tourist events, such as national conventions, the failed Olympics, the Country Music Awards, and so on, the LMEC would rely, not so much on local events and initiatives, but rather on attracting image-branding events of international recognition and weight. Hence, on the LMEC website, it is the New York International Latino Film Festival (2004), the Latin Alternative Music conference (2005), both of which gathered Latin American and nationwide Latino producers and productions of national and international appeal, or the "First Fiesta Cup Soccer Game" between the "two international powerhouses" of soccer, Argentina and Peru (2004), and most recently, the live broadcast of the Latin Grammys, that are most prominently showcased as examples of the LMEC's mission.[8] The relevant word here is "International." In other words, the LMEC vision was dominated by an outwardly image-conscious strategy, a commercial and global version of Latin culture that would be highly tourist friendly but not easily aligned with East Harlemites' needs.

Predictably, the gap between the LMEC's vision for the Uptown's Latin cultural component and that of East Harlemites' became a contentious issue of debate. A year into the project, few East Harlemites had been consulted about what exactly would be included in the cultural component project, while the project was fast tracked over and beyond other community-originated proposals. Area cultural institutions felt excluded and deliberately kept at bay.[9] Glimpses of the project's elitist orientation and top-down vision, however, were more than apparent. In particular, they were revealed at a private event hosted by the LMEC and Merrill Lynch as early as June 2005. The event was closed to the press, though *Marketing and Medios* reported the "unveiling of a vision for a Latin Entertainment District in New York City," the scope of which was evident in the perceptive comments of Afro-Latina actress and singer Daphne Rubin-Vega, who was one of the selected attendees. While not a resident of East Harlem, her comments were evocative of the type of statements that would be heard among East Harlemites: "It's a utopian idea, and utopian ideas are good by definition. They mean well, but the concept didn't originate with the Latino community of El Barrio; the people involved don't necessarily live there. I'm not saying it's going to suck—if you don't mind buying *Guayaberas* designed by Isaac Mizrahi, I guess it's a good idea."[10]

The entertainment district would never be fully unveiled to East Harlem residents. Not until December 2005 did the LMEC hold an informational meeting to discuss a proposal for the "city of dreams." But only selected guests were invited. A preliminary architectural proposal, dated January 2006 and kept at the offices of East Harlem's Community Board, however, revealed that plans for the glitzy entertainment space were well under way. This was so, despite the well-attended July 2005 meeting where East Harlemites had expressed opposition and demanded community input.[11] The proposal, titled "Ciudad de Sueños," identified the City of New York as its client and was developed by none other than JERDE, the

LA-based architecture and design firm, well known for their experiential designs in retail and entertainment such as the Mall of America in Minneapolis and the Universal CityWalk in Los Angeles. JERDE's philosophy is one of authenticity in their place-making design, though the tourist bubbles that result have long been criticized as "cordoned-off spaces [that] play up fake realities to replace real ones, while the public must pay to experience them."[12] These words could well describe the firms' design for East Harlem's "Ciudad de Sueños." The proposal revolved around a small city within a city with a brick-covered street-level plaza that sought to resemble New York City brownstones transitioning into facades of modern glass and light. Never mind that tenement buildings, not brownstones, dominate East Harlem's landscape! Flickering neon ads of Latin celebrities such as Shakira and Jessica Alba adorned the design's views of the middle court, resembling a circular Times Square–like futuristic center. The city within the city could well have fallen directly from Mars onto East Harlem, given its nonexistent resemblance with the local landscape.

The Nebulous Mega Project and the Challenge of the Local

The fact is that a year into the project's planning process, it was difficult to sort out spin from reality. I was told by residents that the Uptown Project's Latino cultural component was highlighted when the project was presented to primarily Puerto Rican and Latino audiences and avoided altogether if few were present. In fact, the entire project had a smoke and mirrors quality throughout. The project's website, for instance, featured an almost undetectable picture of the proposed project's design, a vague description of its contents, and no drawings detailing specific plans (the prompt under "drawings" remained under construction during the year the project was being presented to the community). Nor did anyone from the project's development team ever seem to be available to answer questions and phone calls.

East Harlemites responded. As early as July 2005, a public scoping meeting held by the City's Economic Development Corporation (EDC) at the Julia de Burgos Cultural Center attracted over 250 East Harlem residents opposed to the project. The project's lack of transparency was also a catalyst to the creation of eastharlempreservation.org, the first website dedicated to issues of preservation and development in East Harlem. Founded in 2005 by Marina Ortiz, in direct response to her own frustrations over the lack of concrete information about the project, the website would play a central role in bringing the project to public scrutiny and debate. As she recalled: "They would put up their easels with plans, but would take their presentations after the meeting, and there was no place where people could study and read and grasp the magnitude of their proposals."

Indeed, the shrinking of Puerto Rican physical space in East Harlem has paralleled the growth of website portals purposefully concerned with the marking of Puerto Rican history onto the far cheaper realm of virtual space. Among them: Virtualboricua.com, Mibarrio.org, and eastharlem-preservation.org. Ortiz, the founder of eastharlempreservation.org, had first-hand experiences with issues of displacement and gentrification and had had enough. Her vision was that East Harlem Preservation would serve as a clearinghouse and an advocate for community needs vis-à-vis this project, and others to come. As she described, she had to hound all pertinent parties for information and cut through much bureaucratic red tape to collect information that was supposed to be public and widely available, but through her efforts, memos, documents, studies, and even testimonies read at different hearings on the project were summarily posted for everyone to see.

Eastharlempreservation.org quickly became a key space for documenting East Harlem's everyday happenings, as pictures from public meetings, cultural events, and street fairs and festivals quickly found their way onto the website. But most important, it also became the one space where anyone interested in the Uptown N.Y. Project, and any other development in the community, could find information, serving as a catalyst for community involvement in whatever new project would come their way. But there were also other key actors concerned about the Uptown Project. By the fall of 2005, Melissa Mark Viverito, an East Harlem activist who months earlier had publicly called for community input in the project, had been elected as the new councilwoman, becoming East Harlem's first Puerto Rican councilwoman. There was also a new Borough of Manhattan president, and new members of the local community board, who, having been recently elected, brought renewed sensitivity to community concerns and insisted on bringing the project to public debate.

The leverage these actors have in their dealings with developers is obviously limited. At the same time, development is never as immune to local intervention and debate as many developers would like it to be. In fact, contemporary development strives on the existence of mechanisms for community representation. In New York City, community input into development and land-use issues is provided by the local community boards, made up of appointed volunteers whose recommendations are not binding, but rather advisory, but need to be consulted in most public land-use decisions as required by the City Charter. Their role is to express community concerns and dissent, but foremost they help to facilitate development by fostering acquiescence in the guise of community participation.[13]

Awareness of the limitations intrinsic to the workings of the community boards is central to understanding the limited scope of the Uptown N.Y. Project's Task Force. Indeed, there was much good will from elected officials who demanded that the project be developed anew and the community consulted at every stage of the process. Yet, like the community board, the task force could do little to enforce or oblige developers to comply with community concerns. Most specifically, the task force's activities were limited to drafting a list of "elements of consensus" for the project's RFP (Request for Proposals), following the model of the community benefits agreements that are becoming increasingly common for obtaining residents' approval of large-scale projects. These agreements are negotiated between developers and communities, and often involve giveaways of space, facilities, and other "community needs" to the community in exchange for approval of projects that would otherwise be rejected because of their ill effects with regard to quality-of-life issues, such as traffic, the environment, or a project's sheer size.[14] Except who sits at the bargaining table to represent the "community," what elements are deemed worthy of compromise, and who enforces the agreements, oftentimes remain nebulous and ill-defined. In fact, these key issues are rarely specified and are much less subject to accountability, making the entire "community agreements" process easily dismissed, in the words of one critic, as a "public front to a backdoor deal."

For instance, the involvement of the staff from city agencies in the task force meetings and the fact that elected officials, such as the borough president and the councilwoman, served as ex-officio members quickly cast shadows on the task force's relative autonomy and on its ability to voice dissent. Most troubling, it was demanded that task members maintain confidentiality about meeting proceedings, which greatly hindered their ability to function as community advocates and liaisons, turning them, instead, into virtual partners if not accomplices for the project. The task force's realm of debate was also quite limited. As explained by Mr. Wambua: "The people at the table have a sense of feasibility. They acknowledge that it's going to happen and that it has to be economically feasible. That it is an economic-oriented project, and that we have to be realistic about how much of the stuff that is not so commercial can be included. The task force has recognized that to get a developer, he has to have a profit."

In fact, the task force would find itself functioning more like a marketing focus group than as an urban planning body. As one of its members sardonically put it: "It's like they are telling you that they are going to buy this very expensive gift and that they want to involve you. They want to ask you what type of wrapping paper they should use." I heard similar comments, that the project was a "done deal," that their function was too limited to make a difference. Ardent critics of the project stopped coming to meetings altogether.

The task force included the who's who of East Harlem's economy, cultural and social life, along with members of the community boards, and residents of the immediate area that would be most affected by the project. However, pro-development members outnumbered project critics, which were predominantly represented by African-American residents of the East Harlem triangle, living in the immediacy of the project's proposed site. What is more, their criticisms were not limited to NIMBY type issues. Rather, they responded to the essentialist ethnic politics triggered by the equally essentialist visions of development that dominated the New York City Economic Development Corporation vision for the entire Harlem area.

Recall here that the Latino component had been conceived as the one element of the Harlem-wide "River to River" plan that would target Latinos or represent Latino culture throughout the corridor. Except that developers entirely ignored that, although the project was indeed located in the mostly "Latino" East Harlem, the actual site—the northern section of East Harlem—is in fact recognized by most East Harlem residents as a predominantly African-American hub, whose residents would not necessarily embrace that the project's cultural component be "Latino" by default. In other words, the citywide plans for marking Latino and black sections of Harlem alongside the 125th Street corridor did not quite match East Harlem's actual demographic makeup. Instead, they presented a no-win situation to Latino and to African-American residents, if for different reasons.

Because the plan crossed two districts historically associated with black and Latino culture and tourism, it created pressures for including a Latino component along the 125th Street corridor, lest Latino culture be altogether excluded from the plan. In other words, the plan was presented as the

single largest and glitziest opportunity to showcase Puerto Rican and Latino culture. Yet, the Uptown cultural component was far from the first Latino theme development ever proposed for East Harlem. This honor goes
to a project that was often contrasted to the Uptown N.Y. Project, whose
lingering status evoked much frustration and rancor about the possibility
that Latino culture would find a permanent physical location in East Harlem. I'm speaking of the revitalization plans for La Marqueta, which have
been lingering since the 1980s. La Marqueta is the historic market stretch-
ing under the Park Avenue subway railroad from 111th to 116th Streets created in the mid-1930s under Mayor Fiorello LaGuardia to accommodate
pushcart vendors. In its heyday, the market served as the default location
for the purchase and sale of all types of Latin food, vegetables, spices, and
wares, attracting hundreds of vendors and customers from throughout the
city. Numerous proposals to return La Marqueta to its original glory were
rejected, with some critics decrying the need for a premier place to buy
plantains now available throughout the city. Rather, proponents of the revitalization envisioned La Marqueta as the premier Latin food market, a
venue for restaurants, specialty and health foods, surrounded by spaces
for culturally relevant entertainment. But to little avail. The project had
been plagued with accusations of mismanagement and political haggling
and patronage—the $20 million revitalization budget it received under
the Dinkins democratic administration, for instance, was slashed to $1.4
million under Republican mayor Giuliani, while rumors abounded about
political favoritism in the selection of local agencies to be charged with its
development.[15] Controversies aside, I want to focus on what is true and
uncontested: La Marqueta is a primarily publicly funded and publicly oriented project, and despite having wide support from politicians and the
community at large, not to mention it being widely recognized to bear a
"Puerto Rican stamp," as a project that Puerto Rican residents have been
invested in developing, it has nonetheless lingered for years.

La Marqueta represents the type of publicly oriented project that is becoming more and more of an impossibility in the luxury city. Nelson Garcia, the director of East Harlem Business Capital Corporation (EHBCC)
that is in charge of the project, explained: "La Marqueta is not conducive
to a Gap type store, it is unattractive to investors. As city-owned property
it is subject to all the 'claws of bureaucracy,' yet has limited governmental
funding, and a cultural and public orientation that is unattractive to profit-
oriented investors." La Marqueta's cultural component is a case in point.
The proposal is targeted primarily to local cultural groups and vendors.

Murals are planned for the structure's interior, as well as a historical photo exhibit of La Marqueta's pushcart era, along with a hall of historical figures around a space for live performances and crafts vendors.[16] This is a far cry from the flashy, high-rent post-production units and commercial theater that anchor the Uptown Project's entertainment center. Garcia also noted the difficulties of limiting costs to $20 to $25 per square foot, to ensure participation of local vendors. For comparison purposes, as of 2006, the cost of Harlem's retail space was upwards of $75 per square foot, and midtown space ranged from $130 to upwards of $300 per square foot. In other words, La Marqueta is at a disadvantage precisely because of that which makes it so special and innovative. "It is not a cookie cutter project," said Thomas Lunke, an urban planner with Harlem Development Corporation. It can't provide large venues for retailers like the Uptown N.Y. Project would. It is exactly this difference that has stalled its development and that may hinder its ability to keep costs down for tenants. One pending fear is that the project's ultimate costs will make it impossible for the EHBCC to recruit and subsidize the type of local grocers and tenants needed to create and maintain the Latin market's experience.

The point is that the Uptown N.Y. Project was far from the only opportunity to anchor Latin culture and tourism in East Harlem. That it was treated and spearheaded as such by the New York City Economic Development Corporation above and beyond initiatives that remain dormant, despite receiving community support, was therefore a clear signal of the type of Latino-themed development that would be favored by citywide urban planners. It was a clear message to tourist enthusiasts that only highly profitable commercial development, not more publicly oriented projects, would prevail.

For their part, African Americans were being told that their African-American and multicultural understanding of their immediate Triangle area was insignificant, that if they wanted economic development in their immediate community they would have to join the bandwagon of larger tourism demands. And those called for a Latin, not an African-American development. In the words of the African-American president of the Community Association of the East Harlem Triangle: "This is about a political favor that is owed to Puerto Ricans after Giuliani took away all their money for projects in El Barrio, but it should not be paid at the cost of our own back." To add insult to injury, she bemoaned that her organization, the 41-year-old and primarily African American Community Association of East Harlem Triangle, which stands in immediate proximity to the project, had been entirely ignored while the Puerto Rican leadership was wooed and seduced with the Latino entertainment theme.

"It's a slap in the face," she said. Not only were they entirely ignored, but the project lacked minority contractors or subcontracts in the plan, there were no minority engineers, architects, or partners, no response about environmental effects on the community. An open statement prepared for the Spring 2006 hearing additionally expressed their outrage over the lack of an "Afro-centric design or flavor of which we can relate to, we are opposed to what we believe is prejudice and discrimination to the African-American people in particular and to the Puerto Rican community of which we have great respect and support for."

I want to call attention to the statement's assertion that Puerto Ricans would also be excluded from the Latino "casa de sueños" that East Harlemites were being promised. I do so because it evidences that dissent from African-American residents of the East Harlem Triangle area cannot be so simply reduced to an issue of their not wanting "a Puerto Rican–controlled development" in "their area," a claim some residents used to dismiss their position. This interpretation is way too facile and on too many counts. As we saw, the project was far from a locally generated project, much less a "Puerto Rican development"; that it was viewed as one by some is only indicative of the relative success of the project's marketing maneuvers against the highly charged context of gentrification. Instead, their dissent is more fruitfully read in relation to the old hierarchies of culture, development, and space made so readily evident by a proposal to develop a "glossy Latino entertainment center" in a primarily working-class and racialized community. Being the most directly challenged by the impending project, African-American residents became the most ardent critics of the elitist undertones of a Latin mini-project that would have to conform to the sensibilities of white developers and the new audiences for which the project was ultimately intended. In other words, their dissent was a call that Puerto Ricans would also be erased and their culture subdued if a Latino-themed project ever came to be, if it did not in fact dissipate after approval was gained for the project as its most expendable part.

Sorting Through Spin: Or, Show Me the Money!

As noted, the role of the task force was highly limited, left as it was with the job of simply assessing "how much noncommercial stuff" could be included in the project. This translated to their drafting a laundry list of "elements of consensus" that would be included in the Request for Proposals for prospective developers. At the same time, in their limited role, the task force's list of recommendations is a stark reminder that East Harlemites were not entirely blinded by the spin and were more than ready to make concrete economic demands from the looming project.

Indeed, after the first round of community task meetings, the list of demands could not have been more utopian and far-reaching. At a hearing in the spring of 2006, organized by the community board, the councilwoman, and the borough president, the list of demands included: the involvement of local developers, affordable housing, home ownership and rental opportunities; that affordability be measured by local standards, that they don't use eminent domain but rather incorporate current establishments; that no Wal-Mart type of retailers be allowed; that bus depot air emissions be cleaned before expelling to the community, that buses use green technology; that local institutions be involved in the cultural component; that there be a Latino theme, but assurance of a multicultural content; that construction be sensitive to the archaeology of the area believed to include Native American sites and African burial grounds, among other demands many residents admitted they would have little ability to monitor.

As such, the list received mixed reviews at the highly anticipated hearing. People cheered at its most community-protective measures, but skepticism pervaded the room—and rightly so. East Harlemites have had ample experience with similar forums where promises always abound, but where they never receive any assurances of accountability. Boos were heard at measures demanding the cleaning of bus-depot exhaustion, a clear sign of public doubt that such a measure would be possible, or even sufficient to keep down the area's high rates of asthma. Residents lined up frantically to testify after the task force presentation, especially to express doubts of the feasibility and enforceability of its demands. There were special concerns about the definition of affordability used by the task force. The comments of an African-American tenant and 30-year resident of East Harlem drew laughs of recognition at the shifting and forever unreachable definitions of affordability residents are continually exposed to by new developments: "I've been here for 30 years. . . . Anytime I got a raise, a developer got a raise." The formulas used to designate affordability in housing were especially contentious. The task force used the recommendations from Community Board 11's Affordable Development guidelines, drafted in 2005, which designated the area's median income as $62,800 and low income as $18,840, based on New York city, state, and federally designated statistics, not on local figures, which in 2000 listed the area's median income at $21,480.[17] A speaker at the hearing put it starkly: "If the low is $18,000, and you make $8 or $9 an hour you don't make it, even at $10 an hour you barely make it. And I don't know people here who are making $50,000." Immigrant families make even less, noted Flor Bermudez, the executive director of the Mexican advocacy organization Esperanza del Barrio, about $13,000. As she noted: "I'm an attorney working for a not for profit, and I don't make it. Are you going to let 2-3 families to a building? That's how people are making the $1,200 rent. We all work here. You have to include them in the housing and in the commercial space."

For their part, members of the Community Association of the East Harlem Triangle demanded a 25 percent partnership in the project, asserting their entitlement to as much control of any development that came to their immediate community. This ludicrous request in the world of planning and development, where partnerships demand direct financial investments, was a stark challenge to the view that it is money, not people or community considerations, that should determine development partnerships.

Ultimately, mounting opposition led to the removal of Urban Strategic Partners as the default developer, and a promise by the city that a new Request for Proposals would be developed to meet concerns voiced both by community and the task force. The highly publicized victory was announced by all major newspapers, and hailed as a rare challenge to the Bloomberg administration—an example of the achievements of community-based planning.[18] But the celebration was far too premature. By the fall of 2006, the task force list of demands represented more of a compromise that an outright demand, while most of the publicly stated community stipulations had been tamed or altogether excluded. Yes, the project's RFP showed that it had been downsized; it included less commercial space, and housing units had been designated for moderate- and low-income housing. The involvement of local developers with a proven track record in East Harlem was also recommended. But as residents would soon learn, the victory would turn out to be more spin than reality. The task force's "achievements" were announced at a town Hall meeting at Taino Towers in September 2006, where the tone was professional and technical. A jazzy PowerPoint presentation introduced the recommendations, which were highly editorialized: "We are at a very different space from last year when the project was dropped on us. The city has now treated us with respect. They have certainly embraced us. We believe that this is an altogether new project, a very different project. The Uptown is a thing of the past," said the Vice Chair Robert Rodriguez. Congratulatory statements were repeated by task force members. "The City has heard our community loud and clear," said Councilwoman Melissa Mark Viverito, as details of the new project were unveiled.

Yet the new RFP, drafted after months of task force deliberations, had not changed much at all. For one, the project was still defined as a mega-development; a huge chunk of East Harlem would still be given out to one developer, and once developed, the community would have little control or ability to demand accountability. Racism was obviously central to the conception of this project. Defining such high density and inordinate amount of square footage as part of the same "development track" and allotting it to a single developer spoke volumes about its relative value. As Gary Johnson, a member of the community board, pointed out during the Town Hall meeting: "Why is it that Cornerstone projects can be distributed to multiple developers, why is it that Battery Park City can be sliced and diced for multiple developers, but Uptown NY must go to one developer? . . . Why one developer?"

The massive allotment to a single developer resonated with the times of Robert Moses when East Harlem and other communities were gobbled up to facilitate slum clearance and New York City's "development." Ironically, while Moses' legacy had been long exposed as destructive and biased of the poor and communities of color, as confirmed by the important works of Robert Caro and Jane Jacobs, the Uptown N.Y. Project coincided with a revisionist tide of Moses' legacy among urban planners, evidenced in a number of exhibitions at Columbia University, the Queens Museum, and most important, the major exhibition at the Museum of the City of New York. Located right in East Harlem, this exhibition became the catalyst for numerous discussions throughout 2006 and 2007 where, to great public dismay, Moses was praised as the master builder and there were calls for a new builder with as grand a vision and great will as Moses. The myriad of broken communities and displaced residents now surfaced as necessary collateral costs that time would prove secondary to the grandiosity of the facilities and the monuments built.[19] These are projects that, in the view of development cheerleaders, will eventually—like Moses' previous plans—be seen as visionary as they benefit future generations.

The lackadaisical manner in which the Uptown N.Y. Project's massive scale had been conceived thus remained the greatest elephant in the room throughout the entire community consultation process. For the project's

Fig. 8. Members of Positive Workforce, a workers' group, demanding that any new construction in East Harlem hire local workers, not outside workers' contractors. Members wore their helmets to the Town Hall meeting on the project, to emphasize their position. Photo courtesy of East Harlem Preservation. http://www.eastharlempreservation.org/.

size and scale was taken for granted throughout the task force RFP process, kept purposefully outside the scope of consultation and debate.

Most significantly, the task force recommendations remained vague, and far too open-ended to assure that any real commitments would be secured from developers. The cultural component is a good example of this. As we saw, its initial designation as "Latin" had become too racially charged. It had polarized East Harlemites, as it seemed to exclude the African-American residents of the East Harlem Triangle area, as well as the area's multicultural history. It also seemed too glitzy and removed from local cultural initiatives. "This is not the place where our local artists would perform at any time soon," acknowledged a Puerto Rican task force member.

The new task force recommendations still listed a cultural component. But it was now vaguely described in the PowerPoint presentation as one that would "embrace culture and engage community." Cafes, restaurants, live performance space, cinemas, and art gallery spaces were all included in the wish list, but the lack of specification of what makes or defines "the local East Harlem culture" rendered the list susceptible to a wide range of commercial interpretations—easily translated to the development of a Cinemaplex and a Starbucks, for instance. In other words, attempts to represent the community's multicultural and diverse legacies had failed, or simply had no room in the planning process. Too complex to be easily incorporated into the dichotomous black-West Harlem versus Latino-East Harlem tourist demands, it simply did not fit the succinct PowerPoint presentation, and was consequently altogether obviated, facilitating the whitewashing of this important component of the project.

By the fall of 2007, the city's EDC had yet to make public its choice for a developer, though all signs suggest that it will not be one that complies with the communities' recommendations. For now, I want to conclude with some lessons gained from the debate over the Uptown N.Y. Project hereby described. First is the role the politics of scarce resources, needs, and representation plays in fueling people's dreams and hence support and acquiescence to gentrification. As we saw, residents' initial openness to the Latin mini-city was fed by the diminishing space for projects that mark Puerto Rican and Latino culture onto space in the face of gentrification. Developers and the city's economic team were more than eager to fill this void, but with their own version of what is most suitable to be showcased in the luxury city—a commercial and glitzy Latin component at odds with community needs.

I also want to point out the prevalence of essentialist race and culture paradigms in New York City's tourism and urban development. As we saw, the black-West/Latino-East Harlem divide was central to the city's conceptualization of this project, and is likely to continue to be summoned by developers regardless of the continued displacement of African Americans and Puerto Ricans in the area. This highlights the continued need for unpacking the politics of ethnicity and race as they play out in the context of urban development. It is worth remembering, for instance, that after all was said and done, the "Latino community" was reduced to being simply a mere reference to development projects, instead of a participant in the development process. In other words, to see any "Latino/a"-themed project as providing the same level of participation and inclusiveness because it references Latin culture is to become complicit with neoliberal interests and forces and, ultimately, to foster distinctions and inequalities among Latinos. In this case, there were major distinctions between the upwardly mobile Latinos that will more likely benefit from the project and those who will not. There were differences as well with regard to the vision of Latino culture advanced, where only an international, profit-oriented, and prepackaged tourist vision that was more aligned with commercial developers than local residents was included in the project.

It is also worth noting the growing rentability and co-optability of Latino culture as showed by development of entities such as the Latin Media and Entertainment Commission and the role they are likely to have in defining the type of projects that should be allowed to come to particular communities. The seeming inclusivity of a project defined as "Latino" and its promotion by a panel of "Latino entertainment experts" hid the fact that it was a top-down development with no minority partners regardless of whether they were residents of the area. The Uptown N.Y. Project hence warns us to be more sensitive to and critical of contemporary representations of Latin culture, and of its ongoing resignification for projects that advance capital, neoliberal agendas, and in this case gentrification with little consideration of local needs.

And finally, there remains the issue of urban planning processes functioning as a public relations tool. Perhaps the best example of this is the add-insult-to-injury situation of having the task force almost disbanded by the requirement that its members be excluded from the bidding process. The task force had demanded local participation and ownership of the project. However, it was task force members who had the most experience in urban development, who had the greatest chance of becoming part of a development team. But their participation in a bid required their resignation. Suddenly the task force became further neutralized and weakened by the resignation of some of its key members, leaving project proponents in a more powerful position than ever before. For one, former critics were now potential partners in the development—even if as "minority" and secondary members of some of the bidding teams. Most important, the planning process channeled community protest into a formalized, contained, and confidential process, one that was highly technical and disengaged from public scrutiny.

Hence within a year, by 2007, the once anticipated public meetings on the project were barely attracting an audience. The general lack of criticism and probing questions from the audience had turned the meetings into a tedious and predictable affair. Project supporters were quick to interpret the sorry attendance at these meetings as evidence of mounting community support. Critics, however, attributed it to poor publicity of when and where the meetings were held. Another saw a larger plot involved in it all, and I could not disagree with her assessments: "It's been so long. People are exhausted, they have gotten used to the project, they hear it's a 'done deal.' They're sick about it. They want it done, and gone." Some were angered, though not surprised, to learn that the city had selected proposals that ignored important task force recommendations. The proposals were so vague that many wondered if developers had even bothered to read the RFP. In the words of Benjamin C. Zitron, managing director of Breslin Realty Development Corporation, the only developer I was able to contact because, having already been disqualified, he was no longer bound by the city's confidentiality rule: "The ultimate irony of the CB 11 2005 victory is that the EDC further fostered the myth [of participation] by ostensibly requiring in the subsequent East Harlem Project RFP (attached in my prior email) that local interests be recognized and affiliated with by the Developers; and then proceeded to select final participants despite the fact that they had made no such affiliations. Furthermore, the RFP review process was a sham, providing zero due process, open disclosure, or competent technical or social-impact evaluation. And there is much more to this disturbing story."

In hindsight then, the task force and the community consultation process had worked too efficiently. The process successfully resignified the massive development as accountable to the community, neutralizing its most fervent critics, while exhausting others. For no one could deny that "the community" had been "consulted" and included in the process, as spurious as this process had turned out to be. Yet, this is not to say that community consultations are intrinsically flawed.

As I was concluding this chapter in the fall of 2007, and far from the debates over the Uptown Project, the Movement for Justice in El Barrio, an immigrant community organization, was organizing the first ever NYC Encuentro for Dignity and Against Gentrification in El Barrio. MJB had been waging battles with private developers, and had previously organized a community consultation process, "La Consulta del Barrio," to identify the key problems that the organization should tackle. In addition to gentrification, the almost 1,000 votes cast for La Consulta identified jobs that pay minimum wage, the proposed immigration laws, high costs of public transportation, police abuse, among some of the most pressing needs affecting what remains a primarily poor and, increasingly, a largely immigrant constituency. The open and festive Encuentro underscored the banality and inefficiency of institutional politics most forcefully when children lined up to break a "neoliberal piñata."[20] The enemy was clearly identified; and for once, there were no euphemisms, no doubletalk, no technical language, no marketing ploys nor spin. How wonderful, if politicians could simply listen.

5

From Barrio to Mainstream
On the Politics of Latino/a Art Museums

The relationships between museums and the communities they seek to represent are often contentious. Since the 1990s, however, cuts in state and federal funding for the arts and neoliberal cultural policies emphasizing privatization have exacerbated the tensions. These cuts have pushed many cultural institutions to turn away from grassroots constituencies toward more profitable ones—a shift that has generated multiple debates within the world of U.S. Latino/a culture and the arts.[1] One vivid example discussed below is the debate over El Museo del Barrio (literally, the museum of the neighborhood or community) in East Harlem, an area also known as El Barrio, upon its shift from representing its original Puerto Rican constituency to showcasing all Latino and Latin American cultures in the United States.

The debate spans the mid-1990s, when the museum first shifted direction, but peaked in 2002, after a local resident discovered trash bins filled with catalogues from the museum's early exhibitions. The trashing of the catalogues, which contained important archival documentation of El Museo's past, struck many as symbolic of the institution's expunction of its Puerto Rican history. The incident was reported to East Harlem's Community Board's Cultural Affairs Committee, whose meetings are open to the public, and it was through the board that residents, activists, and artists from within and beyond East Harlem gathered to debate El Museo's direction around the suggestively named "We Are Watching You" campaign.

It is important to note that most "Latino" arts institutions in the United States were the outcome of civil right struggles over representation in the late 1960s and early 1970s. As such, they invested in alternative and empowering views about the relationship of art and communities, emphasizing community involvement and accountability. Like many other community cultural spaces founded at this time, Latino arts institutions were also primarily government-funded, bolstered by state redistribution programs in response to community demands. In the West, they were founded by Chicanos and in the East by Puerto Ricans, the dominant Latino constituencies of the times. Such is the context within which El Museo del Barrio was founded—after pressure from Puerto Rican parents, artists, and educators. Given this history, debates over the involvement of community input in El Museo del Barrio have haunted the institution on a cyclical basis almost from its onset, especially at times of rapid change and increased mainstreaming (Ramirez 2007).

Forty years later, Latino populations have grown more diversified, pressuring these institutions to represent a changing constituency at the same time that a growing popularization of all things "Latino" in the United States has rendered the task ever more difficult. For one, self-identified Latino/a cultural institutions are now coveted arenas for a variety of local and transnational interests, adding to the contests over their mission, direction, and outlook, as they face pressures to become more "global" and marketable, not to mention more tourist- and audience-friendly. Put simply, pressures to "Latinize" and privatize the operations of Latino institutions have presented added challenges to these institutions' original grassroots and community missions.

In New York City, the Latinization of El Museo del Barrio has been particularly successful. It has allowed the institution to make connections with an increasingly diverse Latino population and to attract a more diversified source of government and corporate funders eager to cater to this highly heterogeneous population. The less visible costs of this shift, however, are many and extremely revealing of contemporary Latino cultural politics, and of the very meaning of "community" that is evoked by the institution's name and mission.

This chapter examines the renewed activism over El Museo's mission and direction that I witnessed and supported in 2002–2003, when I was conducting research on the gentrification of East Harlem/El Barrio (Dávila 2004). Specifically, I examine this debate in relation to the greater social and economic pressures cultural institutions face in an era of privatization.[2] These include a sharpening of the already tense relations between museums and communities, now compounded by pressures for the mainstreaming and bureaucratization of arts institutions, and the contradictions involved in the adoption of supposedly more inclusive strategies in order to expand audiences and funding sources. I also address the contrasting systems of evaluation at play in the "ethnic" and "artistic" realms. Accordingly, Latino-identified institutions are consistently valued on imposed standards, never on their own terms, a trend that keeps ethnically identified institutions at bay from mainstream art recognition. Also contentious are enduring hierarchies of representation affecting the enactment, definition, and representation of Latino and Latin American art. As I note, in the shift toward more global and inclusive missions, all that is truly "global"—that is, less narrowly identified by nationality, in this case, diasporic, Latino, Puerto Rican, and Nuyorican art—is consistently marginalized, exposing the contradictory and double-edged nature of many more marketable initiatives.

On the Hierarchies of Latino/Latin American Art

The debate over El Museo must be seen in the larger context affecting the categorization, promotion, and exhibition of Latin American art, particularly the inclusions and exclusions generated by the rising interest in Latin American art and culture in the United States since the 1980s.[3] At this time, while still marginalized in comparison with mainstream art, Latin American art began to be the subject of more attention and exposure, though this interest did not benefit all "Latin American artists" equally. In particular, art scholars were quick to note that U.S. Latino/a artists, that is, artists who were born in the United States or have lived and worked most of their lives here, and who are therefore likely to be considered bicultural U.S. minorities rather than citizens of Latin America, were especially bypassed by the "Latin art boom." (Gómez-Peña 1996; Yúdice 1996). Considered neither truly American nor truly Latin American, these artists were sometimes included and at other times excluded from the category and circuits of "Latin American art," including the literature and major exhibitions and collections. The Museum of Modern Art's 1993 show, *Latin American Artists of the Twentieth Century*, for instance, exhibited only one Mexican American and two U.S.-born Puerto Ricans out of more than 90 featured artists, triggering criticisms about its bias and lack of representation of U.S.-based Latinos (Horton 1993). This exclusion is also reflected in the most important compendiums of "Latin American art" that make minimal or no mention of U.S. Latino artists, with the exception of Chicano art, which is presented, at best, as a marginalized addition (Lucie-Smith 1993; Traba 1994; Sullivan 2000).[4]

The study of Latino art has remained "at an incipient stage," having been historically excluded, in fact obviated from the canonical history of

"American art" as well as from the growing research on Latin American visual arts (González 2003a; Ybarra-Frausto 2005: 9). This invisibility of Latino art and artists from both the Latin American and North American art history canons explains why the "Latin Americanization" and mainstreaming of many spaces originally founded to focus on U.S. Latino art remain so troubling. In other words, at the heart of the debate over El Museo's Latin American turn is the very spuriousness of a constructed category heavily marked by inequalities. "Latin American art" encompasses works and artists that are differentially valued by museums and the market according to a range of factors, but that mainly fit within the confines of the primarily European aesthetic tradition that provides the dominant standard in museums and the market. After all, the field of art production is still largely predicated on Western-centered precepts upholding art's intrinsic value and its separation from the cultural and social context in which it develops. Accordingly, what is defined as art is that which is given autonomous aesthetic value and is able to transcend the immediate for the "universal," even though such evaluations are very much socially produced and grounded in culturally established hierarchies and institutions.[5] An ethnically marked category, Latin American art is already less transcendent and thus marginal in relation to the non-ethnicized "universal," although in comparison to "Latino" art it is far more studied, collected, and institutionalized and hence more invested with notions of high culture and universality.

These hierarchies are at the heart of El Museo's formal shift toward Latin American art. While Latin American artists were always part of the museum's programming, a formal move in focus and mission paralleled the museum's so-called professionalization and institutionalization along more mainstream standards. As noted by María-José Moreno (1997), this transformation—evident from the late 1970s and institutionalized in the mid-1990s—was intended to subvert the institution's marginal position in relation to mainstream art by vesting it with a more mainstream and international image.[6] For instance, the institution's turn toward Latin American art was accompanied by the almost exclusive exhibition of the "high art" version of the visual arts, as well as by a move away from early exhibitions that included historical materials, folklore, and multimedia educational materials. Hence the recommendations of the We Are Watching You campaign that there be more cultural and historical exhibitions to represent the diversity of Latino cultures, including shows focusing on Latinos and baseball, on the development of salsa music in New York, and on cultural exchanges between African Americans and Latinos, as well as a permanent multimedia exhibition of the history of El Barrio and the Puerto Rican diaspora.

The differential evaluation of Latin American art along axes including genre and themes of content is also evident in the relegation of Puerto Rican fare to permanent folkloric and pre-Columbian programs and exhibits rather than "art" exhibitions. Another trend is the gap between "public programming" that is aimed at Latino communities and the art-related programming that is directed at "audiences." The latter are connected to particular art exhibitions, whereby community programming such as the Three Kings Day Parade, celebrated every year in honor of the Nativity, and the Day of the Dead Family Celebration, are marketed as community and family events. The lack of Puerto Ricans on El Museo's curatorial staff, and their concentration in the areas of education and community relations, is yet another indication of these distinctions. East Harlem activist Eric Canales put it bluntly during the heavily attended and highly emotional town hall meeting organized as part of the We Are Watching You campaign. Open to the public, the Town Hall provided an opportunity for the museum's director and board to address residents and activists, and the latter to confront the museum's directorship with their criticisms. At the event, Canales described being "tired of having our culture presented out of the back of a dump truck," referring to the trucks-turned-into-floats during the Three Kings Day parade. The parade remains one of the institution's most popular and populist events and the one most identified with El Museo's Puerto Rican history. Yet Canales bemoaned that the event had been relegated, and had to struggle for resources on a yearly basis, hence figuratively demoted to the back of a "dump truck."

The issue at the core of El Museo's "Latinization," then, was never simply one of "Puerto Ricans versus other Latinos," as it was often depicted in the press. Neither was the issue about the "growing pains" of an institution moving away from its "humble origins." Instead, the controversy revolved around the exclusions that were slowly yet expediently manifested along with El Museo's transformation. Yet throughout 2002, the local press was quick to frame the issue in terms of facile dichotomies of "Puerto Ricans versus Latinos," or purported divisions between those who wanted to keep El Museo as a "ghetto or barrio museum" and those who sought its development into a "world-class museum."[7] These simplistic dichotomies fell far short of representing local demands for equitable, mainstream, and even global recognition of Puerto Rican culture and El Barrio's history, to be judged on their own terms and not by imposed standards against which they would always be considered deficient and flawed. Indeed, for artists and activists I spoke with, the museum's original mission as an institution that would be run by and for working-class people of El Barrio, and that would provide alternative avenues of validation for local artists, was never a "humble" mission. In fact, it was considered a highly empowering and cosmopolitan vision (Ramírez 2003).

Poignantly, the debate coincided with El Museo's first blockbuster exhibition: the Gelman Collection of Mexican masterpieces, featuring works of the internationally renowned artists Frida Kahlo and Diego Rivera (2002). This exhibit brought new and "mainstream" audiences from all over the city to El Barrio, national recognition to the institution, as well as accolades in the *New York Times* and artistic circuits alike. For proponents of the museum's new direction, the well-received exhibition was ample proof of their success. But "We Are Watching You" activists felt otherwise. Some believed that the event underscored the institution's growing distance from El Barrio, while artists in particular interpreted it as another sign of the continued dominance of Latin American over Puerto Rican and U.S. Latino artists in the museum's exhibition roster. Public statements by the chair of the museum's board of trustees about the need to transform El Museo from a "community" or "barrio" institution into a "world-class museum," and even find a new location outside of El Barrio that would attract new audiences and more supporters, were also contentious. El Barrio residents were quick to interpret these statements as a direct challenge to the institution's history as an outgrowth of their struggles to counter their exclusion from mainstream museums. Such statements highlighted the renewed exclusion that accompanied the expanded mission, in particular the subordinate and "dispensable" status of some types of "Latin American art," making activists ever more vigilant about the uses and misuses of discourses of Latinidad.

Reflecting these concerns, the goals of the We Are Watching You campaign were ambitious and many. Activists sought to recover a community voice in El Museo and to reconfigure its board to include community representation. They favored policies—such as a plan to distribute rather than discard old catalogues—to ensure that the institution would remain true to its Puerto Rican past and its community mission. "Community" is obviously a contentious word that can be used to mask hierarchies and imply commonalities. In the town hall meeting and meetings of the We Are Watching You campaign, however, "community" was usually used as a synonym for all that is Puerto Rican, diasporic, or working-class. In other words, the community was never simply tantamount to the geographically bounded space of El Barrio/East Harlem, though references to El Barrio as a poor community and as the historical core of Puerto Rican and Latino New York surfaced often in the context of appeals for the institution's original grassroots orientation. This use of "community" highlights that the debate was as much about class and outlook as it was about nationality. But it was around nationality that inequalities were most apparent, as El Museo's move from Puerto Rican to Latin American art was in fact signaled by the nationalization of its artists, exhibitions, and programs.

It is worth recalling that, notwithstanding all the talk about hybridity and transnationality within the world of Latino and Latin American museums and the arts, targeting museum programs to pay special attention to particular countries remains one way, if not the easiest, to "represent" different Latino/a constituencies. Hence the continued emphasis on artists' nationalities and backgrounds in museum exhibitions, catalogues, and labels. According to this logic of representation, a South American show would necessarily feature South American–born artists and samba, leaving salsa and the mariachis for the "Puerto Rican" and "Mexican" shows, respectively. In other words, in the Latinized museum, Latin American artists and programming are never fully shorn of their Mexican, Brazilian, or Puerto Rican identities. Even shows that espouse a "postmodern" approach to Latin American art by shunning national identifications are not entirely free from these dynamics. The 2006 *TRANSactions: Contemporary Latin American and Latino Art* and exhibition, organized by the Museum of Contemporary Art in San Diego, an institution located near one of the busiest sections of the U.S.-Mexico border, comes to mind. Discussing a show intended to showcase art "across and beyond borders," the curator Stephanie Hanor makes repeated references to notions of diversity, hybridity, and transculturation in the exhibition's catalogue (Hanor 2006). Yet all of the artists are identified by background (such as Mexican or Chicano) or by nationality. We are told that James Luna is of mixed Mexican and Luiseno/Diegeno Indian descent; that Manglano-Ovalle was the child of a Spaniard and a Colombian; that Ana Mendieta draws from her Cuban heritage; that Adriana Varejao references Brazil's history; and that the two artists from Colombia examine their country's drug violence. The museum's director addresses the topic more directly when in the catalogue's Preface he tells us that most of the artists come from the south of San Diego's border (Mexico) and that "Brazil and the United States contribute eight and nine artists respectively; Cuba, six; and Argentina, Chile, and Colombia are each represented by two artists. One artist was born in Spain and one in Belgium" (Davis 2006: 10). In this way, hybridity becomes a "concept" that artists may examine in their own work, but that the homogenizing practices of U.S. museums and its politics of identification do not allow us to fully grasp in relation to the background and identity of Chicano and U.S. Latino artists (Davalos 2001).

The result is the continued consolidation of Latin America rather than the experiences of U.S. Latinos as the reference for authentic representations of "Latinness." As we have seen, "Latino" is not easily slotted into such simple national-origin categories. The value of an identity that can potentially challenge and transpose narrow nationalistic identification with fluidity, openness, and mixing, is effectively challenged. Another problem of conceptualizing Latin America in terms of discrete national identities is the attention it brings to the dominance of particular countries over others, and the ensuing judgments over the value, richness, or depth of particular cultures. In other words, museum staff can strive very hard to achieve representativity. Seldom, however, can they hide or fully address the continued dominance of artists of some Latin American countries over others, a dominance dictated by the political economy of the art establishment, by market forces, and even by international politics.

Conversations with art dealers and museum professionals in the mid-1990s, when I first researched this topic, confirmed these hierarchies. More often than not Mexico is placed at the top, along with South American countries such as Venezuela, Brazil, and Argentina. The second tier contains the Andean and Central American countries, with the Caribbean Islands at the bottom of the hierarchy. It is not hard to see that such distinctions reflect the political-economic configuration of the region, favoring the wealthier, more Europeanized and modern countries with stronger national elites and thus stronger art markets. Indeed, scholars of Latin American art have long noted correlations between wider political and economic trends in the area and the development of art in particular Latin American countries. In particular, art critics and historians have begun to point to the relationship between the unequal promotion of Latin American countries' art and the wider cultural, political, and economic interests of governments, art collectors, and corporations (Goldman 1994; Yúdice 1996). Yet in my conversations with art dealers and museum staff, the political and economic factors affecting the differential development and assessment of Latin American art were consistently hidden behind evaluations of quality and value. In fact, the explanations I was given about the dominance of artists from Mexico, Argentina, Brazil, and Venezuela in galleries and art shows in New York City often involved evaluations of the richness of these particular countries' artists or cultures. These countries were said to have greater and longer art traditions, or to have been historically more "open to international art movements," or simply to have "better artists." Marta Traba (1994), for instance, makes a distinction between "open-door" and "closed-door" countries. She attributes the supposedly greater artistic development of artists from Brazil, Mexico, and Argentina to the fact that those countries have received more European immigrants and thus have more contact with European art trends than the Central American and Caribbean countries. Similarly, a dealer pointed to Mexico's long artistic history, dating back to the origins of Spanish colonization, and to the "openness" of the Southern Cone countries to European immigrants and European art currents, as having helped preserve these countries' artistic lead.

The racist underpinnings of these hierarchies of Latin American countries are quite apparent. What is baffling is that they continue to be veiled by notions of artistic "quality." Also veiled is the role played by Latin American collectors and nationalist economic elites in determining the marketability of Latin American artists (Goldman 1994; Ramírez 2002). Observers of this market note that fluctuations in the sale of Latin American art in major U.S. auction houses almost always reflect financial and political situations in Latin American countries, which affect the participation of Latin American collectors. For although Latin American art is increasingly sold across national boundaries, Latin American dealers and collectors remain the largest buyers of this art, and thus are important figures in the promotion and validation of Latin American artists in the international market (Seggerman 1995). And not surprisingly, what Latin American collectors most often come to the United States to buy is art from their own countries, a shopping trend that is invaluable to the promotion and validation of "their" artists in the New York market. A staff member at Sotheby's Latin American division described to me the "nationalist" tendency of art collectors to buy art from their own countries as a means of protecting, building, or strengthening their own art markets.

The promotion of Latin American art is also increasingly led by Latin American corporations, embassies, and ministries of culture, many of which are directly or indirectly tied to the national imagery of individual countries. Granted, their contribution is not comparable to that of

U.S. transnational corporations, which are becoming some of the largest funders of art programs and exhibits. Nevertheless, it is increasingly common to see these entities sponsoring shows in which the national interests and images of particular countries are represented. Such a trend predates the Latino/Latin American art boom, as noted by critic Shifra Goldman, although it emerged more strongly after the 1980s. A prime example is the 1990 blockbuster traveling exhibition, *Mexico: Splendors of Thirty Centuries,* which had major support from the Mexican government and Televisa, Mexico's largest transnational media outlet. To many critics this event was a nationalist assertion on the part of Mexico as well as a promotion of the Salinas de Gortari government's economic privatization policies (Goldman 1994). The role of the Mexican government in promoting its culture in the United States is expected to heighten as a political medium in a context of increasingly policed boundaries, with a network of Mexican consulates, tourist boards, and private ventures like Banamex fueling the process (Kinzer 2002). For their part, transnational corporations and marketers have also joined the fore: HBO, JP Morgan, American Airlines, American Express, Sony, Citigroup, and Coca-Cola are some of the many companies that in recent years have targeted Latinos through art exhibitions and museum events.

The involvement of investors, collectors, and corporations is welcomed news. But it raises key concerns about the impact their tastes and funding criteria may have on the evaluation and promotion of Latin/Latin American art. In particular, the paucity of research on Latino/a art, the lack of curators, and dearth of institutional spaces to show it, exacerbate their influence relative to curators, researchers and museum educators (Atwood 2003; González 2003a, 2003b). Small institutions like El Museo del Barrio are particularly susceptible in this regard given that their lack of curatorial staff makes them especially reliant on traveling exhibitions curated or initiated through the sponsorship of these more powerful agents. These dynamics affect the equity of representation, as noted by Yasmin Ramírez, a former curator at El Museo who was also involved in the We Are Watching You campaign. Reviewing recent exhibitions at El Museo, she found that: "Artists from Latin American countries with a strong art market such as Brazilians, Venezuelans, Mexicans, Colombians, and Argentineans have had more success at getting exhibitions at El Museo even though their populations in New York are relatively small. By contrast, artists of Dominican descent, who comprise the second-largest Latino population in New York and in Puerto Rico, are rarely exhibited and have no representatives on the board. U.S.-based Mexican Americans and/or Chicanos are also infrequent visitors on the exhibition roster" (Ramírez 2003).

Obviously, El Museo del Barrio is not the only legitimating institution for Latin American art. But it is important to note that its location in New York City, an international epicenter of art and culture historically influential in the validation of trends, artists, and cultural products, makes it an unavoidable stopping point for most Latin American artists and for the different interests involved in their promotion. Hence the heightened frustration experienced by Latino artists, who were de-territorialized and not identified as belonging to the national imagery of a specific Latin American country, and therefore remain the most needy of validation by alternative and "Latino-specific" museums.

The artists I spoke with, for their part, are very aware of the nationalist underpinnings of the representation and promotion of "Latin" art and try to deploy it to their advantage whenever possible. During my conversations with New York–based Puerto Rican artists, many stressed the importance of maintaining their national identity and links with Puerto Rico as a way to attain more recognition as "Latin" artists and perhaps more attention for island-based collectors and galleries. Yet for most of them, identifying themselves with the island was only a limited solution. Puerto Ricans' U.S. citizenship, the island's colonial status, and the long history of transnational flows between the States and the island function as permanent obstacles to the identification of U.S.-based Puerto Rican artists within any single or stable identity category. This in turn affects their evaluation within the construct of "Latin American art." Additionally, few U.S.-based Puerto Ricans can achieve complete acceptance or recognition on the island, where many of them are considered only partially Puerto Rican at best. Indeed, although most Puerto Rican artists come to the United States to become legitimized by American universities, programs, and galleries, there are significant differences in status and access to contacts and resources between Puerto Ricans born or raised on the island—many of whom come from middle- and upper-class backgrounds and who often have good connections with the island's art establishment—and those born or raised in the United States. At the same time, because Puerto Rico is legally a U.S. commonwealth, the Latin American identity of both groups is oftentimes similarly suspect. Even Juan Sánchez, who has gained national and international recognition since the 1980s, pointed to this trend when he shared how most museums and mainstream galleries did not know what to do with him. As a black Puerto Rican artist, he, like many Afro-Latino artists, faced particular problems in establishing his identity. As he explained: "There was once an emphasis to identify me as a Latin American artist, but I have given up trying to justify my identity in the art world." In this way, artists indicated their awareness of the subordinate status of what is Puerto Rican, regardless of their efforts at self-representation. Puerto Rican artists repeatedly complained that the island's ambiguous colonial status limited their ability to market themselves in a context where identity can be a marketable asset, but only for some artists—especially for those with access to national collecting elites and a strong artistic infrastructure—but not for others.

Strategizing through Latinidad

> We hope you agree to adopt our recommendations. We deserve
> to be respected. Our art deserves to be respected and this com-
> munity deserves to be respected. Tell our story properly. Don't you
> remember what it is like to be marginalized? That is what started
> this museum, and here we are after thirty years, still marginalized.
> —Debbie Quiñones at the "We're Watching You" town hall meeting

Considering the extent to which art galleries and collectors can influence the recognition of particular artists, it is understandable that Puerto Rican artists and community activists were concerned about the transformation of El Museo. This transformation was seen as resulting in the loss of a space for asserting and taking pride in an identity still largely subordinated in the world of culture and the arts. It was also seen as part of a strategy of gentrification intended to "deny Puerto Ricans their roots," and an erasure of the progressive goals of past struggles they had waged and witnessed in El Barrio.

At the same time, culture and museums are complex issues around which to organize (Zolberg 1992; Lippard 2002). For one thing, the artists and cultural activists who are the most involved in museum activism are also often the most dependent on these spaces for exhibitions, consultancies, and representation, limiting their leeway to criticize them openly. This explains why the We Are Watching You campaign was generated initially from within the cultural affairs committee of the Community Board. It later brought together artists, residents, activists, and scholars who had worked in El Museo as consultants or volunteers, including some artists involved in its founding. Their public statements stressed their love for and commitment to an institution that they felt had lost its critical and transformative essence. They emphasized that their efforts were in good faith, countering the museum board's claim that they intended to hurt the institution through "bad publicity" after all the good spin it had received during the Rivera-Khalo blockbuster show.

The very creation of the We Are Watching You campaign was a feat in itself. Disheartenment over an institution that had been "long lost" was in fact one of the most difficult challenges encountered by Debbie Quiño-nes and Erica González of the cultural affairs committee of East Harlem's Community Board, when they tried to mobilize people to attend the town hall meeting and write letters to elected officials and to El Museo's board. Once the issue was raised, however, old wounds quickly surfaced, turning the debate into one of dignity, identity, and respect. During the 2002 town hall meeting, the long-time Puerto Rican activist Yolanda Sánchez even demanded the resignation of the board for having betrayed the values on which the institution was founded. As she noted:

> The questions raised in the 1960s about self-identity and about the histor-ical and current status of citizens of non-European descent, folks like me, are questions that are still valid today, when we people of the diaspora, from places other than Europe, continue to be marginalized. This society seeks to impose other values. A hundred percent of cultural institutions that are supported by public funds, by your taxes and by mine, are run by Eurocentric values. Their board members are WASPS [white Anglo-Saxon Protestants] and their museum holdings and shows project their conviction that quality, for the most part, is a European invention. If you had bought into the notion that Puerto Ricans cannot develop a quality museum and that a focus on Puerto Rican creativity will diminish the museum, it is time for those to renounce and open the way to those of us who are secured in our identity. The development of a Puerto Rican mu-seum only enhances the quality of art in the city, it does not diminish it.

Sanchez's statement struck the core of the problem: the view that a Puerto Rican focus constitutes a liability and an obstacle to El Museo's greater scope and visibility. As we have seen, Puerto Rican activists challenged this notion by upholding the intrinsic value of all that is Puerto Rican, alternative, diasporic, grassroots, and community. But El Museo's board saw the issue differently. For them, raising the museum's profile entailed a reconfiguration of El Museo's past and of its very identity. As we saw, it required inserting the institution into the more recognized category of Latin American art, as defined by art historians, collectors, and curators. This is a path that leaves mainstream standards unchallenged, while placing the burden on culturally specific museums to legitimize themselves and what they stand for within a field that continually marginalizes the people they propose to represent. The result is what Fusco and Gómez-Peña (1995), discussing the prospects of dialogue between U.S.-based Latino artists and their Latin American counterparts, describe as a continued form of colonization. By this view, Latino artists are placed in a peripheral position within the field of Latin American art, and pressed to seek validation and recognition from the institutions that represent this art, while these institutions often reject any association with U.S.-based Latinos to avoid being marginalized by the politics of U.S. multiculturalism.

It is important to point out that, for the most part, the "We Are Watching You" activists were not opposed to establishing a connection between El Museo and mainstream museums nor with extending its exhibitions to include Latin American art. Their main concern, rather, was how and on what terms this would be done, and that it not be at the expense of local artists or communities. Instead, they demanded equal collaborations and exchanges between Puerto Rican, Latino, and Latin American artists in ways that would invert rather than consolidate hierarchies of representation. Hence, the recommendations that El Museo complement their then upcoming exhibition of MOMA's collection—noted for its lack of U.S. Latino artists—with an exhibition of Latino artists or with a selection of El Museo's holdings, giving them equal prominence alongside MOMA's collection.

Not everyone involved in the We Are Watching You campaign or otherwise critical of El Museo's position held the same views. Some sought a return to the institution's original mission of encompassing only Puerto Rican culture. Older artists and activists, particularly those who had contributed to the institution's early growth, tended to be more nationalistic on this issue. They were angered that the decision to change the museum's mission had been taken independently by the board, behind closed doors, with no community input. As artist and long-time Barrio resident José Morales demanded during the town hall meeting: "How can you change the mission of an institution without communicating to the community that created that institution?" Younger people, particularly college-educated professionals and scholars who supported the campaign, myself included, were more embracing of a mission that would include all Latinos. In general, however, there was agreement over the need for the institution to truly adhere to its mission to represent Puerto Rican and Latin American culture in the United States, but in an equitable and grassroots-oriented fashion that would honor the institution's original and alternative mission. There was also a shared concern over the increasing devaluation of Puerto Rican culture vis-à-vis the Latin American construct so favored by government and corporate entities. Activists and artists held a commitment to reinstating, not diluting or undermining, what Puerto Ricans had struggled so long to obtain: an open cultural space attentive to the needs of local communities, one whose value would be measured by its success in fulfilling its original mission of empowerment, not necessarily by the number of patrons and tourists it would attract. In the words of one campaign sympathizer: "This museum was built for my children, so they know and learn to appreciate their history. It was not built so that some people can advance their careers, socialize or drink champagne."

Unfortunately, the views expressed in meetings and public debates on this issue were always more complex, open, and politically charged than what was reported publicly. This was seen in press coverage of the appointment of Julián Zugazagoitia, who is Mexican, as director of El Museo del Barrio. The appointment coincided with appeals from the We Are Watching You campaign for community representation on the museum's board of directors. The board was then made up primarily of Puerto Rican members, yet as Yolanda Sánchez noted, activists felt that members had lost any community orientation and resented its elitist vision for the institution's future. Criticisms of the board, however, were publicly constructed as an "anti-Mexican" position that had no place in the "Latinized city," veiling the fact that criticisms were aimed at the mostly Puerto Rican board, rather than at the appointment of the director, and that they predated his appointment. In other words, the class dimensions of the issue were effectively muted.[8]

The distinctions Puerto Rican artists and activist sought to make were therefore directly related to the inequities masked and obviated by the board's facile deployment of Latinidad. Again, history surfaced once more as a strategy of reevaluating their position, this time highlighting their persistent role in challenging Euro-centered definitions of art. As Nitza Tufiño, an artist involved with the museum since its founding, recounted during one of my first interviews on this subject back in the mid-1990s:

We have to be aware that El Museo del Barrio has a distinct history which is the result of struggles and battles that have not been waged by Cubans, or Venezuelans, certainly not by Argentineans, but by Puerto Ricans from here and from the island. We put a lot of effort and bloodshed to establish that place. Should we now hand this place on silver plates to people who have not struggled?

Part of this discourse on claims and entitlement involves making distinctions—based on nationality, length of time in the United States, and class background—among artists who are broadly categorized by both mainstream and culturally specific institutions as simply "Latin American" or "Latino." Even though many of my Puerto Rican artist interviewees are from middle-class backgrounds, have pursued college and graduate art degrees, and in some cases have traveled internationally, they still distinguished themselves from "Latin Americans." As we saw earlier, these distinctions are informed by the aforementioned hierarchies in the Latin American art world, associated with privilege, class, and opportunity, while "Latino" or "Puerto Rican" art was associated with struggle and marginality, and with art invested in a more radical and social perspective.

At the same time, with some important exceptions, such as older generations of Puerto Rican artists who had been involved in the artistic and cultural movement of the 1970s, such as José Morales, Nitza Tufiño, Fernando Salicrup, Marcos Dimas, Diogenes Ballester, and Juan Sánchez, artists remained a minority within the We Are Watching You campaign. It was El Barrio residents, members of the local community board, and area activists that dominated, a pattern that is suggestive of the preeminence of class-based universalist frameworks at play in the field of art production, limiting many artists' activism. Miguel Luciano, an artist with whom I discussed this, agreed: "Many Puerto Rican artists don't want to show in Puerto Rican spaces, because of the stigma. Others depend on it. Most of the exhibiting Puerto Rican artists I known in New York are from the island. Many don't have the same social experience to know about the need of these spaces for connections and for the history of our community." His words are especially revealing of the class dimensions that were largely lost in the debate: that fact that many Puerto Rican artists themselves refuse or have difficulty identifying with Latino-identified institutions and that most artists, irrespective of nationality and background, are well aware of the stigmatized status afforded to race and identity by the mainstream art world. After all, they have been already indoctrinated in art schools that encourage them to downplay their ethnicity in favor of "universal" subjects. They are also familiar with reviews of El Museo's shows published by mainstream newspapers. They know that artists receive accolades when they "cast a wide net" and are associated with dominant currents like conceptualism, and are chastised when they draw on identity themes. This indeed was evident in the *New York Times* review of *The S-Files*, the one show since 1999 that has featured emerging and primarily local artists at El Museo del Barrio (Cotter 2003).

But the fact remains that Latin-oriented institutions and museums are still the primary exhibition venue for Latino artists, limiting the overt criticisms of these spaces and making artists accomplices of the same forces that promote their exclusion. In other words, irrespective of national background, class, and other such characteristics, they are still largely promoted through culturally specific shows and museums, or as one told me, "whenever they need a Pérez or Rodríguez." This explains why, as critical as artists may be of the hierarchies involved in the promotion of Latino and Latin American art and institutions, most realize that these spaces remain the most recognized niche for anything Latino in the U.S. art market. This strategic self-representation, however, while accommodating the dominant framework of Latin American art, has always involved active negotiation.

One powerful strategy involves reconfiguring the meaning of "Latin American art" by ridding the term of its class connotations. Thus, Juan Sánchez emphasized the common position of marginality that Puerto Ricans share with the new Latin American residents of El Barrio, mostly working-class Mexican immigrants: "Right now El Barrio is going through a transformation, but this transformation has not, in any way, involved a change in this community background of poverty. Because El Barrio may be changing from ethnic and cultural background as the Salvadorians and Mexicans are also moving here, but it is still poor people living there. El Barrio continues being 'el barrio.'" El Barrio is currently undergoing a process of rapid gentrification. Yet its economic profile remains well below the average for the borough of Manhattan, with higher unemployment rates, lower income levels, and a higher proportion of residents receiving public assistance. By bringing attention to the area's poverty and including the Latin American residents of East Harlem in that scenario of deprivation, activists were involved in reshaping dominant meanings of what is "Latin American." They pointed out that it is not Latin American elites, but immigrant workers who constitute the highest percentage of new residents of El Barrio. There is thus a disjunction between the primarily working-class Mexican and Latin Americans immigrants in the area and the cultural initiatives directed at them by museums and mainstream institutions. In this way, the "Latinization" of cultural institutions, justified as a response to changing demographics, is revealed as a move that fails to enhance the lives of local residents, who have little in common with the educated and mostly middle-class artists and audiences who dominate the art shows.

Highlighting the area's poverty, however, is not solely a rhetorical tool. Latinos in East Harlem are backing up their vision with actions, founding a variety of alternative cultural projects, galvanized by the threat of the area's gentrification. Like early initiatives almost 40 years before, these seek to place culture at the center of empowerment rather than as the centerpiece of museum display. They include the poetry and music jams at the Julia de Burgos Latino Cultural Center and Camaradas Restaurant; the bomba and plena workshops of Los Pleneros de la 21; the programming of Art for Change; and PRdream, among others. Indeed, there is no shortage of alternative visions of Latinidad to counter those promoted by museums, galleries, and art historians. Their energy is impressive, though their future is quite uncertain.

For one, changes in government financing for the arts, such as those initiated by Mayor Bloomberg in 2006, threaten to pose additional challenges to smaller community-based cultural initiatives. Bloomberg's new cultural policies emphasize "meritocracy and accountability" and are intended to limit the amount of "lobbying" involved in distributing government funding for the arts, especially the involvement of local-level politicians, such as councilmen. Under new guidelines, art groups will be pressed to compete for the same funding pool on the basis of such marketing criteria as audience development and financial planning. Citywide competitions, however, are likely to lead to greater bureaucracy while adding challenges for smaller institutions which lack the staff, the resources, and the infrastructure to comply with these requirements. The future of smaller local institutions, which may be well known within their immediate community, but may fall short of proving their "worthiness" at a citywide level, is likely to be especially endangered.

Meanwhile, El Barrio continues to be El Barrio, a more diverse but still marginal and largely working-class community, and thus an unlikely source of inspiration for U.S. museums and institutions. As we saw, Puerto Rican artists and residents, faced with this exclusion, responded with cultural nationalist demands. Yet, when assessed against the variety of interests that seek to profit from the popularization of anything "Latino," I believe that these responses represent less of a petty nationalist response than a challenge to the neoliberal trends that now shape museum representations of Latino/Latin American art. Lamentably, community responses as represented by the We Are Watching You campaign can barely challenge the multiple interests that provoke such contests within museums, art institutions, and the art market. But this does not mean that they are fruitless or ineffective. The We Are Watching You campaign became pretty much inactive within a year. Political pressure from elected officials; the removal of Debbie Quiñones as chair of the cultural affairs committee; the dependency of artists and cultural activists on the museum; the dawdling bureaucracy of El Museo; discrepancy of members about what the campaign priorities should be, all contributed to its dismantling.[9] Yet, in hindsight, the campaign was extremely successful in bringing attention to the need for more local exhibitions, and greater outreach and accountability on the part of El Museo. It even led to the development of more Puerto Rican, community, and U.S. Latino–centered programming, some of it developed on a volunteer basis by some of the very cultural workers involved in this and previous protests.

In other words, the campaign created fissures and spaces for intervention through which to value and assess the past and look ahead to the future. Undoubtedly, this is a largely undetermined future. But for now, the We Are Watching You campaign brings many lessons to the fore. First is the contradiction of strategies that seek to expand audiences and patrons but fail to address the ensuing inequalities. Second are the ways in which the political gains of the past inform the present, how memory is always resilient, and most important, the fact that people can never be so easily or entirely separated from ethnic-centered cultural initiatives, whether as actors, participants, or constituencies. And perhaps most significantly, the We Are Watching You campaign is a call for museum and art professionals to listen carefully to community demands; that ethnic-based claims that embrace a community vision may constitute one of the most important challenges to the Eurocentric orientation still dominant in the world of culture and the arts.

6

The "Disciplining" of Ethnic Studies
Or, Why It Will Take Goya Foods and J.Lo to Endow Latino Studies

For over 30 years now, some lucky university students have had the opportunity to take a course in Latino studies. What better sign of mainstreaming and of "making it" for Latinos, one may think, than becoming a university subject? The state of Latino and ethnic studies in American universities, however, is a good sign of the status of the "people" that we are supposedly learning about and of our ability to talk publicly about ethnicity and race. For what gets taught within the university is determinant. This is supposedly the world of true "knowledge," not spin. In "the Academy" nothing is ever about race, but about universal knowledge, excellence, production, merit, and scholarship—except that this has never been quite the case.

This chapter looks at the state of Latino and ethnic studies in the corporate university through a consideration of both anthropology, the discipline I am most familiar with, and the new interdisciplinary space at NYU that now houses ethnic studies. By no means will I suggest that what follows is unique to these spaces. Disciplines in the humanities and social sciences that still portend to care about people—literature, history, sociology come easily to mind—are susceptible to similar quandaries in their relationship with ethnic studies. And these are good quandaries to face. The ascendancy of rational choice theories in disciplines like economics and political science have distanced them from considering real people in their theoretical models, and from developing a focus on Latino and ethnic studies, as they remain among the most racially and gender-segregated departments within the academy at large. Indeed, considerations of gender and racial equity within the academy remain covert and more so today when inequalities surrounding race and ethnicity are considered remnants of a past superseded by multiculturalism and by the seeming "coming of age" of minority scholars. But their consideration, however challenging, is more necessary than ever.

Specifically, it is important to place this discussion against the ongoing commercialization of university campuses as these strive to become more "efficient" and "entrepreneurial." This is not a new trend, and the commercialization of university athletics is a good example of this, but one that is increasingly pervading every aspect of university campuses. From the growing reliance on low-paid adjuncts, to corporate funding of scientific research that has more "marketable" potential, to the development of more marketable degrees, to the overall branding of the university "image," profit-seeking schemes are on the rise (Bok 2003; Kirp 2003). But so are cost-cutting measures. These trends have exposed the university's multiple dealings with capital and profit, as well as its role in exacerbating social inequalities, while raising concerns about the humanistic foundations of a university education.

In what follows, I examine and extricate the different levels of opportunity, compliance, and accommodation afforded to ethnic studies within the corporate university, and I examine how neoliberal trends in the academy have affected the disciplines' relationship with and overall status of ethnic studies. Specifically, I look at the continued marginalization of minorities in ethnic studies and interdisciplinary departments originally formed to respond to the academy's disciplinary rejection of alternative subjects and knowledges. Far from a panacea to the university's poor record with diversity, these spaces remain the most vulnerable in the corporate university, the most stretched, and the first to succumb to cost-cutting schemes. I further explore the divides between ethnic and regional studies, such as between Latino and Latin American studies, that are maintained and reinforced within the disciplines and "interdisciplines." Among them are neat boundaries between racialized and nationalized others, knowledge and scholarship, as well as between those scholars who should and should not engage in critical work in the United States and beyond, and on what basis.

The Problem of Diversity: Reflections from My Own Discipline

It is amply recognized that anthropology holds a complex relationship with its minority practitioners. In fact, it has been the subject of substantive research. Few disciplines have engaged in the introspective navel-gazing to the extent that anthropology has, leading to a body of research on the role of forgotten ethnic, women, and gay anthropologists and their contribution toward bringing out issues of power and subjectivity, not to mention a range of theoretical and methodological debates on politically engaged ethnography, positionality, and subjectivity (Jones 1970; Handler 2000; Harrison and Harrison 1998). Debates on the discipline's canonical distinctions and history of exclusion are well known, and consequently, for many, too worn out and even "passé" to discuss. This is one of the reasons I turn to the institutional bases of the academy in which we work, since theorizing the discipline's past has done so much to bring about significant change.

What we are certainly more savvy about is how we talk about racialist practices within the academy. Or perhaps not. We're more likely to hear discussions about what Virginia Dominguez (1997) has termed "a taste for the other," or the hyperprivilege in the hiring and packaging of some minority anthropologists as evidence that diversity has been accomplished, than we are to recognize the very racism that feeds such hyperprivilege in the first place. Besides, the American Anthropological Association (AAA) has a 30-year-old section specifically "committed to addressing the entire spectrum of minority issues in anthropology." By now, anthropology should have long solved issues of diversity within its ranks. But has it?

Many of my colleagues, including those who fall under the rubric of "minority anthropologists," will inevitably admit that opportunities have opened up, and that the goal of diversifying anthropology departments is a common concern of their departments and institutions. But most will also admit that many old and new practices of subjectification remain in place, hindering the attainment of this much-discussed goal within the academy. Unfortunately, there is little documentation to speak directly to the issue. The last available Survey of Departments conducted by the AAA, published in 1998, reports that 11 percent of anthropology faculty members in 1997-1998 were minorities and that this figure had remained "virtually unchanged" since 1988. Worth highlighting is that this figure lags behind national averages for minorities at all ranks (from lecturer to full professors), which, according to data gathered by the U.S. Department of Education gathered one year later, stand at 13.94 percent.[1] I found no information about minority hires across academic fields, well known to range widely: minorities are largely absent in science and math and oftentimes concentrated in the low-paying humanities. What this figure does show, and what is also evident in the AAA report, however, is that minorities tend to be concentrated in the lower ranks (assistant and below) versus at the rank of full professors.

Interestingly, in the market-driven academy, we are less likely to hear of these figures than about the so-called greater marketability of minority scholars. I am speaking here of the inflated Cornel West "star" syndrome, or the myth of the hyperprivileged minority scholar, which so directly fuels the resentment from colleagues and programs about their real contributions to their departments and universities. No wonder the *New York Times* had a field day exposing Cornel West's rap CD, and the anxieties it provoked about the legitimacy of his scholarship.

Indeed, interdisciplinary trends and the treatment of students as consumers have presented unforeseen challenges to disciplinary boundaries, in the process blurring some well-established criteria for academic advancement. Long gone are the days when faculty could go about their ways without caring about students' evaluations or the marketability of their courses. Today, ethnic, gender, and sexuality courses of study are often more marketable and coveted by students than traditional subjects, while book-length monographs, especially if focusing on topics of little interest to U.S. popular tastes, can't find publishers in the market-oriented academic publishing industry, with its growing penchant for interdisciplinary and more marketable topics. In this context, opportunities are obviously opened for new and alternative voices to teach and publish. But, I would argue, not without new boundaries becoming congealed in the process. After all, during the tenure review process, outstanding teaching evaluations, and popularity with students, can be easily invalidated as merit criteria by arbitrary assessments around the "disciplinary content of a course," just as they can be with criticisms of the "theoretical quality" of a single publication. Protectionist arguments of this sort represent an expected response to the reduction of intellectual work to market-driven measures; a common way for disciplines to challenge trends prioritizing "quantity" over "quality" as in the number of students/customers serviced and the number of publications produced. But they are not without political significance. They can lead to the further insularization of the disciplines as these shelter themselves from cultural studies, ethnic and other interdisciplinary studies, and other more seemingly "marketable" intellectual trends. Most significantly, these defensive strategies can be used to invalidate the scholarly achievements of minority scholars as the outcomes of market forces, never of "intellectual merit."

Yet even more problematic is the continued concentration, with all of the opportunities and constraints carried by this trend, of minority anthropologists within ethnic–studies and interdisciplinary departments.

This trend was first documented in the report, written in 1973 and still considered to be the most comprehensive, "Report of the Committee on Minorities and Anthropology," which found that "minority anthropologists tend to perform ancillary roles in the profession such as teaching anthropology in non-anthropology departments and teaching ethnic studies programs" (AAA 1973: 32). This segregation was found to constrain their ability to contribute to wider anthropological debates or the development of academic departments or the discipline. One need not be an expert on theories of value to acknowledge the racially fraught context entailed by entering disciplinary appointments through ethnic studies. Born of political activism in the 1970s, these programs have never commanded the "authority" of disciplinary appointments in "universally" recognized disciplines.

Once again, the AAA lacks conclusive information about this much-alluded-to but never-documented recruitment pattern. But my own personal academic trajectory and that of other colleagues and graduate students, who are African American, Latino, or Asian American, along with years of perusing job listings, applying, interviewing, and writing recommendations for academic jobs, etc., allows me to state that minority anthropologists continue to arrive at anthropology primarily through ethnic studies, women's studies, and other interdisciplinary programs, not because anthropology has openly embraced them or the ethnic or interdisciplinary studies that they often pursue. And here I am fully aware of the dangers of equating ethnic studies and interdisciplinary scholars with minority scholars. Racial and ethnic studies increasingly cross racial lines, while many minority anthropologists have and continue to conduct fieldwork outside of the United States. Anthropology has exerted the same pressures on all of its prospective practitioners to investigate "outside" of their realities, ethnicities, and so on, and to maintain a recognizably impossible "objective" relationship with their subjects of study. But it is also no less true that the ability to disengage or do "disinterested" research, as Bourdieu would have it, is foremost a practice of the powerful groups in society, unlike the likelier trajectory of engaged research of many minority anthropologists, often directed at their own ethnic and minority communities. After all, facing conditions of racial and ethnic discrimination is not a choice for minority anthropologists in the United States, a fact likely to be reflected in their choice of research. Similar dynamics of power, though at a different level, explain the disjunctions we find between Anglo and European Latin Americanists conducting fieldwork in

Latin America, and local Latin American practitioners where there is no tradition of venturing outside of one's country and/or communities for anthropological fieldwork. In other words, like it or not, the entry into anthropology of minority anthropologists in the United States and Latin American practitioners contrasts with that of white anthropology practitioners in the United States and abroad. The research of white anthropologists is less likely to be "encumbered" by the racial dynamics affecting minority anthropologists and less affected by their location on the peripheries of the global economy of knowledge prioritizing, among other variables, U.S. academic centers, scholars, and English as the language of scholarship (Mignolo 2000).

To engage with these dynamics, however, is to confront the long-challenged but still pervasive anthropological canons of objectivity, distance, and scientific inquiry, perhaps now more sophisticatedly rehashed as "theoretically informed" or "theoretically driven fieldwork," yet another euphemism for distance. But one task at a time. For the purpose of this chapter, I underscore the canonical beliefs that continue to affect the standing of many minority anthropologists; and their authenticity as ethnographers, scholars, researchers, and theoreticians. The considerably lesser regard for research conducted in the United States, particularly if done by so-called insiders, over that conducted abroad, and the consideration of minority anthropologist as advocates, or else in terms of their ethnicity and nationality, rather than by their professional identity and anthropological expertise, are also part of these dynamics. As a Chicano colleague recruited to teach in a Midwestern state shared with me, "They want to know if one is a 'real anthropologist'"—as if one's ethnicity would by default affect one's anthropological training. A hiring trend that is intended to address diversity but often adds to the view that ethnicity always trumps the scholarly content of a minority candidate, are target-of-opportunity hires. For they imply that minorities won't rise as "the" candidate over and above "regular" candidates, that minorities can only be hired through a specially targeted search. They also imply that minority candidates should come as "freebies" from the university's provost and administration to departments; that they are never worth a regular department line.

Yet it is not only the devalorization of minority scholars that ensues when they are primarily recruited to fill diversity hires or in ethnic studies programs. Most problematic are the breaches maintained between the discipline and critical racial and ethnic studies and interdisciplinary approaches and perspectives. There is plenty of evidence of this in anthropology job descriptions, where one finds that, everything said about globalization and transnationalism notwithstanding, searches are still organized geographically and thematically, with the result that "Latin Americanists" and "Africanists" or "African-diaspora" scholars—a tag that, in contrast to African American or Black studies, indexes non–U.S.-based research—are sought after, but that searches for scholars working on Latino, African-American, or ethnic studies are less frequently initiated by university departments. Instead, the recruitment pattern for these scholars is often through searches initiated by Africana, ethnic studies, and Latino studies programs, or else conditional to whatever department agrees to join in the search, or is forced to do so, as when it is told by a dean that future lines in the department will depend on the hiring of a minority scholar.

One troublesome outcome of this hiring pattern is the pitting of "global others" against local "others" as subjects of research, of monographs, of knowledge, and all at the same time within the U.S. academy. That is, insofar as departments resort to traditional criteria of intellectual validation—be it fieldwork abroad, or carrying out research in regionally bounded areas, or drawing from strict disciplinary-defined debates—they will, even if unintentionally, continue to separate scholars working on U.S. issues from those working abroad. In other words, departments will contribute to the same trends so challenged by transnational and political economy perspectives within the discipline, while simultaneously guarding neat boundaries between racialized and normative others. To make this point, I draw attention to distinctions between Latin Americanists and Latino studies scholars in U.S. anthropology. The history and continued preference of anthropology departments in hiring "Latin Americanists" is a trend that undoubtedly favors white—hence normative—anthropologists in the United States, for whom Latin America is a popular fieldwork destination, over the "raced" Latino anthropologists working in the United States. One outcome is that students are more likely to have access and hence to be exposed to the struggles of Latin American peasants or the "rituals and festivities" of indigenous peoples, but seldom to the realities of those same peoples if living in our midst. Veiled also by the continued segregation of ethnic studies scholars from the disciplines are divides between who should engage in critical work in the United States (U.S. minorities and ethnic studies scholars) and beyond (white and/or normative disciplinary scholars), and on what basis, and for what reasons.

The concentration of minority scholars in ethnic and interdisciplinary programs is evident in New York City's anthropology departments, from Columbia University, to New York University (NYU), to the City University of New York (CUNY). The primary appointment of Ana Celia Zentella, one of CUNY's most prized anthropologists, the first affiliate to CUNY's graduate program in anthropology, and a mentor to many Latina anthropologists, who is now in the University of California-Davis Anthropology Department, was in fact in the Black and Puerto Rican Studies Department at Hunter College. I am the first Latina ever hired to the NYU Anthropology Department (through a joint appointment initiated by American Studies). My colleague Steven Gregory's appointment at Columbia University was also initiated by African-American Studies. Common lore is that minorities are hard to recruit and retain in Midwestern states or small college towns where minorities are isolated from urban centers or minority communities. But in New York City, where more than 60 percent of the population according to the 2000 census was identified as "minority," and 27 percent as Latino, the scant representation of minority scholars in anthropology programs attests that it is not only in "isolated" areas where a lack of diversity is an issue.

A tangential but interesting trend in New York City anthropology departments is the embodiment of racial and ethnic alterity in foreign-born anthropologists, often South-Asian and Caribbean men, while maintaining minimal representation of U.S.-born minorities. Obviously, the hiring of foreign-born scholars by the globally dominant U.S. academy is an important practice. As the global center of modern anthropology, the United States is often the only source for Ph.D. training and employment at a global level. But it is also appropriate to question the accommodation of difference through raced nationals who, because of their class and status as transplanted rather than indigenous minorities, have had less opportunity to be directly subjected to and engaged (or enraged) by U.S. racial politics and racial structures. For one, the status of transplanted nationals is ostensibly less of a threat to the U.S. academy, if only because their research, and embodiment (in their person) of race, provide greater room for distance and comfort. After all, talk of subalterity and postcoloniality is kinder to the ears of mainstream academic culture than talk of racism and inequality, particularly when occurring on our soil, which unavoidably and directly implicates us in their daily reproduction.

I am reminded here of Vijay Prashad's deconstruction of the model minority, or for our purposes here, "model minority," anthropologist as one who is the direct product of U.S. immigration policies favoring the educated, technical, and professional migrants to the United States (Prashad 2000). Of course, "getting down to business," these distinctions are largely irrelevant in the U.S. academy: a minority is a minority is a minority, making the way in which this identity is strategically deployed to de-center and challenge racism, the thing that should matter most. But awareness of the different politics and multiple deployments of identity that could progressively be made through discourses of Otherness should not come at the cost of exposing the unequal operations and structures of power among different "minorities." Neither should we ignore the particular contexts that render some distinctions of class, race, or nationality more or less relevant as axes of inequality. We should at least be concerned with how these distinctions are strategically used and veiled by U.S. racial/ethnic hierarchies, and be aware that the U.S. academy has embraced and will continue to embrace and exploit these distinctions in uncritical ways. In other words, we should be cognizant that deconstructing plays and powers of positioning are complex matters, but foremost, as Virginia Dominguez so rightly notes, "minorities are not born, they are made" (Dominguez 1997: 337). Specifically, she reminds us that the demand for the minority anthropologist is constructed by the real conditions that create the scarcity—that is, by the continued racialization of minorities, and the lack of educational opportunities and privilege, that remain largely unattended. Indeed, a study recently documented what are very well known dynamics in many elite university campuses, the prevalence of black immigrants over African Americans, and that of first- and second-generation blacks, Asians, and Latinos over their native-born counterparts (Massey et al. 2007). Again, it is not immigrants' "drive and spirit" that explains these dynamics, but rather the education and human capital that selected their parents for immigration versus the diminished opportunities afforded to many native minorities in the United States.

These dynamics are evident even within the construct of "Latino/a" scholars. Now that Latinos are hot in U.S. popular culture, anyone with a Latin last name seems eager to embrace or invoke the category, not to mention those with a stake in Latinos as a market. But even among Latino scholars, differences of class, race, language, nationality, length of residence in the United States, and history, among other variables, actively mediate their identity and, most important, how they live, perform, and experience Latinidad. Even among the small cohort of Puerto Rican/Latino/a scholars, a category in which I include myself, there are

important differences that speak to dynamics of race, class, and nationality that are easily veiled in the U.S. academy. The dominance of lighter
skinned, island-born and -raised Puerto Rican scholars, such as myself,
over U.S.-born Puerto Ricans, is testament to these dynamics. Far from a
mere coincidence, this trend speaks volumes of the U.S.-subsidized middle-class privilege of many Puerto Rican-born and -raised scholars whose
experience was of nationals, even if colonial nationals, versus the racialized condition of the U.S.-born and -raised. It behooves us to ask what
the U.S. educational system is offering minority students, and whether
it is the context that will give rise to minority scholars. This is why it is
extremely important that we be specific about what type of "minorities"
are being hired and retained as full-time faculty in American universities, while also ensuring a diversified body of "minorities" among our
students.

NYU administration, and some of my colleagues, do not like me to say
so (I was quickly sent a booklet featuring the trickle of minorities hired
the year I pointed this out to a dean—not surprisingly, most in nonrenewable, non-tenurable appointments!), but as of 2008, I am the only Puerto
Rican faculty employed in a full-time tenure-track line in the entire NYU
Faculty of Arts and Sciences. This is a fact that is always met with disbe-
lief by my Chicano colleagues on the West Coast. This is New York City—
the so-called historical cradle of Puerto Rican migration! And here, I am
not implying that there are no Latino/a faculty at NYU or that their numbers haven't grown, however slowly. Perhaps there's even a non-identified
Puerto Rican full-time faculty I am yet to know. The point is that the uncritical use of the aggregate category of Latino should not be used to hide
the notorious underrepresentation of Puerto Rican faculty and students
at NYU and at most New York City university campuses. In fact, such a
void was the subject of a policy brief by CUNY's Center for Puerto Rican
Studies, which showed that from 1981 to 2002, the number of full-time
Puerto Rican faculty in CUNY campuses decreased about 25 percent. The
decrease, veiled by the aggregate use of "Latino," which hindered an assessment of the differential hiring of Latino subgroups, was concurrent
with a decrease of over 20 percent in the number of full-time faculty during the same period (Pimentel 2005). Not surprisingly, the report links
the state of Puerto Rican faculty to the overall state of Latino and Latin
American studies in CUNY campuses, which have been the most affected
by state-mandated budget cuts and by administrators who regard these
programs as no longer relevant and unworthy of support.[2]

Before we dismiss this situation as "growing pains Puerto Rican faculty must face in light of a more diversified Latino population," I would like to suggest that the state of Puerto Rican scholars may represent a warning sign of the diminished terrain that is likely to be found by future generations of Latino scholars. As citizens and as the first large-scale Latino immigration into the city, Puerto Ricans have a longer history in higher education, having been in fact behind the foundation of most of the Latino studies programs in the city. If their numbers are presently affected by a diminished number of full-time faculty slots and by the weakening of Latino studies programs, I doubt that future generations of Latino studies and Latino scholars will be spared a similar fate. Put simply, unless we are ready to accept universities mirroring the hierarchy of status and class already at play in the Latino population at large—where mostly white and affluent Cubans, South Americans, and foreign-born upper-class Latin Americans dominate the ranks of our creative economy, as is already evident in Hispanic advertising for instance—we must take notice of what may be learned from the diminished and nonexistent number of Puerto Rican scholars across New York City university campuses. Meanwhile, our university campuses continue to remain white worlds. As George Sanchez announced during a keynote address at NYU, African Americans, Latinos, and Native Americans make up 32 percent of Ph.D. candidates but only 7 percent of all Ph.D. recipients, assuring generations of overwhelmingly white university teachers for years to come (Sanchez 2007).

Returning to the concentration of all minority anthropologists in ethnic and other interdisciplinary departments, it can be safely said that the very fields that were born out of struggles of minorities for recognition— as well as those born of similar struggles, such as women's studies and interdisciplinary programs—have been double-edged swords. These fields have obviously presented employment opportunities, but not without simultaneously segregating minority scholars from the disciplines; while most problematically maintaining the "disciplines" as safely contained apart from other knowledges. One example of this is the disjunction between Latino studies, urban studies, and the anthropological literature on the city, as Latino studies are totally omitted from "high-end" urban studies (Davis 2001). That Latinos are largely absent from most of the literature on U.S. cities except as references, and, most tellingly, that the scholarship of Latino studies scholars, long preoccupied with urban issues, has seldom been engaged by this literature, is a vivid example of the subordination of Latino scholars and Latino studies. This trend also evidences the divides between "theory," scholarship, and ethnic studies that continue to taunt the contribution of minority scholars. Academic publishers and libraries don't help this segregation when they consistently exclude publications on African American and Latino studies from disciplinary and cultural studies listings and bookstore stalls.

But a more pragmatic outcome of the hiring of minority scholars through "programs" or joint appointments is the additional barriers for tenure and promotions that these positions represent. These scholars are required, sometimes over and above their discipline-housed counterparts, to prove their anthropological credentials, by participating in the discipline, publishing in its journals, and participating in two academic units, including serving on committees and participating in events, for the same compensation as their discipline-housed counterparts. And these are the visible parts of this balancing act. Mentoring minority students, becoming the de facto minority and diversity advocates and officers for the universities, that for the most part remain white worlds, are additional, invisible tasks required of minority scholars as part of these arrangements.

I recall the comments of a senior colleague who, upon my third-year review at Syracuse University, dismissed anything I did for Latino studies on campus (when in fact I had been initially hired as a target of opportunity because the university needed minority faculty and students were demanding a Latino studies program). My strategically placed anthropology journal publications were also dismissed on the grounds that I had failed to meet the department's primary expectation: the teaching of large introductory courses in anthropology, and with a standard textbook. My use of Renato Rosaldo's *Culture and Truth* and attempts to deconstruct the concept of culture in the course "Peoples and Cultures of the World" were not going to attract majors to the department. Foremost, an anthropology canon must be conveyed, not criticized or engaged.

Obviously, a tenure-track appointment in the U.S. academy is a feat in itself in a tight academic market increasingly relying on adjuncts, temporary appointments, and other cost-cutting measures. I am also fully aware that similar disciplining and subjection strategies are commonly experienced by most junior anthropologists, irrespective of race and ethnic background. We cannot call attention to the operations of institutional racism in the academy without also recognizing the arbitrary assessments that are deployed to weed out many talented scholars, oftentimes women, gays, older and working-class or politically active scholars. The goal should be to counter all structures that subordinate "difference," both in the academy and beyond. But this includes debunking the view that minority anthropologists have no right to complain about prejudicial assessments because, supposedly being more "marketable," they "always" have a job in a coveted market, or because such trials are to be expected from senior colleagues and administrators as part of the price we must all pay for "tenure." It is in this spirit that I share the anecdote above: to underscore the total disregard of my contributions to Latino studies (for which I had originally been hired) in the anthropology review process. Separations such as this one are insidious, not only because of the effects they have on minority anthropologists, but most significantly for hindering the incorporation and acceptance of alternative approaches and subjects of study into the discipline.

In hindsight, these experiences seem suggestive of wider dynamics concerning the incorporation and management of difference within university campuses. These trends have placed multiple pressures on less powerful departments such as anthropology, which many times are expected to solve the university's problems with diversity through target-of-opportunity hires or demands that they contribute to developing multicultural curricula. The fact that some of the most influential departments such as economics or political science remain more racially homogenous, with little self-critique and examination, or pressure from administrators, should not escape us. It should, instead, help galvanize anthropologists and other scholars in the "lesser disciplines" to advance university-wide reforms that embrace diversity, and not solely at the cost of some departments over others.

Latino Studies, Ethnic Studies, and the Neoliberal Campus

> Until a Goya Foods or a J.Lo endows Latino Studies, these programs will have to compete for scarce financial resources. They should never lose sight that they need a strong, vocal and activist support that they need to cultivate and maintain links with the Latino community beyond the campus . . . , if they hope to survive.
> —Luis Cancel, during a panel on the Future of Latino Studies, John Jay College, New York

I have discussed the segregated and unequal relationship between the disciplines, particularly anthropology and ethnic studies. But I cannot end this discussion without examining the status of ethnic and Latino studies departments in light of neoliberal trends at play in the American academy. Namely, once born out of struggles for social representation and parity by blacks and Latinos in the 1970s, these programs are becoming "mainstreamed" with all the paradoxes involved in the process. Yes, there are many more stakeholders of Latino and ethnic studies, but the institutionalization of these programs, as with the mainstreaming of most ethnic studies, has come at a great cost (Butler 2001; Marable 2000). One outcome has been their insertion in more "utilitarian" projects within the university, including in multicultural management—in order to appease Latino students on campus—or else to provide multicultural literacy as part of the general curriculum. Jane Juffer's (2001) perceptive critique of this trend is relevant here. She documents the increasing use of Latino studies as resources to manage diversity while providing multicultural literacy about this growing minority group who will make up students' future "consumers" and "employees." In this context, she notes, Latino and ethnic studies are increasingly marketed and consumed as "service courses" rather than scholarship, detracting from the alternative knowledge and significant theoretical and methodological contributions intended in the very project of Latino studies. In other words, Latino studies is becoming mainstreamed, but newly subordinated in the very process. In need of probing then, are the contexts in which cultural diversity is produced, by whom, and for whom, never assuming that its coming of age on university campuses equals a change in academic structures (Urciuoli 1999).

At NYU, Latino studies was until recently the missing link in an institution that housed Africana and Asian Pacific American studies, and there is much more still to be done to build a major and degree-granting program. Still, I have had ample opportunities to reflect on how my Latino studies courses are consumed by students and about how I may be unwittingly contributing to the mainstreaming of Latino studies. The mostly white student body of 135 enrolled in my Contemporary Latino/a Cultures course at NYU comes to mind. I was asked to design this course under the rubric of the university's core curriculum, and its requirement for a course in "Worlds Culture," and was immediately enthused that my course was approved as a requirement of the core liberal arts curriculum. I had overcome the long-standing problems of ghettoization, I thought. What better way to lend validity to Latino studies than to develop a course that all NYU students, not solely students interested in Latino studies, would take and what's more, that would fulfill the university's World Cultures requirement, as troublesome as that regionally and geographically bounded category may be. But as I would soon learn, the course's inclusion in the core requirement meant that students would bring their own considerations to bear: what best fit their schedules, or seemed sexier and easier to pass, or even provided the most multicultural competency for their future career paths. And given that Latino and ethnic studies content courses are not inserted into most students' regular departmental curriculum, this course would likely be the be-all-and-end-all of their exposure to Latino studies. In this context, I could not help but connect the lack of Latinos enrolled in my course with the lack of Latino enrollments in the university at large. I also could not stop to reflect about the future use of the knowledge, critical terminology, and concepts I introduce in my class by the "future leaders of this country." This is the university campus where, in 2007, the College Republicans organized the "find the Illegal Immigrant," a game staging an immigrant hunt, which raised heavy student criticism; and the "Affirmative Action Bake Sale" one year earlier, where students of color where charged less for their cupcakes, which went largely unnoticed. Race is certainly a contested issue on this and many other university campuses; one that merits careful discussion, requiring more than an introductory lecture course could provide. Am I contributing to normalizing Latinidad, rendering it safe, apolitical, and unthreatening by the very development of an introductory course providing minimal competence in the history and dynamics of U.S. Latino/as? When I challenge and deconstruct Latinidad, am I giving students recourse to dismiss Latinos as a real entity, not just a social construct? Do I contribute to making students immune to the operations of racism when I repeatedly highlight its multiple operations and how they affect Latinos in everyday life? Can my lectures in fact compete with the glossy pictures they have learned to associate with Latinidad in the mainstream media?

Welcome to the academic mainstream and to the predicaments accompanying a coming of age! Yet the greatest challenge facing Latino studies is not how they may end up functioning, or being consumed as "service" outlets by students. Most troubling are the challenges that follow from administrators' demands that they function as fiscally efficient and "productive" programs. Within the neoliberal university, this has meant cuts and takeovers in the name of greater fiscal "efficiency," accompanied by a growing hostility from university administrations to the existence of ethnic-identifiable units. This last point is not unrelated to the "out with race-and-ethnicity and in with globalization" equation on which neoliberalism and color blindness are so often predicated. If different subject matters touch on Latino issues, and if we live in a transnational and hemispheric world, what is the rationale for creating distinctive programs of study? So goes the reasoning behind the institution of "makeshift" programs, drawing a Latino studies program from American, Latin American, and Spanish departments with little attention to Latino studies as a distinctive area of study.

Yes, Latino and ethnic studies are broad endeavors. Latino studies has long been at the vanguard pushing the boundaries of American, ethnic, and other geographically bounded areas, additionally touching on comparative and transnational studies. What cannot escape us is that it is far cheaper for administrators to convert and repackage their already hired Latin American, Africanist, and Asian-American studies faculty into Latino and ethnic studies scholars than it is to hire newly minted Ph.D.s working in these areas into full-time faculty lines. Thus, before we take too much pride on the breadth and scope of our interdisciplinary engagements, we should recall the economies involved in the politics of academic hires. I doubt, for instance, that administrators would be as willing to demand that faculty working in "disciplinary-sanctioned areas" stretch out and pass their "expertise" for that of others within their discipline, however related their fields of studies may be. After all, specializations and subspecializations provide the heart and rationale of any university. The university simply could not exist if it could not claim the exclusive sale of "expertises" embodied in particular disciplines and scholars, the spuriousness of which could be debated to the point of exhaustion. What I seek to point to is the racist and ghettoizing assumptions that guide the view that some areas of study are deserving of specificity, protection, and cultivation (namely, those harbored within disciplines or within geographically bounded studies) but others are not (ethnic and interdisciplinary studies). These are the types of hierarchies that, across university campuses nationwide, allow established disciplines like English and history to justify the need to hire multiple faculty specializing in different subjects and subcategories, according to periods and genres (an early medievalist working on drama versus a late medievalist working on poetry, for instance), or even national countries (French literature), or even to have multiple Europeanists divided by country and period, (medieval, early modern, modern), etc. In other words, these are the assumptions that allow thematic, theoretical, methodological, and even topic and focus differences to be recognized and signaled during hires initiated by disciplinary departments, even among faculty working in the same country and region. In sharp

contrast, in many disciplinary departments, whoever does anything related to ethnic studies becomes the stand-in for all "minorities," regardless of the period, genre, or other differences commonly recognized by
the discipline, while in history and anthropology the entire continents of
"Latin America," "Asia," and "Africa" continue to be treated as "expertise"
areas, not worthy of the type of period and national subdivisions afforded
to European and American history. Ethnic studies are at the bottom of
these totem poles, the free-for-all and amorphous subject that, in the view
of many faculty and university administrators, is devoid of real content
and scholarship, and hence undeserving of their particular hires, much
less of any differentiation.

Through practices such as this, Latino and ethnic studies are rendered
as peripheral undertakings, destined to remain contained, not unlike the
turn to "multiculturalism" in the 1980s was once reduced to the inclusion
of some "seminal subaltern" texts into the core disciplinary curricula. In
particular, the university's penchant for analytic "frameworks" and "concepts" makes Latino studies especially vulnerable to being reduced to a
matter of the savvy use of constructs of border culture, transnationalism,
movement, flows, and instability. These are concepts that are increasingly
interpellated from different disciplines and interdisciplines, at the same
time that Latino and ethnic studies become delegitimized as fields of inquiry spanning different methodologies and approaches, yet requiring
particular "knowledge," and most important, a continued reference to a
people. This last point is especially troubling as it involves a de-linking
of Latino studies scholarship from Latino/as, as a real and living entity,
with a history and an ever-changing reality of their own. I thus share the
concerns expressed by many Latino scholars who warn that critical attention to globalization, fragmentation, and difference should not function
as a hindrance to examining class, exploitation, the workings of capital-
ism, and how Latinos are inserted into the U.S. political economy (Darder
and Torres 2003). This is the concern that the professionalization and institutionalization of Latino studies does not lead to its depoliticization or
to a decline in the activist roots, or to its commitment to social transformation and connections to living communities these programs had originally espoused.

In part, these concerns are as old as the very enterprise of developing ethnic studies in university campuses. After all, the university is an
utmost conservative space, where scholarship, like art if you will, is foremost defined by its distance from concrete people and events, and by its

putative universal value—far from a welcoming space for ethnic studies to strive and succeed. What is new is how these tensions are exacerbated by the growing consolidations apace in the neoliberal campus, and the questions they raise around the legitimization or further ghettoization of these programs.

Within Latino studies, two of the most common types of consolidations involve merging Latino studies with Latin American studies or with other pan-ethnic comparative units, as in the growth of centers for hemispheric studies, or centers for the study of ethnicity and race (Cabán 2003). Both alternatives represent conversations already taking place within Latino studies which is increasingly characterized by broader comparative and transnational perspectives. The questions they raise, then, pertain not to the nature of these conversations, but rather to the effects of these institutionalized consolidations. Will they tame and limit the long-standing quest of these types of programs to transform, not simply to become accommodated, into the academy? Isn't transformation of the academy and of dominant criteria at play for validating scholarship still essential to overcoming the continued marginalization of ethnic studies?

I ask these questions with the understanding that, in the corporate university, it is not pedagogical and intellectual but foremost financial considerations that often constitute the greatest impetus for these consolidations. And this is exactly the problem: not where Latino and ethnic studies is positioned. As Professor Ricardo Ortiz noted at a panel on the subject: "It could be in a Russian or Math department if given the proper financial and faculty resources!" The issue is that current consolidations are envisioned with an eye to stave off investments, and downgrade their resources and university profile.

This was my experience at NYU, when in 2006, the ethnic studies units, including Africana, Latino/a and Asian Pacific American studies, along with the interdisciplinary programs in gender and sexuality, metropolitan studies, and American studies were consolidated into a new department, the Department of Social and Cultural Analysis. Many of us, with a long history of informal collaboration with each other, welcomed the opportunity to "formalize" such arrangements, as well as the protection of a department that would facilitate hiring in these units. Many also bought into the dean's presentation of this cluster as the only way to "save the ethnic studies units," which were said to be untenable and "no longer viable" in their current autonomous state. What was not easy to deny, however, is that it was the administration's starving of these programs

from hires and resources that had made them "untenable"—Latino studies had never been funded by the administration, yet its foundation was
now presented as conditional to the creation of this cluster. Also impossible to deny are the multiple challenges that individual units, especially
ethnic studies, will now face if they seek to grow and strive within the
new "confederate" environment.

Not surprisingly, consolidation into the department of Social and Cultural Analysis (SCA) came in the midst of the university attacks of GSOC,
the graduate student union, the ensuing strike, and the administration's
aggressive union-busting measures and refusal to renegotiate a contract.
Predictably, the strike dominated student organizing and faculty concerns
throughout 2005-2006. And by the end of the academic year, the union
remained unrecognized, while ethnic studies were no longer independent
programs but were "functioning" as units within the newly created SCA
department. Poignantly, with the exception of a number of Africana faculty who refused to be part of the new department, entirely destabilizing
Africana's presence in SCA, the elimination of ethnic studies as freestand-
ing units went largely unnoticed. In fact, their demise as independent
units was hardly mourned, a stark sign of the weakened and mostly disenfranchised status under which these units were consolidated into SCA.

Returning to the politics of academic hires, it is worth noting that
within the new department, faculty searches within the units are to be carried at the "intersection" of these areas, not in particular units. SCA is a department, we are now being told; the strengthening of the individual units
is simply a "narrow," and in fact a futile concern, hindering SCA's growth
and success. Hiring at the "intersections" of fields is certainly innovative.
Still, given the unequal status in which such disparate units as gender and
sexuality, American studies, Africana and others joined the cluster, and the
scarcity of resources, I am skeptical that collaborations rather than competitions can be the most natural outcomes of these arrangements. For one,
it is important to remember that hiring at the "intersections" is economically efficient. These appointments allow deans to claim that they do support ethnic studies on campus, but to do so through cheaper and flexible
appointments, to be shared by different units. Not surprisingly, many of
these appointments come in the form of the more downgraded-part-time-
nonrenewable position of faculty fellows, or else as temporary and highly
flexible "loans" of already existing faculty that deans may allow to transfer
from other departments into SCA, rather than in the form of what's most
needed: altogether new and full-time faculty hires.

Perhaps this downgrading, including the inability to offer separate majors rather than "concentrations" under SCA, is not much of an issue for units like metropolitan studies or American studies. These areas are already well represented within traditional disciplines in the humanities and social sciences. Units such as these stand to gain a lot from their more direct involvement with ethnic studies. But for the ethnic studies units founded after long struggles to carve a space within the academy, the prospects are more dire. Let us not forget that ethnic studies has always been intersectional and interdisciplinary. In contrast, not until recently have race and ethnicity become central concerns of more established interdisciplinary spaces. Unfortunately, it is the field of ethnic studies that is most often downgraded as most "insular" and lacking in intellectual merit by administrators and even by colleagues, a disregard that serves as testament to their unfamiliarity with the ethnic studies endeavor. The fact is that, more than ever, ethnic studies requires and demands the necessary specializations to engage in the substantive intra-ethnic comparative and transnational dimensions that characterize its work. In other words, a setting that demands that Latino and ethnic studies stretch themselves in the service of other units in which it may be clustered will necessarily be less conducive to their success as one that facilitates more substantive and contextualized understandings at the very "intersections" of these already heterogeneous areas of study.

Unfortunately, consolidations like those presented by SCA are likely to present fewer opportunities to hire specialized faculty, unless in consultation with the needs of other units, and hence less ability to bring in the necessary expertise in the various fields, areas, and genres that make up "Latino" or any other "ethnic" studies. All the while, the disciplines' continued specializations and subspecializations and their divorce from ethnic and racial studies remain unaddressed. It is worth noting that while the ethnic studies units were being downgraded from autonomous programs to SCA units, new institutes and centers in geographically bounded areas continued to strive at NYU, including the Center for European and Mediterranean Studies and the Institute for French Studies, while others such as as the Africa House and Asia House were being established anew.

These are some of the reasons why, despite my critical engagement with anthropology, I eagerly moved 50 percent of my appointment toward this department, where only 25 percent of my line had been appointed, against pressures from the administration that faculty within SCA units move 100 percent of their line to SCA. I had spent eleven years of my career maintaining multiple appointments in anthropology, American and Latino and Latin American studies. Yes, I resented not experiencing the safe comfort and the easier workload provided by a single disciplinary appointment. Still, I considered it a politically significant move to participate actively and simultaneously in all of these areas—part and parcel of my quest to legitimate my work in the marginal areas of Puerto Rican, Latino, and comparative ethnic studies within the more disciplinary spaces. And, unlike other colleagues with split appointments, I had been quite fortunate. I had been tenured and promoted in anthropology while holding these multiple engagements, a position from which I could now intervene in the advancement of ethnic studies for years to come. Embracing the fuzziness of a not yet defined administrative unit that to me was guided foremost by financial considerations, and abandoning my links with an established department, was simply not an option I would consider. It is after all within the disciplines that my contributions in Latino and ethnic studies are less recognized and hence more politically relevant; where students are least exposed to Latino and ethnic studies, and where there should be more, not less, faculty working in these areas.

Most significantly, the assumption that interdisciplinary spaces are always inherently progressive and can guarantee a more intellectually enlightened space than any disciplinary space simply did not ring true to my experiences as a faculty holding appointments in both a disciplinary and an interdisciplinary unit. Indeed, those of us who tread interdisciplinary spaces often take too much for granted: that our struggles are one and the same, that we know each other's projects and are in a better position to avoid and prevent the types of power plays and hierarchies that plague the American academy. But I beg to differ. Anthropology may have a bad reputation as the "Handmaiden of colonialism," after Kathleen Gough's famous 1968 article exposing the discipline's historic ties with colonialism. But this history is acknowledged and debated, and the discipline has not shied from self-critique. Assumptions of progressivism and political enlightenment which are often taken for granted in interdisciplinary spaces in ways that can so dangerously hinder our self-reflection and critique do not come so easily when one treads a disciplinary space.

Yes, SCA may represent an edgy space of openness and intersections—it is certainly the only department where white male faculties are a minority, and where people of color predominate. Perhaps this will be the exemplary and determinant space that transforms the academy from now until ever. And perhaps this chapter may even help to bring about equity in resources, respect, and support for ethnic studies within SCA, and for the entire SCA endeavor. But I have reasons to be skeptical. Most pressingly, I fear that these types of consolidations at the edges of the disciplines, along with the "flexibilization" they foster in matters of faculty hires and curriculum, may present undue pressures to the most marginalized scholarly spaces in the academy, while simultaneously helping to maintain the traditional departments, and the university at large, as protected white-only faculty worlds.

I want to end by considering the suggestion voiced by Luis Cancel, a participant in a panel on the future of Latino Studies at CUNY's John Jay College, that it will take a corporate power of Goya food or J.Lo to ensure the survival of Latino studies.[3] A former commissioner of Cultural Affairs under David Dinkins, and former director of the Bronx Museum, and current director of the Clemente Soto Velez cultural center, Cancel has had ample experiences with the challenges of inserting Latino culture into public space. Most recently he had been waging a campaign to defend the Clemente Soto Velez which, located in the trendy Lower East Side of Manhattan, had been threatened by gentrification.

As he reminded participants, it was not by the grace of administrators, but rather through the political muscle of student mobilizations, that ethnic studies was founded. But now, students have become part of the "mainstream," they are not burning like "our generation," who was starved to learn about our culture. It was up to us, he added to make Latino studies relevant to a changing community and to develop a political base, otherwise, "we better pray that J.Lo or Goya Foods come down and save the entire endeavor."

That students are not "burning" but are instead concerned with training in the most profitable careers is not surprising. They are neither immune to the corporate university nor to the demands of the contemporary job market, even when, let's face it, students learn very marketable skills when they take Latino studies courses. The fact is that Latino studies grew out of civil rights and community movements and it would be naïve to attribute their decline simply to trends in the corporate university. Instead, we need to account for the larger dynamics that affect the formation of vibrant Latino political movements in the present, foremost of which is the growing disregard of race and ethnicity as variables not only affecting social equity but also informing progressive politics. The greatest problem, however, is that it is not only university administrators, politicians, and pundits who uphold the lessening utility of race and ethnicity, but increasingly ourselves who tread Latino and ethnic studies. Connecting with communities, defending the integrity of Latino and ethnic studies, and developing social and politically relevant research, are risky endeavors in a neoliberal academy that promotes the distance of "globalization" and the obtuse and obscure language of "intersections." In other words, the engagements Cancel felt were needed were exactly those that seem to pose the greatest risk to the gains for which ethnic studies scholars have struggled for so long in their quest to challenge the scholarship versus activism divide that has troubled our validation and that of our work within the academy. These are real concerns given the already disenfranchised status of ethnic studies within the academy. But they are also troubling, for they make us complicit with the same disciplinary canons that have long been used to maintain hierarchies of academic knowledge. Most problematically, it dawned on me, these canons are no longer only imposed on us. Rather, we are imposing them on each other as we become complicit in the spurious battle for academic distinction, and as we are pressed to validate ourselves and our research.

Still, the Latino and ethnic studies endeavor is irrevocably informed by particular living communities, however broad, changing, and diverse these communities may be. This fact is not so easily veiled by intellectual trends or university policies. By necessity, then, our scholarly engagements in Latino studies are prone to confront us with race and the operations of racism in all of its guises. With hope, this confrontation will guide us toward an active questioning, not only of the way in which we talk about race, but also with its functioning in the academy and the institutional structures we inhabit. And with even more hope, this realization will also involve a vigilant re-theorization of our politics and practices as we tread the increasingly disciplined path of disciplinary, and interdisciplinary, boundaries.

Conclusion

On the Dangers of Wishful Thinking

I believe we are arriving but in arriving let us be sure that we always remember our historical point of departure . . . , and let us be sure that in arriving we transform that destination that we are starting to reach.

—José Limón, address at the Smithsonian, Washington, D.C.

Are we trying to participate in the system as is? Or will we want to change it? Will we see ourselves as part of the system and involved in social change or become just another interest group involved in the political process?

—Angelo Falcón, address at the Tomas Rivera Policy Institute, Los Angeles

As Latinos do "make it," or are said to "make it" in the American mainstream, abiding questions remain. Will we remember our historical roots and help transform the destination we are starting to reach? Or will we be part of the same problems that have long hindered our "coming of age"? I pose these questions with the belief that the Latinos' coming of age is more spin than reality. Yes, more Latinos are joining the ranks of the middle class. Many have long been part of, while others identify with or are joining, the ranks of America's political, economic, and institutional mainstream. Yet as I have repeatedly shown throughout this work, as a group that is at once both living and socially imagined, Latinos continue to occupy a marginal position in society, even when they are joining the ranks of mainstream culture. This predicament frames and informs the terms and implications of their coming of age, as evidenced by the ongoing and heated debates over Latinos' supposed impact on "American culture."

At the core, these debates communicate that Latinos are not "properly" American, that they represent a challenge to mainstream (white) society; that their effect will be adverse and should be contained.

For years, such misguided yet ingrained assumptions have fueled the contradictory politics of wishful thinking in which Latino pundits and advocates respond to these imagined threats by showing that Latinos are safe, that they can even have a positive and re-invigorating effect on American culture. These responses are important and necessary. Through such efforts, attention is finally and deservingly given to the significant everyday contributions Latinos make as citizens, as workers, as consumers—the same contributions that are continually dismissed in public discourse. Yet, as we remake ourselves for public approval, we cannot ignore the dangers of engaging in this type of response uncritically. One such danger that must be considered is the impact this coming-of-age discourse may have on the state of Latino and African-American relations. I focus especially on this relationship because African Americans often serve as the never mentioned but always present reference to how these representations of Latinos are constructed and publicly interpreted. It is important to remember that alongside the increased public debates over Latinos, the state of contemporary black and Latino relationships are increasingly presented as polarized, nonexistent, and challenged. Implicitly and explicitly, then, this discourse pits blacks and Latinos against each other in a contest to win approval of a dominant (white) society.

Such polarized and competing representations were especially notable in discussions of the 2000 census showing Latinos "outnumbering" African Americans, and have continued to be fueled by the immigration debate where Latino immigrants are routinely described as threats to African-American jobs, communities, and economic well-being. This competitive discourse has also been fueled by Latino pundits bemoaning African Americans for acting as gatekeepers of Latino progress, and as hoarders of political power that should rightfully belong to Latinos because of their "numbers."[1]

Part of the problem is that in a nation whose racial formation has been constructed along a black-white dichotomy, African Americans have long served as reference to stories of immigrant upward mobility, the one group everyone is supposed to distance themselves from as they claim Americanness. If people couldn't be white, in other words, they could at least claim to be not-black. However, over and above other ethnic groups in this country, Latinos have shared African Americans' position on the lowest rung. Like African Americans, Latinos have been stereotyped as crime-ridden and poverty-stricken, and both groups share similar socio-economic statistics with regard to poverty, education, and discrimination indexes. Additionally, in many barrios, Latinos have long shared space and struggles with African Americans and jointly participated in the creation of commonly shared popular cultural expressions such as hip hop; not to mention the fact that many Latin American immigrants share a common African legacy with their African-American counterparts and increasingly identify as Afro-Latino.[2] Most important, with the exception of some Latino groupings such as the first wave of Cuban exiles, Latinos have seldom been branded as "model minorities," as have some Asian Americans. The model minority dynamic is problematic in its own right, and I do not have space here to discuss important Asian-Latino and Asian-African-American alliances that have emerged in any number of instances. Here, my point is that there are significant and even overwhelming similarities that have sustained common political alliances between blacks and Latinos; many of these were stamped by civil rights–era policies and institutions.

Despite these strong similarities, alliances between these groups were never entirely secured. Today, they can seldom be taken for granted. On the one hand, these groups are increasingly recognized as being internally heterogeneous; on the other, there is the growing recognition of existing differences among "blacks" and "Latinos." Together, these factors make coalitions challenging within members of each group, not to mention between them. Meanwhile, the attending discourse of color blindness continues to undermine "ethnicity" and race as variables for organizing progressive politics. But most of all, I believe that the prospects for black and Latino relations are being affected by the economics of numbers so prevalent in the contemporary neoliberal climate, and by the preeminence given to "culture" and "values" when establishing identifiable constituencies that can be easily accounted for, ranked, and valued.

U.S. racial politics, and arguably all cultural struggles, take place within a defined racial/national hegemony. That's why they are often characterized by zero-sum games, where the gains of one group are believed to unavoidably result in a loss for another. All the while established racial hierarchies remain intact, or else are transformed to cement established hierarchies of power. As anthropologist Brackette Williams has shown, at the heart of these cultural struggles is a dominant nationalist ideology against which groups are ranked according to how closely they resemble the dominant national identity at play (1989). Criteria for establishing degrees of belonging are seemingly limitless. Race, language, religion, class, and gender are always at play, but so are values and dispositions through which the politics of culture and race are actively played out. Groups can one-up one another based on values that may be considered to "belong" to some groups more than others, and that may serve as a source of privilege and status, however short-lived. The cultural struggles continue, however, as long as the dominant racial hegemony remains intact, making racial and cultural contests most revealing of the abiding racial and cultural hierarchies at play. In other words, inter-and intra-ethnic contests, be they among Latino subgroups or between Latinos and African Americans, are most revealing of the prevalence of whiteness. These contests remind us that, however transformed and changed its definition may be, whiteness continues to be reproduced through values, ideologies, and institutions as normativity—the one guarantor of belonging everyone is judged against and hence must strive for. Hence, my interest in exposing the linkage of Latinos to the values of conservatism, docility, and other model minority myths in Chapters 1 through 3, as well as my attention to how Latino/a culture becomes "whitewashed" when reconfigured for greater consumability in institutional spaces as varied as museums and urban planning, as discussed in Chapters 4 through 6.

In the contemporary neoliberal context, however, contests over the "values" people are given as constituencies are more than ever exacerbated by the spin created by marketers and political pundits. And in these realms, Latinos are more than ever recognized to be the one group that will provide institutions and marketers with the most consumers and constituents. Not only are Latinos profitable because of their numbers, but they are also profitable because their so-called identifiable culture and language allow marketers and politicians to target them without upsetting white audiences. An entire industry and global media industry sustains "Hispanics'" profitability, an industry that as I noted in Chapter 3 has become more powerful and exclusive because of ongoing media consolidation trends. The result is that Latinos are courted ad nauseam by marketers seeking to capture billions of Latino dollars, while at the same time they are demonized in public discourse as an economic liability who take jobs, benefits, and resources from "regular Americans."

Marketers' continued favor of Latinos was openly displayed during a panel discussion of the importance of using ethnic media when targeting minorities as political constituencies during the First National EXPO of Ethnic Media held at Columbia University on June 9, 2005. The topic of the panel, entitled "Use It or Lose It—Capturing the Swing Vote through Ethnic Media," was the role played by "ethnic media" when targeting minority constituencies. But it was the gains of Latinos as political constituencies that dominated the discussion. Lionel Sosa and Sergio Bendixen, the two Latino political entrepreneurs we met in Chapter 2, emphasized Latinos' growing numbers, and how political parties could tap into their conservative values, greatly overshadowing presentations on the African and Asian American vote. Panelists representing these constituencies sat at opposite ends of the table, visually marking their peripheral role in the discussion. I spoke to James Bernard, founder of *Source* and *XXL* magazines, who discussed African-American voters. He had been in similar meetings where the value of African Americans had been relegated to the margins, although not intentionally, he noted. Instead, the effect was always implicit in the overt interest Latinos raised among business and media types, versus the almost invisible space African Americans occupied in these types of discussions. He was especially critical of the conservative, traditional, and family value descriptions of Latinos that dominated presentations by Sosa, particularly his "Nos Conocemos" ad for Bush that was discussed in Chapter 2 and viewed during the panel discussion. When the ad was played, members of the audience broke into laughter, mocking the ad, while others sat quietly, responses that confirmed the power of the emotionally laden message of Latinos coming of age. But there was another message as well. In Bernard's words, "When you hear things like this, it's like an album you play backwards and you notice that it is saying something else. That African Americans are gone. It's an implicit critique, that you lazy Negroes can't hold your families together. That Latinos are reasonable and we're not. That we don't matter. It's the old conquer and divide thing."

I spoke with a number of African-American civil rights leaders who, like some of their Latino counterparts we heard from throughout this book, are involved in social advocacy and research, about the role they believe Latinos are increasingly given vis-à-vis African Americans. What I found was a common recognition of the old divide and conquer theme that played implicitly at the aforementioned panel. As Roderick Harrison, the founding director of DataBank at the Joint Center, the largest African-American think tank, explained: "We have a history in the U.S. of comparing blacks and European immigrants and now Hispanics are brought in as model minorities to prove that opportunities are there, and to show that groups can be successful if they have the right values, and if you sacrifice.

And we use Hispanics as part of this morality story that 'If you don't make it, there must be some problems with your culture and people.'" The problem, he noted, is that this is done in ways that erase commonalities and needs among black and Latino organizations and constituencies which, with the exception of immigration to which I turn later, are practically the same: more money for schools, job opportunities, health care, and equal employment opportunities.

As problematic as it is that the Latinos-as-model-minorities view is often purposefully deployed against blacks and to bring about divisiveness between these groups, this trope is, unfortunately, quite pervasive. What is more, these "model minority" representations have taken on special urgency within debates over immigration as pundits have sought to represent Latinos as a constituency that will not hurt this country but rather help to refurbish it. Clearly these representations operate as a form of counter-narrative to the dominant view of Latinos as "America's" greatest economic and social liability. As Chapters 1 through 3 showed with regard to marketers and political pundits, these representations are troubling for reducing Latinos' entry into the mainstream to a very narrow path: namely, as a tame and unthreatening group that can be "more American than the Americans"—because of their (supposedly) social conservative values.

Yet this view of "Latinos-as-more-American-than-the-Americans" has implications beyond marketing and politics. As we are told by Roberto Lovato's perceptive essay on the Latino right, the military, the church, and the criminal justice system are three important conservative and right-leaning socializing institutions that are becoming among the surest and easiest paths for Latino mobility in light of diminished sources of employment and economic opportunities (Lovato 2007b). Each of these institutions caters to Latinos through similar conservative messages, which, as Lovato argues, could turn up a "Latino politic in the service of empire."[3] I share Lovato's concern with the number of institutions that are eager to feed into and target Latinos through conservative messages, though I am a bit more hopeful. "Conservative" values and messages of family, hard work, and patriotism are not the property of any particular institution; they could be strategically embraced to bring about progressive policies for more equitable social welfare, as in the resurgence of sanctuary churches in the fight against deportation in Los Angeles. Further, and as pondered by the epigraphs by anthropologist Jose Limón and policy advocate Angelo Falcón, the effects of Latinos' entry into important governmental and private sectors of society is potentially up for grabs; Latinos could perhaps even help to transform these spaces and become agents of positive social change. One example is the border mayors/governors who refuse to buy into homeland security plans to enforce the border without comprehensive immigration reform. In other words, the problem is neither one of "values" nor of the sectors where Latinos gain entry and employment. Instead, it is the narrowing of the meaning of "values" in contemporary society, alongside the pressures exerted on Latinos to conform and overcompensate by aligning with power uncritically that is deserving of more scrutiny. Additionally, these "model minority" representations are most dangerous for depoliticizing Latinos by presenting them as a safe and easily accommodated constituency from the point of view of the dominant, white "majority." These portrayals have the unfortunate effect of disavowing Latinos' history and everyday acts for civil rights and equity, both within their own communities and alongside African Americans.

Gary Sheffield, the major league baseball player, may have been criticized in 2007 after noting that in contrast to African Americans, Latinos are easier to control than blacks, which explains the growing number of Latinos in the major leagues alongside the stark decrease in black players. "It's (about) being able to tell (Latin players) what to do—being able to control them. . . . Where I'm from, you can't control us." He was called a racist for generalizing about Latinos (ESPN 2007a). Yet, his comments are extremely suggestive of what as we have seen is a widely held view, certainly among marketers and political pundits—the invocation that Latinos constitute a more "tamable" constituency than blacks. This view not only generalizes the structural vulnerability of the undocumented Latino worker onto the entire Latino population, but also, and most problematically, turns such vulnerability into a "positive" character trait. In fact, this is the same view that Eddie Perez, a Latino player and former teammate of Sheffield, was eager to reproduce in response to his comments: "It's not because they like us—it's because we're doing good. When we play, we play hard. You don't hear too many Latin players talk a lot of trash" (ESPN 2007b). Obviously, Perez's comments were informed by the "good" Latinos stereotype so widely marketed by many Latino pundits.

Indeed, black-brown relations are permeated with stereotypes. Like most Americans, blacks and Latinos are not exempt from thinking about themselves and each other in terms of the same dominant stereotypes that circulate in greater society and that inform ideas about who is more or less likely to be loud, aggressive, submissive, hard-working, athletic, and so on

(Mindiola et al. 2003). Given this, Latinos need to be especially cautious to not fall for the stereotypes of the hard-working and submissive Latino embedded in the model minority myth, and careful of not embracing it in ways that veil and reproduce racist attitudes against African Americans. Doing so would implicate Latinos in the same immigrant hard-working tropes that immigrant groups have long used to claim whiteness by distancing themselves from blacks. We must remember that this move has never quite worked for Latinos, and that Latinos have failed to be fully "saved" and "whitened" by long-standing attempts to associate them with these tropes. Instead, and more likely than not, Latinos have been subjugated by these views, especially when they are used to turn them into a "model" but depoliticized constituency. In other words, this view asks too much from Latinos, while providing very little in return.

At the same time, stereotypes are just stereotypes, whether positive or negative. For sure, they justify injustices, and bring about misunderstandings, and consequently should always be questioned and probed. However, to exert inequalities, stereotypes require access to power and institutions, which neither blacks nor Latinos control fully. This is why it is important to turn our attention to the political economies of culture as played out in particular institutional spaces. Only then can we begin to appreciate the economic logics that are always hidden from view, but that I believe are centrally involved whenever inequalities and tensions surface between and among members of racial and ethnic groupings.

Indeed, lost in the scandal over Sheffield's comments are important insights about the political economy of baseball, specifically the leagues' penchant for Latin American players, their investments in baseball schools in Latin America rather than in the inner-city barrios, and the cheaper costs of hiring and courting Latin American imports. In other words, his comments were most revealing of the political economy of baseball, the same economy that, in the words of Ozzie Guillen, the Latin coach of the Chicago White Sox, allows the signing of "one African-American player for the price of 30 Latin players" (Feinsand 2007). These important dynamics were central to his comments, but were nevertheless lost from public view when Sheffield's remarks were spun into a news bite about a "black player being racist against Latinos," and the ensuing scandal his comments triggered.

The point is that media representations of black-brown relations and collisions are, more often than not, incomplete and misguided. Unfortunately, this truism cannot be repeated enough. Broadcast media is not known for its nuance when sexier bylines are at stake, nor is it known for seeking sources beyond the most easily accessible and available talking heads and pundits who are often involved in setting the agenda of particular debates. Such is the case with much of the news on "black and brown" relations that reached the media throughout 2007, a year when "gangs" and the immigration debate dominated "black and brown" news. Then, it was not rare to find the same spokespeople quoted over and over, often the spokespersons holding the most extreme or more easily scandalized positions. Among them, Nicolas Vaca, author of *The Presumed Alliance: The Unspoken Conflict Between Latinos and Blacks and What It Means for America*; Earl Ofari Hutchinson, author of *The Latino Challenge to Black America: Towards a Conversation Between African Americans and Hispanics*; and to a lesser extent, activist Ted Hayes of *Choose Black America*. Adding insult to injury, their stands were represented by the simplistic and marketable titles of their books and positions, reifying instead of elucidating or probing their bases.

But I want to return to the importance of examining the political economy informing contemporary representations of race. In this regard, I believe that focusing on particular institutions may be especially revealing of how the ranking and evaluation of racial others takes place in the contemporary neoliberal moment, where race seems so skewed and its discussion is so elided from public debate. Chapters 4 through 6 introduced this type of analysis around a Latino and Latin American museum, urban planning, and the corporate university. With the exception of Chapter 4, these chapters did not focus on dynamics that directly affect black and Latino relations. However, in exposing the working of some institutional spaces involved in producing and representing Latino/a culture, and in examining how they reproduce, justify, and conceal distinctions and inequalities among Latinos, and that which is deemed to best represent Latinidad, they bring attention to some of the key intersections between capital and race that underlie these distinctions. Recall the economic dynamics that affect the exhibition of Latino and Latin American art, and how they favor artwork hailing from Latin American countries with strong art collectors, elites, and institutions like museums and embassies, whereas Latino art continues to be obviated from the Latin American and American artistic canon. Economic considerations were also involved in the continuous relegation of ethnic studies within the corporate university in ways that favor the established disciplines and geographically bounded subjects such as Latin American studies and so on over U.S. ethnic studies. Last, in the realm of urban planning, Latino culture is relegated to being a mere theme, while residents are excluded as stakeholders and beneficiaries of new developments. Each of these chapters highlights the accommodation and insertion of Latino culture within "mainstream" institutions, showing that inclusion does not necessarily equate with equality or with legitimate belonging and entitlements.

These chapters also show that cultural struggles and conflicts are never simply rhetorical. Instead, they have genuine cultural, political, and economic sources and foundations that can be addressed, be it through less elitist definitions of Latino/Latin American art and programming in Chapter 4 and/or through investments in local communities in Chapter 5. Thus, with regard to black and Latino tensions, it is equally important to look at the economies behind the "spin" in order to expose whose power is being cemented and what interests are benefiting most from inter- and intraracial politics. Only then will debates over the transformation of neighborhoods that used to be black and are now Hispanic, and jobs that used to be held by blacks and are now held by Hispanics, not be reduced to a problem posed by Hispanic immigrants and their "effects," but instead begin to account for the structural factors that underlie these changes. More often than not, these are the same structural factors that affect both groups: the penchant for cheap vulnerable labor and the lack of investment in social infrastructure, and the racism that continues to limit the real and meaningful "coming-of-age" of people of color in this country. This realization could perhaps move us from the current impasse, where immigrants are treated as scapegoats, especially regarding the economic fate of African Americans, and instead direct our attention to a government that continues to disinvest from the welfare, education, health, and economic well-being of its residents, whether they are citizens or not.

Recognizing that race and racism are centrally involved in determining which groups are accepted into America's mainstream, however changed and transformed this mainstream is considered to be, and which ones are considered its perennial and potential threats, is especially paramount for contextualizing the current immigration debate. Currently, the immigration debate has fueled an uncritical nativism where "citizenship" is reified as the guarantor of rights and entitlements and the ultimate mark of privilege and status, hiding the fact that citizenship has never conferred equal status and privileges to racial others. Indeed, today more than ever citizenship should serve as a point for connection, rather than contention, between Latinos and African Americans. For one, the second-class citizenship long endured by Puerto Ricans and many U.S.-born Latinos is not dissimilar to the second-class citizenship long awarded to African Americans and to many others who have never been vested with the full benefits of citizenship because of their race, gender, or sexuality. Placing citizenship under such critical scrutiny could be especially effective in tempering the rise of nativist anti-immigration positions while galvanizing a movement toward the expansion of true citizenship rights for all. In particular, awareness of the uncertainties of citizenship should make us especially skeptical of claims that present nativist anti-immigrant positions as "anti-racist" on the count that they are motivated by the need to defend our "black population" who are deemed to be the ones most hurt by immigration, in ways that turn anti-immigrant discourse into a buffer for expressions of racism. After all, it may be more palatable to say one is "anti–illegal immigration" than it is to say one is anti-blacks and anti-Latino or anti–people of color. Yet we should not forget that Hispanic immigrants are primarily mixed-race and colored, not white. And it is this very fact that creates most anxiety, and that causes nativist anti-immigrant positions to be imminently racially driven, and hence consequential for blacks, as they are for Latinos and for anyone who is not considered to be unquestionably "normative" or Anglo-American.

Finally, I have spent considerable time and effort dispelling public discourse that serves to whitewash and align Latinos with projects that advance normativity, while creating inequalities among Latinos along the lines of citizenship, class, and other variables. I hope to have shown the significance of examining how Latinos are being appealed to, and the type of projects advanced on their behalf in order to resist their co-optation into projects and policies that can affect not only Latinos but all Americans. In this regard, I repeat Mari Matsuda's well-known call to the Asian Law Caucus, when addressing Asian Americans' potential to serve as a racial middle that supports white supremacy, that "We will not be used!"[4] Like her, I plead that Latinos remain informed of our past, the same past that is linked and relived in others' present, and that we remain committed to social justice in our alliances and politics. Toward this goal I hope that this volume serves as a warning that projects and policies that claim to advance a "Latino/a" agenda are not always inclusive, referencing "Latino/a" culture provides little guarantee of a lack of complicity with neoliberal interests and forces, and that distinctions and inequalities among Latinos are not being reproduced and fostered. At the same time, my hope is that a greater awareness of how racial and cultural hierarchies operate through discourses, institutions, and policies may help to bring about more recognition of commonalities across Latino subgroups as well as with African Americans and other ethnic groups. If we recognize the hurdles that hinder Latinos' rightful inclusion in the nation, because of who they are and what they are seen to represent, irrespective of their education, class, even citizenship status, we could perhaps all take less refuge in our "privileges," and be more likely to establish meaningful alliances across class and citizenship statuses. This task requires that we suspend our uncritical celebration of Latinos' coming of age, and instead anchor our understanding of their past, present, and future in the ever-changing but pervasive politics of race.

Notes

INTRODUCTION

1. See Kolata 2007 for a recent exposé on the "Hispanic paradox" which, while identifying numerous socioeconomic reasons for Latinos' longer life span, ends with the characteristic mention of Latinos' "happy-go-lucky" attitude as a primary reason for their health.

2. See Gonzalez 2007 for an overview of how these "positive" discourses are related to the debate over immigration.

3. See for instance debates around Nava's 2004 exposé of black and Latinos' "presumed alliance."

4. This last view ignores a long-standing literature documenting how Latin American mestizaje has long functioned as an "all-inclusive ideology of exclusion" given its inevitable insertion and use by a range of nationalist ideologies and projects (Stutzman 1981).

5. On Latinos as white, see Waterston 2006, and on their refiguring the meaning of "mainstream," see Hayes-Bautista 2004.

6. Alonso-Zaldivar 2004; Tafoya 2004.

7. Alonso-Zaldivar 2003.

8. The literature documenting racism in Latin America is extensive. See Sheriff 2001; Twine 2006; Telles 2006b for some important works challenging the myth of Latin America's racial democracy, looking in particular at the case of Brazil, which has figured most prominently in debates about the supposedly greater racial inclusivity at play in Latin America.

9. In his discussion of race and the politics of representation, Stuart Hall identifies race as a floating signifier to highlight its lack of fixity and its social construction. He does this to call attention to the multiplicity of meanings that can be "fixed" to particular signs. I use his concept here a bit differently, to highlight the vacuous state of indeterminacy that precedes the affixing of meaning to a particular sign (Hall 1997).

CHAPTER 1

1. As Garcia 1989 tells us, there is very little research about organizations during the 1930-1950s. This period is often obviated and disdained by the over-attention given to the more radical and since highly romanticized Chicano movement. Even less is known about Puerto Rican organizations in the East. Garcia, however, shows us that the accommodating stance of middle classes in this period was never as assimilationist as it has been described. Cultural plural-ism better describes the aspirations of this group.

2. See Haslip-Viera et al. (2005) for assessments of Puerto Ricans' engagement with changes in the political/economic policy climate from the 1960s to the 1990s.

3. I discuss this in greater detail with regard to the development of Hispanic marketing (Dávila 2001b).

4. For a discussion of the trajectory of analyses on the "Puerto Rican excep-tion," see Melendez Velez 2005.

5. See Gregory Rodriguez's website in the New America Foundation: http://www.newamerica.net/index.cfm?pg=Bio&contactID=62.

6. For a discussion of predatory lending practices and how it affects Latinos, see reports by the Center for Responsible Lending, May 2006, and the Annie Casey Foundation (2005).

7. TRPI spring 2007 conference description at http://www.trpi.org/update/events_spring_1.html.

8. Arguably other factors may be at play, such as New York's immigrant his-tory ethos. The key issue is the regionally specific factors that may affect the po-liticization of citizenship around issues of class. Another interesting point of con-trast is the intersection of citizenship/class in Chicago, which is also connected to the specific histories of immigration and economic insertion among Mexicans and Puerto Ricans in the area (De Genova and Zayas 2003). See also Smith 2005 for a discussion of citizenship and race with regard to Mexicans and Puerto Ri-cans in New York.

9. See Wright 2005 for a discussion of different approaches to class analysis, and Ortner 2003 for class as a "project" always in motion and transformation.

10. On the regional and national dynamics affecting Latinos' identifications with regard to class issues, see Vila 2000 and Pulido 2006.

CHAPTER 2

1. See National Council of La Raza (November 16, 2004) Memorandum, How Did Latinos Really Vote in 2004? and William C. Velasquez Institute (undated), "The 2004 WCVI National Latino Election Day Exit Poll" by Dr. Henry Flores of St. Mary's University. Both reports were presented at the National Latino Exit Poll Briefing, organized by *Demos* on December 6, 2004.

2. See, for instance, *La Prensa* 2004: 8A; Radelat 2004; Juan Gonzalez 2004; Johnson 2004; Kasindorf 2004.

3. These views were described by pollsters working with Latinos. But they are also represented in the National Town Halls on issues concerning Latino voters in 2004 conducted by NALEO (NALEO 2004). See also Fraga et al. 2006 and Bendixen 2007.

4. Since then, Latino youth have been targeted by voter mobilization campaigns such as that launched by the bilingual youth-oriented Mun2's "voto Latino." But Mun2 is limited in reach as a cable station and is not available in all the markets.

5. In fact, some observers found that, contrary to past elections, the Democrats' Spanish-language ads emphasized values and family even more than the GOP (Connaughton et al. 2007).

CHAPTER 3

1. Larmer 1999. See also Dávila 2001b for an earlier discussion of Latino marketing hereby updated.

2. Chavez 2001 and Santa Ana 2002 provide some recent examples of the types of metaphors that have dominated coverage of immigrants as economic burdens or liabilities to the national community.

3. See Ong 1999 and Williams 1989 for notions of racialized ethnicity as the outcome of processes of homogenizing difference and othering of marginal subjects within nationalist projects. For a discussion of Latinos' construction as permanent aliens within U.S. nationalist discourse, see Oboler 1995; and Honig 1998 for discourses of foreigners as embodiments of national democratic values.

4. The sections below draw primarily from my previous work, especially from Chapter 2 of *Latinos Inc.* (Dávila 2001b).

5. The campaign mobilized activists and state officials from New York City and beyond and, For an insightful assessment of the connections between Murdoch's lobbyists and local activists, see Gonzalez 2004.

6. Napoli (2006: 30).

7. Rincon and Associates 2004.

8. See "Policy Review Paper Assessing the Nielsen and Rincón Study on Latino Television Viewing Prepared by The Tomás Rivera Policy Institute," 2004 by Rodolfo O. de la Garza, Ph.D., Louis DeSipio, Ph.D., Jongho Lee, Ph.D., and Harry Pachon, Ph.D.; and "Scholarly 'Confusion' Evident in Review of Latino Television Study by Tomas Rivera Policy Institute," press release by the National Latino Media Coalition, July 12, 2004.

9. See Change the Sample.com.

10. Advertising Age 2006.

11. On media consolidation, see Ballvé 2004.

12. Eric Dash "Tapping Into the Hispanic Market," *New York Times,* April 14, 2006.

13. Derek Turner and Mark Cooper, "Out of the Picture: Minority and Female TV Station Ownership," www.freepress.net. October 2006.

14. Pinon 2007.

15. Castañeda 2007.

16. The New York meetings were organized by the National Association of Hispanic Journalists and the National Hispanic Media Coalition with the cooperation of Free Press. For more information about FCC hearings held in Texas, Los Angeles, Washington, Philadelphia, and other cities, see http://www.stopbigmedia.com/=hearings.

17. As of November 2007, the project is still in the works. This discussion is based on the presentation by Carl Kravetz at the 2006 AHAA 21st conference in Miami.

18. See Kravetz 2006.

19. See Horwitz 2006 on the linkage between the myth of the black legend and the current immigration debate, as well as Kanellos 1998.

20. Association of Hispanic Advertising Agencies POV on the Economics of Integration, The Dollars and "Sense" of the Immigration Debate. http://www.ahaa.org/media/Immigration%20Forum/Immigration%20POV.htm.

21. See Grow et al. 2005 for the feature article.

22. See for instance the comments of economist James P. Smith to Newsweek, http://www.msnbc.msn.com/id/12599439/site/newsweek/.

23. "The Multicultural Economy 2007" Selig Center for Economic Growth, Terry College of Business, University of Georgia, 2007.

CHAPTER 4

1. I provide more background on East Harlem's urban policy issues in Dávila 2004.

2. See Dávila 2004 for discussions of the Empowerment Zone's tourism initiative and NYC Department of City Planning for an Overview of the River to River Project, http://www.nyc.gov/html/dcp/html/125th/125th4.shtmlr dis.

3. http://www.nyc.gov/html/lmec/html/about/about.shtml.

4. Brash 2006.

5. Ibid.

6. Ibid.

7. Ibid.

8. Get the Latest News from the NYC Latin Media and Entertainment Commission: http://www.nyc.gov/html/lmec/html/news/news.shtml.

9. Mayor Bloomberg, Latin Academy of Recording Arts and Sciences, Univision Network, and NYC Big Events Announce NYC to Host Latin Grammy awards for First Time Ever, Press release, April 11, 2006.

10. Big Plans, Bucks, For a Hispanic Mini-City, Mariana C. King. *Marketing and Medios*, June 1, 2005.

11. JERDE 2006.

12. Bengal 2001.

13. As David Diaz's (2005) study of Chicanos and urban planning in the Southwest shows, similar community advisory boards were initially made up of elected members, who yielded more power than developers had anticipated. The move from an elected to an appointed membership, he notes, was a key way through which elected officials curtailed their power by controlling their membership through the appointment process.

14. Terry Pristin, "In Major Projects, Agreeing Not to Disagree," *New York Times*, June 14, 2006.

15. *New York Times* 1996; Arce 1995.

16. Zaretsky 2005.

17. See Community Board 11 (2005), and Community Board 11 (2007).

18. http://www.mbpo.org/press/pressreleases/news_item.2006-05-03.5302584681, El Barrio Residents Win One, *El Diario/La Prensa*, May 6, 2006; Facing Neighbors' Concerns, City Kills Huge East Harlem Project, by Timothy Williams, *New York Times*, May 4, 2006; 'Uptown' Plan Down and Out, by Bob Kappstatter, *New York Daily News*, May 3, 2006.

19. See Powell 2007 for a discussion of this revisionist turn and its major voices. A presentation promoting a gentle "moses effect" was discussed in a panel, Best Laid Plans: Planning New York's Future: A Discussion of Urban Planning in Robert Moses' Time and Today, Tuesday, March 20. Panel discussion at the Museum of the City of New York, especially by Rohit T. Aggarwala, director of the Mayor's Office of Long-Term Planning and Sustainability.

20. Walking, We Ask Questions, by R. J. Macconi, http://www.narconews.com/Issue42/article2037.html].

CHAPTER 5

1. A study by the New York Foundation for the Arts reported declining shares of state and federal government funds in overall funding for the arts, and highlighted the resulting inequities among organizations that obtain or fail to obtain support (NYFA 2001). Citing a study by the Alliance for the Arts, the foundation noted that government funds as a share of all arts funding in New York City dropped from 28.9 percent in 1982 to 11 percent in 1998. Corporations and private foundations filled the void to some extent, but failed to make up for the decline in government funding. The inability of many arts institutions in New York City to access city funding has led to higher ticket prices for cultural events, which in turn have made them inaccessible to much of the population, particularly youth.

2. This chapter is based on original research and on my recollections as a staff member at El Museo del Barrio and at the former Museum of Contemporary Hispanic Art (MoCHA) in the late 1980s and early 1990s. I conducted interviews and conversations with artists, curators, and art administrators in New York City in the late 1990s (see Dávila 1999; 2004). This early research coincided with an initial wave of activism in 1997–1999 by a group of artists then organized as "Puerto Ricans for the New Millennium." Their concerns were similar to those of the We Are Watching You campaign, in which many of these artists later became involved. I was one of other scholars involved in the We Are Watching You campaign; I coordinated an open letter in support of the Community Board's position and the We Are Watching You campaign. The letter was drafted and signed by a group of university professors, curators, writers, and doctoral students in solidarity with community groups (signers included Luis Aponte Pares, Juan Flores, Gabriel Haslip-Viera, Wilson Valentin, Miriam Jiménez Román, and Arnaldo Cruz-Málave). The letter was published in El Barrio's community newspaper *Siempre* and in *El Diario*, New York's Spanish-language daily, in August 2002.

3. Some of the factors associated with this rising interest include the popularization of multiculturalism as a political discourse, the marketing strategies of transnational corporations seeking to ingratiate themselves with a growing Latino market by funding exhibitions, and the internationalized commercialization of Latin American art (Goldman 1994; Fusco 1995). Some traveling exhibitions linked to this art boom" in the late 1980s include *Hispanic Arts in the United States: Thirty Contemporary Painters and Sculptors,* organized by the Museum of Fine Arts in Houston; *The Latin American Spirit: Art and Artists in the United States, 1920–1970,* by the Bronx Museum of the Arts; and *Art of the Fantastic: Latin America 1920–1970,* by the Indianapolis Museum of Art.

4. Most Latin American artists have at some point traveled, studied, or lived in the United States, a back-and-forth movement that challenges strict differentiation between Latin American and U.S.-based Latino/a artists. Distinctions abound in their treatment, however; hence, even the most recent such work, Edward Sullivan's (2000) *Latin American Art in the Twentieth Century,* while unique in devoting a chapter to Chicano art, otherwise excludes treatment of U.S.-Latino artists. See also Mosquera 1996.

5. For the dominance of Western standards in the evaluation of Latin American art, see Ramírez 1996; Ybarra-Frausto 1991; and Torruella-Leval 1995. On the autonomization of art, see Marcus and Myers 1995. The processes by which art attains autonomous value in opposition to the particular contexts of its production have been described by Bourdieu, Williams, and others writing on the construction of the category of Western art. For instance,

Raymond Williams (1977) notes that by achieving separation from the social context in which it develops—by denying any utilitarian function or economic motive behind its production, or by veiling the power of those distinguishing qualities—art is defined as an "absolute abstraction," valuable in and of itself. These processes are also succinctly described by Bourdieu 1993, for whom the field of artistic production is an "economic world upside down," directly involved in denying the very same processes that affect its evaluation, such as the economic factors and structures impacting the production, circulation, and consumption of artistic goods. I am not implying here that distinctions between low and high art are not made within the category of Latin American art, but that the very field of "art" reproduces hierarchies in which the canons of high art, defined as universal and humanistic, are predominant. See Ramírez 1996 for a discussion of the prevalence of Western-based standards of aesthetic quality, universality, and autonomy in the evaluation both of Latin American art vis-à-vis European traditions, and of different types of art within the category of Latin American art.

6. El Museo's transformation is discussed in greater detail by Moreno (1997: 265), who charts the decrease in exhibitions featuring Puerto Rican artists from the late 1960s to the mid-1990s, when the institution formally adopted a Latin American focus as part of its mission. While this transformation had its origins in the late 1970s, it did not become marked until the Latino/Latin American art boom of the 1980s, and was only recently institutionalized in the museum's mission statement. See Moreno 1997 for more about El Museo del Barrio's history, and see Wilson 1984 for a discussion of the trajectory of MoCHA and other Latino institutions in New York City.

7. See the *New York Times* article by Lee (2002) for an evocative example of how the issue was treated in the mainstream media. *El Diario*, the Spanish-language newspaper, had more even coverage (see for example Vega 2002).

8. See LeBron 2007 for a comprehensive discussion of the debate over El Museo's change in mission that places it against a larger historical context, including the debate over the representation of Puerto Rican identities. This work also discusses the perspective of the museum's staff, which differed from that of the board.

9. The campaign won promises that two seats on the museum's board of directors would be allotted to community representatives—people who would be accountable to the community, rather than simply those able to contribute funds to the museum. However, the replacement of Debbie Quiñones as chair of the cultural affairs committee, in the middle of the campaign, interfered with the selection of such members. And the campaign's demand that board members whose terms had long expired step down and be replaced with new members was never answered.

CHAPTER 6

1. http://Chronicle.com/weekly/almanac/2002/nation/0103202.htm: Number of Full-Time Members by Sex, Rank, and Racial and Ethnic Group, Fall 1999.

2. See Haslip-Viera's 2005 assessment of Latino Studies programs in CUNY. This second report, very poignantly, cites senior administrators at CUNY announcing that these programs have "outlived their mission" and should be disbanded, even in campuses that serve a primarily Latino student population, as do those in the Bronx along with many community colleges.

3. Presenters included Raymond Rocco and Suzanne Oboler. Held at John Jay College, February 21, 2007.

CONCLUSION

1. See, for instance, Vaca's 2004 controversial exposé of conflicts between Latinos and blacks with regard to African Americans' greater control of civil and government jobs.

2. See, for instance, initiatives like the Afro-Latin@ Project, http://afrolatino project.org/site/index.php?option=com_frontpage&Itemid=1.

3. Lovato 2007b.

4. Mari Matsuda, "We Will Not Be Used," *Asian American Pacific Islands Law Journal*, 1993.

Bibliography

Acuña, Rodolfo. 2006. *Occupied America: A History of Chicanos*. New York: Longman.

Advertising Age. 2006. Hispanic Fact Pack: Annual Guide to Hispanic Marketing and Media.

Alba, Richard, and Victor Nee. 2003. *Remaking the American Mainstream: Assimilation and Contemporary Immigration*. Cambridge, Mass.: Harvard University Press.

Alcoff, Linda. 2005. *Visible Identities: Race, Gender, and the Self*. Oxford, New York: Oxford University Press.

Alonso-Zaldivar, Ricardo. 2003. "For Millions Of Latinos, Race Is a Flexible Concept: The Rigid Labels Used By the Census Bureau Often Don't Fit The Beliefs of Their Ancestral Cultures." *Los Angeles Times*, March 11.

———. 2004. "Study Examines How Latinos View Themselves Racially." *Houston Chronicle*, December 6.

American Anthropological Association. 1973. "The Minority Experience in Anthropology: Report of the Committee on Minorities and Anthropology." American Anthropological Association (August), http://www.aaanet.org/committees/minority/minexp.htm (accessed November 3, 2005).

Anderson, Nick. 2004. "The Race to the White House; Parties Seeking to Speak Language of Latino Voters; Both Democrats and Republicans Unveil TV Ads Targeting a Crucial Constituency." *Los Angeles Times* March 6, Part A, p. 14.

Annie E. Casey Foundation. 2005. "Double Jeopardy: Advocasey Explores the High Cost of Being Poor." *AdvoCasey* (Winter): 1.

Arce, Maritere. 1995. "La Marqueta Muere Lentamente." *El Diario/La Prensa* 26 (13): 7.

Association of Hispanic Advertising Agencies. "Missed Opportunities: Vast Corporate Spending in the U.S. Hispanic Market." http://www.ahaa.org/research/Missedopportunities.pdf.

Association of Hispanic Advertising Agencies POV on the Economics of Integration. "The Dollars and "Sense" of the Immigration Debate." http://www.ahaa.org/media/Immigration%20Forum/Immigration%20POV.htm.

"At La Marqueta, Concrete and Enamel." 1996. *New York Times*, December 8, Real Estate section, p. 91.

Atwood, Roger. 2003. "Rediscovering Latin America." *ARTnews* (June): 99–101.

Badillo, Herman. 2006. "One Nation, One Standard: An Ex-Liberal on How Hispanics Can Succeed Just Like Other Immigrant Groups." *Sentinel HC.*

Baker, Chris. 2003. "What Is Middle Class?" *Washington Times*, November 30.

Balibar, Etienne. 1991. "Is There a Neo-Racism?" In *Race, Nation, Class: Ambiguous Identities*, ed. Etienne Balibar and Immanuel Wallerstein. New York: Verso.

Ballvé, Marcelo. 2004. "The Battle for Latino Media." *NACLA Report on the Americas* 37 (4): 20.

Bedolla, Lisa. 2005. *Fluid Borders: Latino Power, Identity and Politics in Los Angeles.* Berkeley: University of California Press.

Bendixen, Sergio. 2007. The 2006 Elections: The Issues and the Hispanic Electorate. Presentation at the Center for American Progress, Washington D.C., February 15.

Bengal, Shanshank. 2001. "Urban Legend." *Trojan Family Magazine* (University of Southern California) Summer. http://www.usc.edu/dept/pubrel/trojan_family/summer01/Jerde/Jerde.html.

Bennett, Jessica. 2006. "'Zero Impact': An economist talks about the economics of illegal immigrants—and why we may be overestimating the significance of undocumented workers." *Newsweek*, May 2. http://www.msnbc.msn.com/id/12599439/site/newsweek/.

Blackwell, Angela Glover, Stewart Kwoh, and Manuel Pastor. 2002. *Searching for the Uncommon Common Ground.* New York: W. W. Norton.

Bok, Derek. 2003. *Universities in the Marketplace: The Commercialization of Higher Education.* Princeton, N.J.: Princeton University Press.

Bonilla-Silva, Eduardo. 1998. *White Supremacy and Racism in the Post-Civil Rights Era.* Boulder, Colo.: Lynne Rienner.

———. 2003. "'New Racism,' Color-Blind Racism, and the Future of Whiteness in America." In *White Out: The Continuing Significance of Racism*, ed. Ashley W. Doane and Eduardo Bonilla-Silva, 271–74. London: Routledge.

Bosquez, Mario. 2005. *The Chalupa Rules: A Latino Guide to Gringolandia.* New York: Penguin.

Bourdieu, Pierre. 1993. *The Field of Cultural Production.* New York: Columbia University Press.

Brash, Julian. 2006. "The Bloomberg Way: Development Politics, Urban Ideology, and Class Transformation in Contemporary New York City." Dissertation submitted the Graduate Faculty in Anthropology. New York: The Graduate Center.

Bright, Brenda, and Liza Bakewell. 1995. *Looking High and Low: Art and Cultural Identity.* Tucson: University of Arizona Press.

Brodkin, Karen. 1999. *How Jews Became White Folks and What That Says about Race in America*. New Brunswick, N.J.: Rutgers University Press.
Brooks, David. 2006. "Immigrants to Be Proud Of." *New York Times*, March 29.
Brown, Michael K., et al. 2005. *Whitewashing Race: The Myth of a Color-Blind Society*. Berkeley: University of California Press.
Butler, Johnnella. 2001. *From Color-Lines to Borderlines: The Matrix of American Ethnic Studies*. Seattle: University of Washington Press.
Cabán, Pedro. 2003. "From Challenge to Absorption: The Changing Face of Latina and Latino Studies." *Center for Puerto Rican Studies* 15 (2): 127–45.
Cardenas, Vanessa. 2007. "The Inexplicably Uncourted Latino Vote." Washingtonpost.com's Think Tank Town, October 13; http://www.washingtonpost.com/wpdyn/content/article/2007/10/12/AR2007101201425.html.
Castañeda, Maria. 2007. "Spanish-Language Media in an Era of Deregulation." In *Global Communications: Towards a Transcultural Political Economy*, ed. P. Chakravartty and Y. Zhao. Landham: Rowman and Littlefield.
Center for Responsible Lending. 2006. "Unfair Lending: The Effects of Race and Ethnicity on the Price of Subprimer Mortgages." Washington, D.C.
Chait, Jocelyne. 2001. "Community-based Planning: Moving Beyond the Rhetoric. Progressive Planning." http://www.plannersnetwork.org/publications/2001_147/Chait.html.
Champagne, Patrick. 2004. "Making the People Speak: The Use of Public Opinion Polls in Democracy." *Constellations* 11 (1): 61–75.
Chavez, Leo. 2001. *Covering Immigration: Popular Images and the Politics of the Nation*. Berkeley: University of California Press.
Chavez, Linda. 1991. *Out of the Barrio: Toward a New Politics of Hispanic Assimilation*. New York: Basic Books.
———. 2002. *An Unlikely Conservative: The Transformation of an Ex-liberal, or, How I Became the Most Hated Hispanic in America*. New York: Basic Books.
Cohen, Lizabeth. 2003. *A Consumers' Republic: the Politics of Mass Consumption in Postwar America*. New York: Vintage Books.
Community Board 11. 2005. "Affordable Housing Development Guidelines." http://www.cb11m.org/info/about.htm.
———. 2007. "Statement of District Needs Fiscal Year 2007." http://www.cb11m.org/info/files/Statement%20FY07.pdf
Connaughton, Dina Nekrassova, and Katie Lever. 2007. "Talk About Issues: Policy Considerations in Campaign 2004 Latino-Oriented Presidential Spots." In Federico Subervi, *The Mass Media and Latino Politics: Studies of Media Contents, Campaign Strategies and Survey Research 1984–2004*.
Consumer Expenditure Survey. 2001. *Consumer Expenditure Survey*. U.S. Department of Labor Bureau of Labor Statistics.
Cotter, Holland. 2003. "The S-Files." *New York Times*, January 17, Leisure/Weekend Desk, Section E, p. 48.

Cruz, Jon. 1996. "From Farce to Tragedy: Reflections on the Reification of Race at Century's End." In *Mapping Multiculturalism*, ed. Avery F. Gordon and Christopher Newfield, 19–39. Minneapolis: University of Minnesota Press.

Curiel, Carolyn. 2004. "How Hispanics Voted Republican. *New York Times*, November 8.

Dabbah, Mariela, and Arturo Poire. 2006. *The Latino Advantage in the Workplace: Using Who You Are to Get Where You Want to Be*. Naperville, Ill.: Sphinx Publishing.

Darder, Antonia, and Rodolfo D. Torres. 2003. "Mapping Latino Studies: Critical Reflections on Class and Social Theory." *Latino Studies* 1 (2): 303–24.

Davalos, Karen. 2001. *Exhibiting Mestizaje: Mexican (American) Museums in the Diaspora*. Albuquerque: University of New Mexico Press.

Dávila, Alberto, and Marie Mora. 2000. "English Skills, Earnings, and the Occupational Sorting of Mexican Americans along the U.S. Mexico Border." *International Migration Review* 34 (1): 33–157.

Dávila, Arlene. 1999. "Latinizing Culture: Art, Museums and the Politics of Multicultural Encompassment." *Cultural Anthropology* 14(2): 180–202.

———. 2001a. "Culture in the Battlefront: From Nationalist to Pan-Latino Projects." In *Mambo Montage: The Latinization of New York*, ed. Agustin Lao and Arlene Dávila, 159–82. New York: Columbia University Press.

———. 2001b. *Latinos Inc. Marketing and the Making of a People*. Berkeley: University of California Press.

———. 2004. *Barrio Dreams: Puerto Ricans, Latinos and the Neoliberal City*. Berkeley: University of California Press.

Davis, Hugh. 2006. Foreword. *TRANSactions—Contemporary Latin American and Latino Art*. Stephanie Hanor, ed. Museum of Contemporary Art San Diego.

Davis, Mike. 2001. *Magical Urbanism: Latinos Reinvent the US Big City*. New York: Verso.

De Genova, Nicholas, and Ana Ramos Zayas. 2003. *Latino Crossings: Mexicans, Puerto Ricans, and the Politics of Race and Citizenship*. New York: Routledge.

De la Garza, Rodolfo. 2004. "Latino Politics." *Annual Review of Political Science* 7: 91–123.

Delmos, Jones. 1970. "Towards a Native Anthropology." *Human Organization* 29: 251–59.

DeSipio, Louis, and Roberto de la Garza. 2002. "Forever Seen as New: Latino Participation in American Elections." In *Latinos: Remaking America*, ed. Marcelo Suarez Orozco and Mariela M. Paez, 398–409. Berkeley: University of California Press.

Diaz, David. 2005. *Barrio Urbanism: Chicanos, Planning, and American Cities*. New York: Routledge.

Dominguez, Virginia. 1997. "A Taste for 'the Other': Intellectual Complicity in Racializing Practices." *Current Anthropology* 35 (4): 333–42.

Elliot, Andrea. 2004. "For New York Evangelicals, a Political Conversion." *New York Times*, November 14, Section 1; Column 2; Metropolitan Desk; Second Front: 35.

ESPN. (2007a). Sheffield Says Latin Players Easier to Control than Blacks, June 3. http://sports.espn.go.com/mlb/news/story?id=2891875ESPN.

———. (2007b). Perez on Sheff's Comments: "That's going to hurt a lot of people." June 6. http://sports.espn.go.com/mlb/news/story?id=2893756.

Ewen, Stuart. 1996. *PR! A Social History of Spin*. New York: Basic Books.

Feinsand, Ozzie. 2007. "Latinos' Love of Baseball the Key." *New York Daily News*, June 5.

Flores, Henry. 2004. "Tio Politico; 'Are Latinos Republicans or Democrats?'" *La Prensa*, December 29, 16 (24): 8A.

Flores, Juan. 1996. "Pan-Latino/Trans-Latino: Puerto Ricans in the "New Nueva York." *CENTRO Bulletin* 8(1–2): 170–86.

Fraga, Luis, John Garcia, Rodney Hero, Michael Jones-Correa, Martinez-Eers, and Gary Segura. 2006. Redefining America: Findings from the 2006 Latino National Survey. Presentation at the Center for American Progress. February 16, 2007.

Frank, Thomas. 2005. *What's the Matter with Kansas: How Conservatives Won the Heart of America*. New York: Owl Books.

Fusco, Coco. 1995. *English Is Broken Here: Notes on Cultural Fusion in the Americas*. New York: New Press.

Fusco, Coco, and Guillermo Gomez Pena. 1995. "Nationalism and Latinos, North-South: A Dialogue." In *English Is Broken Here: Notes on Cultural Fusion in the Americas*. New York: New Press.

Garcia, Charles Patrick. 2006. *A Message from Garcia: Yes, You Can Succeed*. New York: Wiley.

Garcia, Chris F., John Garcia, Angelo Falcón, and Rodolfo O. De la Garza. 1989. "Studying Latino Politics: The Development of the Latino National Political Survey." *PS: Political Science and Politics* 22 (4): 848–52.

Garcia, Guy. 2004. *The New Mainstream: How the Multicultural Consumer Is Transforming American Business*. New York: Rayo.

Garcia, Mario T. 1989. *Mexican Americans: Leadership, Ideology and Identity, 1930–1950s*. New Haven, Conn.: Yale University Press.

Gaspar de Alba, Alicia. 1998. *Chicano Art Inside Outside the Master's House: Cultural Politics and the CARA Exhib*ition. Austin: University of Texas Press.

Goldberg, David Theo. 1993. *Racist Culture: Philosophy and the Politics of Meaning*. Malden, Mass.: Blackwell.

Goldman, Shifra. 1994. *Dimensions of Art in the Americas*. Chicago: University of Chicago Press.

Gómez-Peña, Guillermo. 1996. "The Multicultural Paradigm: An Open Letter to the National Arts Community." In *Beyond the Fantastic: Contemporary Art Criticism from Latin America*, ed. Gerardo Mosquera, 183–95. Cambridge, Mass.: MIT Press.

Gonzalez, Gilbert. 2007. *Guest Workers or Colonized Labor? Mexican Labor Migration to the United States*. Boulder, Colo.: Paradigm.

Gonzalez, Juan. 2001. *Harvest of Empire: A History of Latinos in America*. New York: Penguin Books.

———. 2004. "Don't Count Out Rupe in Nielsen Row." *New York Daily News*, June 3, p. 16.

Gonzalez, Michael. 2004. "Hispanic for Jorge." *Wall Street Journal*, November 8, Eastern Edition, A15.

Gonzalez, Rita. 2003a. "Archiving the Latino Arts before It Is Too Late." Latino Policy and Issues Brief. Los Angeles: UCLA Chicano Studies Research Center, no. 6, April.

———. 2003b. "An Undocumented History: A Survey of Index Citations and Art Historical Resources for Latino and Latina Artists." Latino Policy and Issues Brief. Los Angeles: UCLA Chicano Studies.

Gosselin, Peter. 2004. "The New Deal; The New Dean; If America Is Richer, Why Are Its Families So Much Less Secure?" *Los Angeles Times*, October 10, p. A1.

Grosfoguel, Ramon, Nelson Maldonado-Torres, and Jose David Saldivar. 2006. *Latino/as in the World-System: Decolonization Struggles in the 21st-Century U.S. Empire*. Boulder, Colo.: Paradigm.

Grow, Brian, Adrienne Carter, Roger O. Crockett, and Geri Smith. 2005. "Embracing Illegals." *Business Week*, July 18, 56.

Guinier, Lani, and Gerald Torres. 2002. *The Miner's Canary: Enlisting Race, Resisting Power, Transforming Democracy*, ed. Sandra Jackson and Jose Solid. Cambridge, Mass.: Harvard University Press.

Gutierrez, David. 1995. *Walls and Mirrors: Mexican Americans, Mexican Immigrants, and the Politics of Ethnicity*. Berkeley: University of California Press.

Hall, Stuart. 1991. "The Local and the Global: Globalization and Ethnicity." In *Culture, Globalization and the World System*, ed. Anthony D. King. Binghamton: Department of Art and Art History, SUNY at Binghamton.

———. ed. 1997. *Representation: Cultural Representations and Signifying Practices*. London: Sage Publications and Open University.

Haney-López, Ian. 2005. "Race on the 2010 Census: Hispanics and the Shrinking White Majority." *Daedalus* 134 (1): 42.

Handler, Richard. 1988. *Nationalism and the Politics of Culture in Quebec*. Madison: University of Wisconsin Press.

———. ed. 2000. *Excluded Ancestors, Inventible Traditions: Essays toward a More Inclusive History of Anthropology*. Madison: Wisconsin University Press.

Hanor, Stephanie. 2006." Transactions: Across and Beyond Borders." In *TRANS-actions: Contemporary Latin American and Latino Art*. Museum of Contemporary Art, San Diego.

Harrison, Faye, and Ira Harrison. 1998. "Anthropology, African Americans, and the Emancipation of a Subjugated Knowledge." In *African American Pioneers in Anthropology*, ed. Faye Harrison, 1–36. Urbana: University of Illinois Press.

Haslip-Viera, Gabriel. 2005. "Report on the Status of Departments and Programs in Latino and Latin American Studies and Puerto Rican Studies at the City University of New York." New York: The CUNY Council of Departments and Programs in Latin American, Puerto Rican, and Latino Studies.

Haslip-Viera, Gabriel Falcón, Angelo Falcón, and Félix Matos Rodriguez. 2005. *Boricuas in Gotham: Puerto Ricans in the Making of Modern New York City*. Princeton, N.J.: Markus Wiener Publishers.

Hayes-Bautista, David. 2004. *La Nueva California: Latinos in the Golden State*. Berkeley: University of California Press.

Hero, Rodney, Chris Garcia, John Garcia, and Harry Pachon. 2000. "Latino Participation, Partisanship and Office Holding." *PS: Political Science and Politics* 33 (3): 529–34.

Hispanic Business. 2003. "U.S. Hispanic Consumers in Transition: A Description Guide. A HispanTelligence Special Report." A Hispanic Business Inc. Research Unit, June.

Hispanic Voter Project. 2004. "Bikini Politics: The 2004 Presidential Campaigns' Hispanic Media Efforts Cover Only the Essential Parts of the Body Politic: A Select Group of Voters in a Few Battleground States." Hispanic Voter Project, Johns Hopkins University. September 28. http://www.jhu.edu/advanced/communication/hvp_2004_Interim_Report_Segal.pdf.

Honig, Bonnie. 1998. "Immigrant America? How Foreigners 'Solve' Democracy's Problems." *Social Text* 56, 16 (3): 1–27.

Horton, Ann. 1993. "Conversations with Curator Waldo Rasmussen." *Latin American Art* 5, (1): 40–41.

Horwitz, Tony. 2006. "Immigration and the Curse of the Black Legend." *New York Times*, Op Ed, July 9.

Hutchinson, Earl Ofari. 2007. *The Latino Challenge to Black America: Towards a Conversation between African Americans and Hispanics*. Chicago: Middle Passage Press.

Igo, Sarah. 2007. *The Averaged American: Surveys, Citizens, and the Making of a Mass Public*. Cambridge, Mass.: Harvard University Press.

JERDE. 2006. "Ciudad de Sueños." Proposal prepared for the City of New York, January.

Johnson, Kirk. 2004. "Hispanic Voters Declared Their Independence." *New York Times*, November 9.

Jones, Delmos J. 1970. "Towards a Native Anthropology." *Human Organization* 29 (4): 251–58.

Juffer, Jane. 2001. "The Limits of Culture: Latina/o Studies, Diversity Management, and the Corporate University." *Nepantla* 2 (2): 265–93.

July, Gordon, Avery Newfield, and Christopher, eds. 1996. *Mapping Multiculturalism*. Minneapolis: University of Minnesota Press.

Kanellos, Nicolas. 1998. *Thirty Million Strong: Reclaiming the Hispanic Image in American Culture*. Golden, Colo.: Fulcrum Press.

Kasindorf, Martin. 2004. "Hispanic Voters Paint a New Picture." *USA Today*, November 11.

Karp, Ivan, Christine Mullen Kreamer, and Steven D. Levine. 1992. *Museums and Communities: The Politics of Public Culture*. Washington, D.C.: Smithsonian Institution Press.

Kinzer, Stephen. 2002. "Arts in America: Mexico's Cultural Diplomacy Aims to Win Hearts in U.S." *New York Times*, August 1, The Arts Cultural Desk, Section E, p. 1.

Kirp, David L. 2003. *Shakespeare, Einstein, and the Bottom Line: The Marketing of Higher Education*. Cambridge, Mass.: Harvard University Press.

Kirshenblatt-Gimblett, Barbara. 1998. *Destination Culture, Tourism, Museums and Heritage*. Berkeley: University of California Press.

Kochhar, Rakesh. 2004. "The Wealth of Hispanic Households: 1996–2002." The Pew Hispanic Center, Washington D.C., October 18.

Kolata, Gina. 2007. "Data on Hispanic Immigrants Presents Puzzle on Aging." *New York Times*, January 3.

Kornblum, Janet. 2002. "More Hispanic Catholics Losing Their Religion; Church Hasn't 'Caught Up' with People." *USA Today*, December 12. p. D12.

Korzenny, Felipe, and Betty Ann Korzenny. 2005. *Hispanic Marketing: A Cultural Perspective*. Burlington, Mass.: Butterworth-Heinemann.

Kovach, Gretel. 2007. "Pesos for Pizzas FOR PIZZAS?" *New York Times*, February 19. Vol. 139, Issue 10, p. 8.

Kravetz, Carl, AHAA Chair. 2006. "Latino Cultural Identity Project." Presented at AHAA 21st Conference, September 20, in Miami, Florida. http://www.ahaa.org/meetings/Miami06/presentation/presentation.htm.

Larmer, Brook. 1999. "Latino America." *Newsweek*, July 12.

Leal, David, Matt Barreto, Jongho Lee, and Rodolfo de la Garza. 2005. "The Latino Vote in the 2004 Election." *PS: Political Science and Politics* 38: 41–49.

LeBron, Marisol. 2007. Transboricuas, Sellouts, And None of the Above: Representing Puerto Rican Identities at El Museo del Barrio." Honors Undergraduate Thesis. Oberlin, Ohio: Oberlin College.

Lee, Denny. 2002. "A 'Museo' Moves Away From Its Barrio Identity." *New York Times*, July 21, Section 14, p. 4.

Lewis, Justin. 2001. *Constructing Public Opinion: How Political Elites Do What They Like and Why We Seem to Go Along with It.* New York: Columbia University Press.

Limon, Jose. 1993. "Representation, Ethnicity and the Precursory Ethnography: Notes of a Native Anthropologist." In *Recapturing Anthropology: Working in the Present,* ed.

Richard G. Fox, 115–36. Santa Fe, N.M.: School of American Research Press.

———. 2003. "Have We Arrived? Class, Museum Culture and Mexican-America." http://latino.si.edu/researchandmuseums/presentations/jose_limon.htm.

Lippard, Lucy.1990. *Mixed Blessings: New Art in a Multicultural America.* New York: Pantheon Books.

———. 2002. *Biting the Hand: Artists and Museums in New York Since 1969.* Minneapolis: University of Minnesota Press.

Lovato, Roberto. 2007a. "The Smog of War." *Nation,* April 2.

———. 2007b. "Becoming Americano." *Public Eye* 22 (1): 1.

Lucie-Smith, Edward. 1993. *Latin American Art of the Twentieth Century.* London: Thames and Hudson.

MacFarquhar, Larissa. 2004. "The Pollster: Does John Zogby Know Who Will Win the Election? *New Yorker,* October 18.

Manhattan Community District 11. 1996. "New Directions, El Barrio Spanish Harlem, East Harlem Triangle, Randalls and Wards Island." A 197-A Land Use Plan devised by Community Board No. 11, Borough of Manhattan.

Marable, Manning. 2000. *Dispatches from the Ebony Tower: Intellectuals Confront the African American Experience.* New York: Columbia University Press.

Marcus, George, and Fred Myers. 1995. *The Traffic in Culture: Refiguring Art and Anthropology.* Berkeley: University of California Press.

Marquez, Benjamin. 1993. *LULAC:* The Evolution of a Mexican American Political Organization. Austin: University of Texas Press.

———. 2003. *Constructing Identities in Mexican American Political Organizations: Choosing Issues, Taking Sides.* Austin: University of Texas Press.

Massey, Douglas, Margarita Mooney, Kim Torres, and Camille Z. Charles. 2007. "Black Immigrants and Black Natives Attending Selective Colleges and Universities in the United States." *American Journal of Education* 113 (February): 243–73.

Meléndez Vélez, Edgardo. 2005. "The Puerto Rican Journey Revisited: Politics and the Study of Puerto Rican Migration." *Centro Journal* 17 (2): 191–220.

Mignolo, Walter. 2000. *Local Histories/Global Designs: Coloniality, Subaltern Knowledges, and Border Thinking.* Princeton, N.J.: Princeton University Press.

Miller, Daniel. 1995. *Acknowledging Consumption: A Review of New Studies.* London, New York: Routledge.

Mindiola, Tatcho, Yolanda Flores Niemman, and Nestor Rodriguez. 2003. *Black-Brown Relations and Stereotypes.* Austin: University of Texas Press.

Montejano, David. 1987. *Anglos and Mexicans in the Making of Texas, 1836–1986.* Austin: University of Texas Press.

Moreno, María-José. 1997. "Identity Formation and Organizational Change in Nonprofit Institutions: A Comparative Study of Two Hispanic Museums." Ph.D. Thesis. Columbia University.

Mosquera, Gerardo. 1996. *Beyond the Fantastic: Contemporary Art Criticism from Latin America.* Cambridge, Mass.: MIT Press.

Myers, Fred. 2001. *The Empire of Things: Regimes of Value and Material Culture.* Santa Fe: School of American Research Advanced Seminar Series.

NALEO. 2004. "National Town halls: A Report on issues concerning Latino voters in 2004." Washington, D.C.: National Association of Latino Elected Officials.

———. 2005. *Directory of Latino Elected Officials.* Los Angeles: National Association of Latino Elected Officials.

Napoli, Philip. 2006. "Audience Measurement and Media Policy: Audience Economics, the Diversity Principle and the Local People Meter." Working Paper. Bronx, N.Y.: The Donald McGannon Communication Research Center.

National Council of La Raza. 2004. Memorandum, "How Did Latinos Really Vote in 2004?" November 16. Washington, D.C.: NCLR.National Latino Media Coalition. 2004. "Scholarly 'Confusion' Evident in Review of Latino Television Study by Tomas Rivera Policy Institute." Press release, July 12. New York City 2006 125th Street/ River to River. Department of City Planning. http://www.nyc.gov/html/dcp/html/125th/125th4.shtml.

Nava, Gregory. 2004. *The Presumed Alliance: The Unspoken Conflict Between Latinos and Blacks and What It Means for America.* New York: Harper Collins.

Noriega, Chon A. 2000. *East of the River: Chicano Art Collectors Anonymous.* Santa Monica: Santa Monica Museum of Art.

NYFA. 2001. *Culture Counts: Strategies for a More Vibrant Cultural Life for New York City.* New York Foundation for the Arts.

Oboler, Suzanne. 1995. *Ethnic Labels, Latino Lives: Identity and the Politics of (Re) Presentation in the United States.* Minneapolis: University of Minnesota Press.

Ong, Aihwa. 1999. "Cultural Citizenship as Subject Making: Immigrants Negotiate Racial and Cultural Boundaries in the United States." In *Race, Identity and Citizenship,* ed. Rodolfo Torres et al., 262–94. New York: Blackwell.

Orfield, Gary, and Michal Kurlaender. 2001. "Diversity Challenged: Evidence on the Impact of Affirmative Action." Civil Rights Project. Cambridge, Mass.: Harvard Education Pub. Group.

Ortner, Sherry. 2003. *New Jersey Dreaming, Capital, Culture and the Class of '58.* New Durham: Duke University Press.

Park, Edward J. W., and John S. W. Park. 1999. "A New American Dilemma? Asian Americans and Latinos in Race Theorizing." *Journal of Asian American Studies* 2 (3): 289–309.

Peñaloza, Lisa. 1994. "Ya Viene Atzlan! Latinos in US Advertising." *Media Studies Journal* (Summer): 133–41.

Perez-Torres, Rafael. 2006. *Mestizaje: Critical Uses of Race in Chicano Culture.* Minneapolis: University of Minnesota Press.

Pew Hispanic Center/Kaiser Family Foundation. 2004. *National Survey Of Latinos Politics and Civic Participation.* The Henry Kaiser Family Foundation.

Pimentel, Felipe. 2005. "The Decline of the Puerto Rican Full-time Faculty at the City University of New York from 1981–2002." *Center for Puerto Rican Studies* 2 (3): Hunter College, New York.

Pinon, Juan. 2007. "Azteca America's Strategies of Expansion and the Struggle for the Legitimate Latino Representation." Paper presented at NYU's Culture and Communication Program, February 12, New York.

Political Communication Lab. 2005. Stanford University. http://pcl.stanford.edu/campaigns/campaign2004/archive.html.

Portes, Alejandro, and Alex Stepic. 1993. *City on the Edge: The Transformation of Miami.* Berkeley: University of California Press.

Portes, Alejandro, and Ruben Rumbaut. 2001. *Legacies: The Story of the Immigrant Second Generation.* Berkeley: University of California Press.

Powell, Michael. 2007. "A Tale of Two Cities." *New York Times*, May 6, Section 14, p. 1.

Prashad, Vijay. 2000. *The Karma of Brown Folk.* Minneapolis: University of Minnesota Press.

Pulido, Laura. 2006. *Black, Brown, Yellow and Red: Radical Activism in Los Angeles.* Berkeley: University of California Press.

Radelat, Ana. 2004. "Hispanics Boost G.O.P." *Hispanic* 17 (12): 16–18.

Ramirez, Mari Carmen. 1996. "Beyond the Fantastic: Framing Identity in U.S. Exhibitions of Latin American Art." In *Beyond the Fantastic: Contemporary Art Criticism from Latin America*, ed. Gerardo Mosquera, 229–45. Cambridge, Mass.: MIT Press.

———. 2002. "Collecting Latin American Art for the 21st Century." International Center for the Arts of the Americas. Houston: Museum of Fine Arts.

Ramirez, Yasmin. 2003. "Passing on Latinidad: An Analysis of Critical Responses to El Museo Del Barrio's Pan-Latino Mission Statements." Washington, D.C.: Smithsonian National Research Conference.2002.

———. 2007. "The Activist Legacy of Puerto Rican Artists in New York and the Art Heritage of Puerto Rico." ICAA Documents Working Papers, No. 1, September, 46–53.

Ramos, Jorge. 2004. *The Latino Wave: How Hispanics Will Elect the Next American President.* New York: Rayo.

Rasmussen, Waldo, Fatima Bercht, and Elizabeth Ferrer. 1993. *Latin American Artists of the Twentieth Century.* New York: Harry N. Abrams.

Reynolds, Howard. 2006. "Gary Sheffield: Latinos Are Easier to Control Than Blacks," Latinosports.com, June 4, 2007.

Rifkin, Janey. 1999. "Tomorrow's Middle Class Is Defined as Hispanic." *Hispanic Times Magazine* 20 (5): 54.

Rincon and Associates. 2004. "Latino Television Study." Prepared for the National Latino Media Coalition, February 1.

Rodriguez, Clara. 2000. *Changing Race: Latinos, the Census and the History of Ethnicity.* New York: New York University Press.

Rodriguez, Gregory. 1996. "The Emerging Latin Middle Class." Research Report, Davenport Institute, Pepperdine University, School of Public Policy.

———. 2005. "Why We're the New Irish." *Newsweek*, May 30, 35.

Rodriguez, Richard. 1982. *Hunger of Memory: The Education of Richard Rodriguez.* New York: Bantam Books.

Roediger, David R. 1999. *The Wages of Whiteness: Race and the Making of the American Working Class.* London: Verso.

Sampson, Robert. 2006. "Open Doors Don't Invite Criminals." *New York Times*, Op Ed., March 11.

Sanchez, George. 2007. Keynote Address. NYU Conference: "Humanities or Human Resources? The Future of Ethnic Studies and Labor in the Corporate University." New York University, American Studies Program. April 13.

Sanchez, Jose. 2007. *Boricua Power: A Political History of Puerto Ricans in the United States.* New York: New York University Press.

Sanchez, Leslie. 2007. *Los Republicanos: Why Hispanics and Republicans Need Each Other.* New York: Palgrave.

Sanchez-Korrol, Virginia. 1983. *From Colonia to Community: The History of Puerto Ricans in New York City.* Westport, Conn.: Greenwood Press.

Santa Ana, Otto. 2002. *Brown Tide Rising: Metaphors of Latinos in Contemporary American Public Discourse.* Austin: University of Texas Press.

Santiago Irizarry, Vilma. 1996. "Culture as Cure." *Cultural Anthropology* 11 (1): 3–24.

Sawyer, Mark. 2005. "Racial Politics in Multiethnic America: Black and Latina/o Identities and Coalitions." In *Neither Enemies nor Friends: Latinos, Blacks and Afro-Latinos*, ed. Anani Dzdzienyo and Suzane Oboler, 265–80. New York: Palgrave.

Scott, Janny, and David Leonhardt. 2005. "Class in America: Shadowy Lines that Still Divide." *New York Times*, May 15.

Segal, Adam. 2003. "The Hispanic Priority: The Spanish Language Television Battle for the Hispanic Vote in the 2000 U.S. Presidential Election." Hispanic Voter Project, Johns Hopkins University, February.

———. 2004. "Presidential Spanish Language Political Television Advertising Set Records in Early Primaries." Hispanic Voter Project, Johns Hopkins University, March.

Segal, Daniel, and Richard Handler. 1995. "U.S. Multiculturalism and the Concept of Culture." *Identities: Global Studies of Culture and Power* 1 (4): 391–408.

Seggerman, Helen-Louise. 1995. "Latin American Art at Christie's and Sotheby's." *Art Nexus* 18 (October/December): 198–99.

Sheriff, Robin. 2001. *Dreaming Equality: Color, Race, and Racism in Urban Brazil*. New Brunswick, N.J.: Rutgers University Press.

Silva, Javier, and Rebecca Epstein. 2005. "Costly Credit: African Americans and Latinos in Debt: Borrowing to Make Ends Meet Briefing Paper #5." DEMOS: A Network of Ideas. New York, May.

Smith, James P. 2003. "Assimilation across the Latino Generations." *American Economic Review* 93 (2): 315–19.

Smith, Robert. 2005. *Mexican New York: Transnational Lives of Immigrants*. Berkeley: University of California Press.

Sosa, Lionel. 1998. *The Americano Dream: How Latinos Can Achieve Success in Business and in Life*. New York: Dutton.

Sosa Lionel, with the Napoleon Hill Foundation. 2006. *Think and Grow Rich: A Latino Choice*. New York: Ballantine Books.

Stoler, Ann Laura. 2002. *Carnal Knowledge and Imperial Power: Race and the Intimate in Colonial Rule*. Berkeley: University of California Press.

Stutzman, Ronald. 1981. "El Mestizaje: An All-Inclusive Ideology of Exclusion." In *Cultural Transformations and Ethnicity in Modern Ecuador*, ed. Norman E. Whitten, Jr., 45–94. Urbana: University of Illinois Press.

Subervi-Velez, Federico, ed. 2008. *Mass Media and Latino Politics: Studies of Media Content, Campaign Strategies and Survey Research: 1984–2004*. Hillsdale, N.J.: Lawrence Erlbaum.

Sullivan, Edward J. 2000. *Latin American Art in the Twentieth Century*. London: Phaidon.

Suro, Roberto, Richard Fry, and Jeffrey Passel. 2005. *Hispanics and the 2004 Election: Population, Electorate and Voters*. Washington, D.C.: Pew Hispanic Center.

Tafoya, Sonya. 2004. "Shades of Belonging." The Pew Hispanic Center, Washington, D.C.

Takacs, Stacey. 1999. "Alien Nation: Immigration, National Identity and Transnationalism." *Cultural Studies* 13 (4): 595–620.

Telles, Edward. 2006a. "Mexican Americans and the American Nation: A Response to Professor Huntington." *Aztlan: A Journal of Chicano Studies* 31(2): 7–23.

———. 2006b. *Race in Another America: The Significance of Skin Color in Brazil*. Princeton, N.J.: Princeton University Press.

Tomás Rivera Policy Institute (TRPI). 2001. "The Latino Middle Class: Myth, Reality and Potential." Authors: Frank D. Bean, Stephen J. Trejo, Randy Crapps, and Michael Tyler. TRPI: Los Angeles.

————. 2004. "Policy Review Paper Assessing the Nielsen and Rincón Study on Latino Television Viewing." Authors: Rodolfo O. de la Garza, Ph.D., Louis DeSipio, Ph.D., Jongho Lee, Ph.D., and Harry Pachon, Ph.D. http://www.trpi.org/update/media.html.

Torres, Andres. 2006. *Latinos in New England*. Philadelphia: Temple University Press.

Torruella-Leval, Susana. 1995. "Coming of Age with the Muses: Change in the Age of Multiculturalism." Paper Series on the Arts, Culture and Society. New York: Andy Warhol Foundation for the Visual Arts.

Traba, Marta. 1994. *Art of Latin America, 1900–1980*. Baltimore: Johns Hopkins University Press.

Turner, Terence. 1994. "Anthropology and Multiculturalism: What Is Anthropology That Multiculturalism Should Be Mindful Of." In *Multiculturalism: A Critical Reader*, ed. David Theo Goldberg, 406–25. Oxford: Blackwell.

Twine, France Winddance. 2006. *Racism in a Racial Democracy: The Maintenance of White Supremacy in Brazil*. New Brunswick, N.J.: Rutgers University Press.

Urciuoli, Bonnie. 1996. *Exposing Prejudice, Puerto Rican Experiences of Language, Race and Class*. Boulder, Colo.: Westview Press.

————. 1999. "Producing Multiculturalism in Higher Education: Who's Producing What for Whom?" *Qualitative Studies in Education* 12 (3): 287–98.

U.S. Census Bureau. 1998. *Income 1998. Table A. Comparison of Summary Measures of Income*. http://www.census.gov/hhes/www/income/income98/in98sum.html

————. 2003. *Income in the United States: 2002*. Prepared by Carmen De Navas-Walt, Robert Cleveland, and Bruce H. Webster Jr., U.S. Government Printing Office, Washington, D.C. http://www.census.gov/prod/2003pubs/p60-221.pdf.

Vaca, Nicholas. 2004. *The Presumed Alliance: The Unspoken Conflict between Latinos and Blacks and What It Means for America*. New York: Rayo.

Valdes, Isabel. 2000. "Marketing to American Latinos." Paramount Market Publishing.

Valdes, Isabel, and Marta Seoane. 1995. "Hispanic Market Handbook: The Definite Source for Reaching This Lucrative Segment of American Consumers." Gale Research Inc.

Vega, Maria. 2002. "Una Casa Cultural Blanco de Discordia." *El Diario*, August 29, p. 26.

Vila, Pablo. 2000. *Crossing Borders, Reinforcing Borders: Social Categories, Metaphors and Narrative Identities on the U.S.-Mexico Frontier*. Austin: University of Texas Press.

Wartzman, Rick, and Joe Flint. 2000. "Nielsen Ratings Spark a Battle over Just Who Speaks Spanish." *Wall Street Journal*, February 25, p. B1.

Waterston, Alisse. 2006. "Are Latinos Becoming 'White' Folk? And What That Still Says about Race in America." *Transforming Anthropology* 14 (2): 133.

Weston, Kath. 1997. "The Virtual Anthropologist." In *Anthropological Locations*, ed. Akhil Gupta and James Ferguson, 163–84. Berkeley: University of California Press.

William C. Velasquez Institute. (undated). "The 2004 WCVI National Latino Election Day Exit Poll." By Dr. Henry Flores of St. Mary's University. Both reports were presented at the National Latino Exit Poll Briefing organized by Demos, December 6, in location.

Williams, Brackette. 1989. "A Class Act: Anthropology and the Race to Nation among Ethnic Terrain." *Annual Review of Anthropology* 18: 401–44.

———. 1991. *Stains in My Name, War in My Veins: Guyana and the Politics of Cultural Struggle*. Durham, N.C.: Duke University Press.

———. 1993. "The Impact of the Precepts of Nationalism on the Concept of Culture: Making Grasshoppers of Naked Apes." *Cultural Critique* 24 (Spring): 143–91.

Williams, Raymond. 1977. *Marxism and Literature*. Oxford: Oxford University Press.

Wilson, Patricia. 1984. "Puerto Rican Art in New York: The Aesthetic Analysis of Eleven Painters and Their Work." Ph.D. Dissertation, School of Education, New York University.

Wright, Erik Olin, ed. 2005. *Approaches to Class Analysis*. New York: Cambridge University Press.

Ybarra-Frausto, Tomás. 1991. "The Chicano Movement/The Movement of Chicano Art." In *Exhibiting Cultures: The Poetics and Politics of Museum Display*, ed. Ivan Karp and Steven Lavine, 128–50. Washington, D.C.: Smithsonian Press.

———. 2005. "Imagining a More Expansive Narrative of American Art." *American Art* 19 (3): 9–15.

Ybarra-Frausto, Tomás, and Michael Dear. 1999. "El Movimiento: The Chicano Cultural Project since the 1960s." In *Urban Latino Cultures/La vida Latina en L.A.* ed. Gustavo Leclerc, Raul Villa, and Michael J. Dear, 23–44. London: Sage Publications.

Yancey, George A. 2003. *Who Is White? Latinos, Asians, and the New Black/Nonblack Divide*. Boulder, CO: Lynne Rienner.

Yúdice, George. 1996. "Transnational Cultural Brokering of Art." In *Beyond the Fantastic: Contemporary Art Criticism from Latin America*, ed. Gerardo Mosquera, 196–215. Cambridge, Mass.: MIT Press.

Zaretsky, Aaron. 2005. "La Marqueta Arts and Culture Program." New York: East Harlem Business Capital Corporation.

Zate, Maria. 1994. "The Hispanic Middle Class." *Hispanic Business*, November.

Zogby, Joe, and Rebecca Wittman. 2004. "Hispanic Perspectives." Submitted to National Council of La Raza. Zogby International, New York.

Zolberg, Vera. 1992. "Art Museums and Living Artists: Contentious Communities." In *Museums and Communities: The Politics of Public Culture*, ed. Ivan Karp, Christine Mullen Kreamer, and Steven Lavine, 105–36. Washington, D.C.: Smithsonian Institution.

Index

About the Author

ARLENE DÁVILA is Professor of Anthropology and American Studies at NYU. Her previous works include *Barrio Dreams: Puerto Ricans, Latinos and the Neoliberal City*, and *Latinos Inc: Marketing and the Making of a People*.